Learning from Cases

Learning from Cases

Unraveling the Complexities of Elementary Science Teaching

Deborah J. Tippins

University of Georgia

Thomas R. Koballa, Jr.

University of Georgia

Beverly D. Payne

University of Georgia

Allyn and Bacon

Boston • London • Toronto • Sydney • Tokyo • Singapore

Series Editor: *Traci Mueller*
Editorial Assistant: *Bridget Keane*
Marketing Manager: *Amy Cronin*
Editorial-Production Service: *Omegatype Typography, Inc.*
Composition and Prepress Buyer: *Linda Cox*
Manufacturing Buyer: *Suzanne Lareau*
Cover Administrator: *Kristina Mose-Libon*
Electronic Composition: *Omegatype Typography, Inc.*
Photo Research: *Katharine S. Cook*

Library of Congress Cataloging-in-Publication Data

Learning from cases : unraveling the complexities of elementary science teaching /
   [edited by] Deborah J. Tippins, Thomas R. Koballa, Jr., Beverly D. Payne.
     p. cm.
   Includes bibliographical references and index.
   ISBN 0-205-30588-1 (alk. paper)
     1. Science—Study and teaching (Elementary) 2. Case method. I. Tippins, Deborah J. II.
Koballa, Thomas R. III. Payne, Beverly D.

  LB1584 .L39 2002
  372.3'5044—dc21

                                                  2001053410

Contents

3 *Organizing Meaningful Science Learning Environments*   *32*

4 *Creating a Culture for Learning Science
in the Elementary Classroom*   *49*

5 *Diverse Science Learners in the Elementary Classroom* **73**

6 *Elementary Science Teaching for Understanding* **101**

Preface

Science teaching is a complex and uncertain endeavor, particularly in the elementary grades. Elementary teachers are expected to teach science in ways that enable children to experience and construct meaningful understandings about the world around them. They must do this while also attending to the needs of the developing child, the waves of school reform, and the demands of the other curricular areas for which they are responsible. The knowledge base needed to guide children's science learning experiences in such an ever-changing environment far exceeds what can be deduced from theoretical principles. Rather, it must be constructed from experiences that highlight the situation-specific and context-dependent nature of science teaching and learning in the elementary school. *Learning from Cases: Unraveling the Complexities of Elementary Science Teaching* brings attention to the dilemmas and challenges of elementary science teaching and learning through the narrative cases of prospective and practicing teachers, science teacher educators, informal science educators, and scientists. Additionally, these authors offer suggestions for improving classroom practice and stimulating critical reflection about science teaching and learning.

This book is intended for all who have a stake in the science learning of children, including beginning and experienced elementary teachers, teacher educators, teacher mentors, and school administrators. It is designed for use as a vehicle to foster the development of problem-solving and decision-making strategies. It can be used with pre-service teachers to assist them in developing an understanding of current instructional practices in science at the elementary level and the specifics of science education reform efforts that will affect them. Additionally, the book will be very useful for schoolwide or districtwide professional development as well as graduate-level education courses that focus on science teaching and learning. Schools and universities that are involved in partnerships can use this case book to guide their efforts related to science education.

The book includes eleven chapters. The first chapter introduces the case approach to teaching and provides a rationale for using cases in elementary science education. Chapters 2 through 10 contain three or four cases each and are organized around such topics as assessment, language, inquiry-based instruction, diversity, conceptual understanding, and professional development. Found among these chapters is a mix of open cases, which involve unresolved dilemmas or challenges, and closed cases, in which the authors are able to offer possible resolutions for the dilemmas or challenges described. Each case is accompanied by questions to facilitate reflection and discussion and one or more responses that feature interesting and diverse perspectives on the dilemma or challenge central to the case. Consistent with the range of elementary school configurations, the cases focus on science teaching and learning in preschool through grade 8. The final chapter of the book provides guidance for writing and sharing cases and commentaries to foster reflection and discussion on issues of importance to elementary science teaching and learning.

This book will be particularly valuable to educators who recognize that science teaching and learning occur in a world that is constantly in flux and that teaching is deeply rooted in our personalities and experiences as learners. Classroom cases facilitate exploration of the complex and messy problems and challenges of science teaching. Because the cases are embedded contextually in the elementary science learning environment, they bring a slice of reality to the reader and offer no "right answers" or tidy solutions. They provide the data to provoke careful thought and meaningful discourse, allowing readers to develop the skills of classroom analysis, decision making, and problem solving that are so essential for today's elementary teacher. A classroom case, as the centerpiece of deliberation, can also serve as a foundation for the development of fundamental understandings of science teaching and learning and as a guide for enriching classroom practice.

This handbook should be used interactively and to complement other science teaching and learning resources. It is not intended to be used as a stand-alone science methods textbook. We recommend that individuals read a case and use the Questions for Reflection and Discussion to facilitate their reflective thinking and discussion before examining the case commentaries. Some commentaries offer reflections on the case's dilemma by the case author; others provide an expert's constructive critique of the case. It is hoped that the commentaries will shed new light on the case and provide a different perspective from which to consider the dilemma or the proposed solution. After reading the commentaries, individuals might want to revisit the Questions for Reflection and Discussion.

This book is the product of the thinking and experiences of seventy-six individuals who are dedicated to the improvement of elementary science teaching and learning. We are very much indebted to those who have contributed to this book, and we appreciate the understanding and flexibility they showed us as we edited the content of cases, commentaries, and abstracts for instructional purposes and consistency of style.

Deborah J. Tippins
Thomas R. Koballa, Jr.
Beverly D. Payne

Learning from Cases

1

Using Cases in Elementary Science Education

Consider the context of the teaching environment of a typical elementary classroom: one teacher and twenty to twenty-five unique students living together usually in one small room, six to seven hours a day, five days a week, for 180 days a year. Elementary teachers are required to make judgments; develop and revise plans; implement lessons; be able to use and create knowledge in the context of their own classrooms; nurture; communicate with learners, parents, and other teachers; involve all learners; and much more. They need to remain sensitive to each child's attitudes, values, social adjustment, and cognitive development. They are also expected to have a command of various knowledge bases (content, pedagogical, social, and cultural) and to be reflective, problem-solving professionals. What a challenge!

Teaching has always been a complex and demanding profession, and it has become more so as elementary schools have taken on increased social responsibility, expanding their functions beyond academic learning. Today, elementary schools provide such services as health care, transportation, extended day care, breakfasts and lunches, and counseling and mental health services, to name a few. However, the most important goal of elementary teaching—academic learning— requires that teachers be prepared not only to teach many subjects (e.g., reading, mathematics, science, language arts, social studies), but also to do so effectively with students of different cultural backgrounds, linguistic abilities, learning styles, and special needs. Teachers who are ill prepared to deal with the complexity and ambiguity of teaching often find the demands of the classroom too challenging and may quickly become discouraged or adopt a simplistic view of teaching in which "tricks of the trade" and "recipes" serve as a substitute for thoughtful practice.

WHY A FOCUS ON SCIENCE EDUCATION AT THE ELEMENTARY LEVEL?

Although science is an essential and fundamental subject within the elementary school curriculum, it must compete for time in the curriculum in many school systems. In fact, on average, in the United States, elementary students spend less than 20 minutes a day studying science (Weiss, 1987). One reason so little time is spent teaching science in the elementary school may be attributed to the fact that elementary school teachers often have had only one or two required science courses plus a single course on the teaching of elementary science. Research suggests that many elementary teachers lack confidence in their abilities to teach science (Abell & Roth, 1992; Borko, 1991). And when they do teach science, teachers often view science as a body of facts, definitions, and rules to be learned or memorized. For many teachers of science, textbooks become the major sources of information and knowledge about science and expository methods such as discussion and lecture are the primary means for teaching science. Research also indicates that 75 percent of lower elementary (K–3) and 90 percent of upper elementary (4–6) science instruction involves lecture and discussion teaching methods (Barba, 1998). This overreliance on expository teaching techniques and science textbooks neither promotes nor encourages the development of scientific thinking or attitudes, nor do these books and techniques engage students in applying cognitive processes that are basic to understanding the appropriate content. There is probably no quicker way to discourage student interest in science than to teach science as though it is an organized body of knowledge to be learned in a sequential manner. The textbooks and instructional materials that are traditionally used in elementary teacher education programs and professional development tend to perpetuate the development of elementary science teachers as technical decision makers (Anderson & Mitchner, 1994) moving in lockstep through a series of curriculum activities. Recent studies point to elementary teachers' strengths in language arts and the need to link science teaching and learning with the development of written and oral literacy (Akerson & Flanigan, 2000; Flick, 1995).

We believe, as do most science educators, that the teaching of elementary science should provide students with opportunities to wonder, explore, discover, think critically and practice methods of inquiry, develop conceptions of how the world works, and develop appropriate attitudes and skills to enable them to become scientifically literate citizens in a democracy. Classrooms where such teaching occurs value questions, experimentation, risk taking, and collaborative problem solving. How can teachers create a vision for meaningful science learning that encompasses these ideas? Case-based pedagogy can contribute to the development of teachers' knowledge and growth as science learners. Lee Shulman (1992) has defined cases as engaging narrative stories containing events that unfold over a period of time in a specified place. Classroom cases draw our attention to the dilemmas that characterize the lives of elementary teachers and serve as a vehicle for reflection and changing practice. We will discuss our use of cases in considerably more detail later in this chapter.

In determining what all teachers of science need to know and be able to do, the *National Science Education Standards* (National Research Council, 1996) drew heavily from the document *Science for All Americans* (American Association for the Advancement of Science, 1989). This document emphasizes the need for teachers to do the following:

- Understand the nature of scientific inquiry, its central role in science, and how to use the skills and processes of scientific inquiry
- Understand the fundamental facts and concepts in the major science disciplines
- Be able to make conceptual connections within and across the science disciplines as well as to mathematics, technology, and other subjects
- Use scientific understanding and ability when dealing with personal and societal issues (p. 59)

The use of cases in elementary science teacher preparation, on the one hand, might resemble conceptions of good teaching advocated in these reform documents. These documents call for science teaching that encourages the development of communities of science learners, multiple perspectives, critical thinking, connection of the content and material with the lives of students, diverse approaches to solving problems, in-depth and hands-on science education environments, investigation and inquiry, integration of scientific and pedagogical knowledge, and the teacher as a reflective practitioner. A basic premise of this book is that case-based instruction promotes these recommended types of teaching and learning and can motivate and facilitate science reflection of prospective and practicing teachers. On the other hand, the cases presented in this book should not be thought of as examples of either exemplary or ineffective practice, but rather as "narratives designed to promote a discussion of significant issues, portray a variety of teaching strategies and philosophies, and highlight the complexity, rationality and flaws [or diversity] in student thinking" (Barnett & Tyson, 1993).

CASES AND THE KNOWLEDGE BASE IN TEACHER EDUCATION

Certainly, if we examine many teacher education programs, we will find a mismatch between how science is usually taught in undergraduate and graduate programs and how the *National Education Science Standards* are suggesting teachers perform in science classrooms today. Two different viewpoints exist on how best to improve learning most effectively. Historically, our schools were based on behavioral or objectivist principles, centered on a set of assumptions about the nature of knowledge, how it is acquired, and strategies to ensure that students acquire this knowledge. From this perspective, knowledge is viewed as fully known, inert, transmittable, and waiting to be transferred from the teacher who owns it to students who do not (Bereiter & Scardamalia, 1987). Science teachers, in this perspective, acquire a great deal of important knowledge in the discipline of science and transmit this knowledge to students, who are expected to assume a passive role when science is taught.

An alternative perspective that has gained in respectability over the last two decades is known as constructivism (Driver, Asoko, Leach, Mortimer, & Scott, 1994; Phillips, 1995). A constructivist view of science teaching holds that knowledge is both personal and social and that meaning is constructed by the learner at the intersection of knowledge of the subject matter and personal experience. The fundamental role of the teacher in the constructivist-oriented classroom is to help children generate connections between what they are supposed to learn and what they already know or believe. In this context, teachers provide students with relevant experiences and subsequent opportunities for dialogue so that meaning can evolve and be constructed. Teachers use their knowledge and skills to create science environments in which children explore, construct new knowledge, and then use that knowledge in new situations (Arends, 1994). Learning occurs in the context of current understanding and is facilitated by social interaction as students share their ideas with peers, both in small groups and within the total society of the classroom as the students work with authentic tasks, problems, and questions.

In recent years, the focus on preparing science teachers as technical decision makers has given way to preparing critically reflective practitioners (Anderson & Mitchner, 1994). Rather than allowing actions to be governed by rules and prescriptions derived from professional knowledge, reflective practitioners, according to Schon (1987, p. 39), construct new categories of understanding and ways of framing problems of practice. Reflective teachers perceive their classrooms as living laboratories where the scientific process of gathering data and proposing explanations joins with creative and intuitive abilities to solve problems and promote learning.

The philosophical premise of this elementary science casebook is consistent with the trend toward preparing elementary teachers to function in a constructivist learning environment. Like all learners, teachers need to construct their own knowledge and theory of science learning that is developmental and that is based on experience, reflection, interaction with others, and exposure to effective teaching models. Case-based pedagogy can be supported by the portion of the knowledge base that asserts that teacher's knowledge is (1) contextual, that is, situation specific; (2) interactive, informed, and informing through interaction; and (3) speculative, because much of teachers' work involves uncertainty (Clark & Lampert, 1986). Cases can provide situation-specific circumstances that can help teachers connect theory and practice in a supportive, interactive environment.

THE HISTORICAL EMERGENCE
OF CASE-BASED PEDAGOGY

Cases and case-based pedagogy have been a cornerstone of professional training in schools of law and medicine since the 1880s (Naumes & Naumes, 1999) and are increasingly being used in other professional fields, such as business, political science, journalism (Knirk, 1991), architecture (Schon, 1983), educational psychology and measurement (Silverman, Welty, & Lyon, 1994), and teacher education (Kagan, 1993; Koballa & Tippins, 2000; Redman, 1999; J. H. Shulman, 1992). Instructors use cases in these fields in markedly diverse ways (Cooper & Mc-

Nergney, 1995; Naumes & Naumes, 1999), shaped in part by the kind of knowledge that is believed to characterize each discipline. In law, for example, instructors teach legal principles based only on relevant facts. Original cases are used as a context for group problem solving to learn foundations of judicial reasoning for the purpose of seeking to reach "the correct decision." Legal principles now compose a body of knowledge that has accumulated over time and guides legal practice. Similarly, in medicine, a clearly defined body of knowledge guides the use of cases. A history of an individual, group, event, or decision is presented and includes the results of the actions, as well as the actions themselves. In both these fields, the cases are taught by using Socratic questioning or doubting to lead students to predetermined right answers.

Based on the use of case studies in law and medicine, a similar approach was adapted for use in teaching of management at the Harvard Business School in the early part of the 1900s (Naumes & Naumes, 1999). However, business cases differ dramatically from medical and law cases (Cooper & McNergney 1995; Kowalski, Weaver, & Henson, 1990). Business cases are used to teach students how to analyze problems, develop the ability to separate important facts from less significant ones, and develop skills in identifying a multitude of acceptable decisions. They are carefully constructed to provoke discussion and analysis. In business schools, case instructors question students to think analytically with the possibility of arriving at different conclusions; interaction among business students is promoted and encouraged by the instructor.

From business, the case method spread to the point at which it is used not only in most business programs, but also in other fields, including education. In the Foreword of the book *Who Learns What from Cases and How* (Lundeberg, Levin, & Harrington, 1999), Merseth provides a brief history of the use of cases and the case method in education. She notes that case materials were used in teacher education programs in New Jersey and Massachusetts as early as 1920, and activities related to this approach, while not large or well organized, continued to exist throughout the 1960s and 1970s. Beginning in the 1980s and continuing to the present time, interest in cases and case-based methods by teacher educators has continued to grow as a result of a number of events. Lee Shulman's 1985 presidential address to the American Educational Research Association publicly recognized the case method, professional articles advocating cases began to appear in teacher education literature, and conference workshops and journals sponsored special issues on the topic of cases. Since the early 1990s, articles and commentaries about cases and casebooks have been plentiful.

As the use of classroom cases in teacher education has evolved over the past fifty years, various formats have emerged to illustrate problems or dilemmas in teaching and learning. These formats have included the critical incident, protocols, vignettes, simulations, video cases, and, more recently, interactive video cases. Today, as the use of cases continues to gain in popularity, we see the influence of these earlier approaches on case-based education.

PERSPECTIVES ON TEACHING AND CASE METHODS

The surging interest by teacher educators in cases and case-based pedagogy stems from the increasing belief in their value as a tool for helping prospective and practicing teachers to develop skills of critical analysis and problem solving, acquire broad repertoires of pedagogical techniques, develop higher-order cognitive thinking, and engage in reflective practice. Case-based pedagogy is valued as a context for decision making, involving students in their own learning, encouraging the development of a community of learners, and generating a realistic picture of the complexities of teaching (Merseth, as cited in Lundeberg et al., 1999; Cooper & McNergney, 1995). Although theoretical arguments for the use of classroom cases as instructional tools have expanded rapidly, there is no consensus about what constitutes the definition, purpose, use, and effectiveness of cases in education and science teacher education.

We regard classroom cases, as used in this book, to be examples of the narrative mode of literature. It is useful to make a distinction between a case and the case method. Miller and Kantrov (1998) provide a useful definition in which "case refers to a narrative organized around a key event and portraying particular characters that is structured to invite engagement by participants in a discussion" (p. 2). Lee Shulman believes that the most powerful cases are more than simply narratives of events, they are cases "of something" (1992, p. 17) that represent some larger set of ideas and therefore are worthy of reflection and deliberation. In addition, classroom cases usually include descriptions of the participants, thoughts, feelings, and behaviors (Kagan, 1993). Our approach to case-based pedagogy is similar to the dilemma-based cases proposed by Harrington, Quinn-Leering, and Hodson (1996): "Dilemma-based cases [are] intended to provide students of teaching with opportunities to recognize specific events as problematic; gain an understanding of them; reflect on them and on the consequences of action; and devise sensible, moral, and educative ways of acting" (p. 26).

The cases included in this book are intended to portray dilemmas and contexts that are particular to elementary science teaching and learning. Thus, although the substantive content of each case is crucial, its place as a centerpiece for deliberation and discussion is equally important.

WHY USE A CASE-BASED APPROACH TO SCIENCE TEACHING AND LEARNING?

Anyone who has had any involvement in teacher preparation programs knows that students have a desperate need to know "all the answers" to the complex questions and issues that confound elementary teachers every day in classrooms. Life in classrooms would be so simple, safe, and secure if only teachers could be provided with all the "right answers." Then teacher educators could design the ideal program and channel everyone through it who wants to be a teacher. Unfortunately, life in classrooms is anything but simple. Teaching is one of the most complex and challenging of all professions.

Teaching through cases has an appeal for a variety of reasons. Implicit in studying cases is the understanding that there are no clear-cut, simple answers to the complex issues teachers face. Judith Shulman, in the introduction to her book *Case Methods in Teacher Education* (1992), summarizes Lee Shulman's argument for the use of cases as teaching tools:

> Case-based teaching provides teachers with opportunities to analyze situations and make judgments in the messy world of practice, where principles often appear to conflict with one another and no simple solution is possible. (p. xiv)

Within teacher preparation programs, cases are used in a variety of contexts. Most often, instructors use cases in teacher education or pre-service courses to provide vicarious experiences that bring the reality of the classroom into the teacher education curriculum and enable students to identify issues confronting teachers and students (Kowalski, Weaver, & Henson, 1990; Miller & Kantrov, 1998). If elementary education students are to think like teachers, they might need practice. Students should be provided with opportunities to encounter real-life teaching dilemmas and problems in the safety and security of simulated situations. The case approach allows them to apply principles of teaching and learning and try them out without harming themselves and others in the process (Cooper & McNergney, 1995).

The case approach has also been recommended as a means to contextualize the knowledge that students typically receive in a linear and fragmented way in separate courses, lectures, techniques, and methods during their teacher preparation (Elbaz, 1991; Griffith & Laframboise, 1997; Harrington, 1995). The emphasis on reflection and problem solving in case-based pedagogy leads to the integration of information from multiple experiences that isn't possible with isolated course lectures, discussions, and readings. The case approach is an active pedagogical process as opposed to a passive process that ensues from lectures. Instead of being told how it is done, students learn by performing all the various analyses and activities themselves (Naumes & Naumes, 1999). Similarly, if we believe that knowledge is situated in social contexts and we want teachers to teach in collaborative ways, the manner in which they are taught must reflect processes of community building and inclusion. The use of cases and cased-based pedagogy not only can promote the integration of theory and practice, but can also assist in bridging this gap through collegial dialogue.

Similarly, the case approach is proposed as a means of assisting students of teaching in dealing with the many dilemmas they will encounter in their classroom practice. Traditionally, field experiences of pre-service programs have been identified as the preferable way to provide students with opportunities to develop practical and theoretical knowledge; however, many scholars have questioned this practice (Doyle, 1986; Feiman-Nemser & Buchmann, 1986). Cases may overcome some of the shortcomings of field and clinical experiences by providing prospective teachers with opportunities for reflection while facilitating their professional development (Carter, 1988; Merseth, 1991). As Donald Schon writes (1987), case-based approaches to teaching support a conception of teachers as critical inquirers who reflect on and in practice. Although most elementary science educators would agree that teachers should be reflective, they do not necessarily agree on what is meant by reflection. We believe, as do others (Harrington, Quinn-Lerring, & Hodson, 1996; Schon, 1987; Smyth, 1992; Zeichner & Tabachnik, 1991), that critical reflection is socially mediated. This means that our students' reflections should be open to multiple perspectives; consider the social, political, ideological, moral, and ethical content of their assumptions; and identify options, alternatives, and possibilities for future inquiry.

The case authors in this book have independently and uniquely defined the dilemmas and struggles of their own practice. We encourage elementary science teachers and science educators who interact with these cases to recognize how their own assumptions influence the ways in which they make sense of the dilemmas portrayed in each narrative. Additionally, we ask readers to consider the deep social, moral, ethical, and political structures that surround each case.

RESEARCH ON CASE-BASED INSTRUCTION AND ITS USEFULNESS AS AN INSTRUCTIONAL APPROACH IN TEACHER EDUCATION

The use of cases and case-based pedagogy in teacher education has grown tremendously since 1990. Although carefully grounded in theory, the various arguments for the use of teaching cases are often promotional, based on anecdotal evidence, and involve an assortment of unrelated and noncumulative published studies (Grossman, 1992, Harrington, 1995; Richardson

& Kile, 1992; L. Shulman, 1992). Until the mid-1990s, any empirical evidence of how cases were being used in teacher education and their effects on prospective and practicing teachers was rarely evident. Only recently have teacher educators begun to define an empirical basis of what case-based pedagogy actually means for teachers.

Lundeberg, in her chapter "Discovering Teaching and Learning through Cases" (Lundeberg et al., 1999), constructed a model of research related to the kinds of understanding about teaching and learning that prospective teachers may develop through the use of cases. She presented research evidence to suggest that case discussions can assist pre-service teachers by enabling them to do the following:

- Apply theoretical and practical knowledge to specific school contexts and
- Reason critically about classroom dilemmas and propose courses of action. Through vicarious engagement in case stories, pre-service teachers make discoveries about themselves as future teachers and as learners. As pre-service teachers write about and discuss case situations, they
- Develop metacognition with regard to one's own teaching, and
- Examine their beliefs about teaching. Using cases also enables pre-service teachers to discover how colleagues' perspectives, values, and ideas may influence changes in their understanding of teaching and learning. This influence of learning through social interaction helps pre-service teachers to
- Value social, ethical, and epistemological growth. (pp. 3–4)

PHILOSOPHICAL AND PEDAGOGICAL UNDERPINNINGS OF THIS CASEBOOK

Like many teacher educators, we are enthusiastic about the use of cases and case-based pedagogy in education—and science education in particular. However, because of the many different definitions and assumptions about the effectiveness of cases and their link to theory, it is incumbent on us to make our perspectives on case-based pedagogy explicit. A basic premise of this book is that teachers at all levels are holders and creators of knowledge, which is reflected in personal and social narratives of experience. The narratives in our book were written by educators to describe challenging situations that occurred in the context of elementary science teaching and learning. These stories cannot be wrapped up in neat and tidy packages at the end of each discussion. Instead, they reflect the complexity and ambiguity of teaching and learning science through interwoven scenes and plots. They are stories that are rooted in the lived experiences of children, teachers, and administrators; are mediated by the subject matter; and are situated in diverse communities. These case narratives, as representatives of teacher knowledge, are constructed in the classroom through the interaction of teachers' experience with information derived from the discipline of science. Accordingly, knowledge is not considered to exist as an external body of information independent of humans; nor can it be completely codified to the extent that a complete set of consistent principles or scientific theories drive teachers' classroom decisions. Rather, the creation of knowledge can be understood as an inductive process in which teachers make sense of multiple experiences in contextualized settings. Case-based pedagogy is particularly suitable in light of perspectives that view knowledge as "constructed, built on prior knowledge, coupled with experience, transformable, evolving, and sequential and, thereby, provides students with insight into alternative solutions rather than 'correct' answers" (Harrington, 1995, p. 203).

We view case-based pedagogy as a pedagogical tool that can promote discussion, engage diverse perspectives, and explore critical issues of science teaching and learning. We do not approach the use of cases as models of exemplary or ineffective practice. Rather, we view cases as "windows into science classrooms" (Tobin, Kahle, & Fraser, 1990), where teachers wrestle with the experiences, ideas, issues, and dilemmas of practice.

Miller and Kantrov (1998) use a similar metaphor of windows and mirrors that helps to identify the essential value and variety of cases. Participants in a case discussion reflect on and discuss what they see through the window of the case: the actions, issues, and characters that they find engaging. Participants also consider and talk about what they find reflected through the mirror of the case: their own reactions to what they see and what those reactions tell them about themselves and their own circumstances. Working with others, people learn how what appears through the window of the case is reflected differently in others' mirrors. This awareness of difference opens up the possibility of change (pp. 5–6).

NATURE OF THE CASES IN THIS BOOK

The cases you are about to read describe actual or fictional events that occurred in urban, suburban, or rural elementary science classrooms and other informal science environments. We use an open and closed case format to depict the narratives included in this book. Although each case is characterized by a central dilemma or challenge, multiple story lines interact and bear on one another without clearly defined solutions or outcomes. A second author discusses potential solutions or resolutions to the dilemmas portrayed in each case. In several instances, two respondents offer diverse perspectives from which to consider the story depicted in each case. We describe closed cases as ones in which the author is able to resolve the dilemma in some manner. A second, and sometimes third, author provides a personal interpretation of the case and opinions about the viability of the solutions described in the narrative. We recognize that these open and closed cases do not stand alone in isolation from professional practice. Any case in a book such as this cannot do justice to all the relevant features of the situation, such as the feelings, experiences, and history of the individuals involved. While reading these cases, you might sometimes say to yourself, "I don't have enough information to be able to decide!" However, readers and users of this book are encouraged to think of the solutions to open cases and responses to closed cases from various perspectives, rather than searching for "the right answer." The open and closed cases in this book invite different perspectives and provide opportunities for prospective and practicing teachers to articulate and consider various viewpoints. Participants have the chance both to reflect on their own experiences and to hear another's ideas. Even if prospective or practicing teachers share similar interpretations of cases, these interpretations do not necessarily lead to similar solutions (Nichols, Tippins, & Wieseman, 1997). There is as yet no single commonly accepted strategy for case-based teaching, so be creative and imaginative as you create additional case contexts and explore issues. The discussion of these cases should help you to examine your values, beliefs, knowledge, and problem-solving skills.

Each case in this book is preceded by an abstract that briefly summarizes the case and is followed by Questions for Reflection and Discussion. We suggest that individuals read through a case in its entirety and respond initially to the questions for reflection individually or through group discussion before reading case solutions and responses. We provide specific guidelines for developing open and closed case narratives in the final chapter of this book.

The case narratives, solutions, and responses presented in this book are designed to preserve the insights shared by authors from their unique perspectives. To avoid imposing an interpretation drawn from our own respective worldviews, our editorial work was informed by collaborative dialogue with the authors. Case and response authors come from a variety of positions with respect to science teacher education. Elementary classroom teachers, prospective and practicing elementary science teachers, student teachers, administrators, graduate students, scientists, informal science educators, and college/university-based science teacher educators all contributed to the development of this book. The authors generally relate case narratives that describe experiences embedded within their unique roles as educators. Their stories are characterized by a variety of writing styles, which we believe ultimately "enrich our understanding and are integral to the personalities of these authors" (Kagan & Tippins, 1993).

We believe that the cases in our book meet the criteria described by McNergney, Herbert, and Ford (1994), which state that cases should allow for "multiple levels of analysis and be sufficiently rich to make room for multiple interpretations" (p. 340). In other words, the cases in our book offer opportunities for analysis on more than one level and are sufficiently complex to invite multiple interpretations. In an effort to invite students to explore multiple interpretations, layers of commentary are built into several of the cases. Judith Shulman (1992) initially introduced the idea of building a case with layers of commentary. Our cases are accounts of classroom dilemmas, which are followed by commentaries from other teachers or educational scholars who have personal involvement, knowledge, or insight with respect to the situation. The commentaries raise issues in the case but do not necessarily provide solutions or answers. Judith Shulman (1992) suggests that narratives with layered commentaries can link cases to research, provide multiple perspectives on the same issue, or create a context for action. Our goal for this case book is not to impose a particular view or prescribe the one way to approach a situation, but rather to expose different ways of looking at things. All the stories in this book will no doubt raise more questions than they answer.

References

Abell, S. K., & Roth, W. M. (1992). Constraints to teaching elementary science: A case study of a science enthusiast student teacher. *Science Education, 76,* 581–595.

Akerson, V. L., & Flanigan, J. (2000). Preparing preservice teachers to use an interdisciplinary approach to science and language arts instruction. *Journal of Science Teacher Education, 11*(4), 345–362.

American Association for the Advancement of Science. (1989). *Science for all Americans.* New York: Oxford University Press.

Anderson, R. D., & Mitchner, C. P. (1994). Research on teacher education. In D. Gabel (Ed.), *Handbook of research on science teaching and learning* (pp. 3–44). New York: Macmillan.

Arends, R. I. (1994). *Learning to teach* (3rd ed.). New York: McGraw-Hill.

Barba, R. H. (1998). *Science in the multicultural classroom* (2nd ed.). Boston: Allyn & Bacon.

Barnett, C., & Tyson, A. (1993, April). *Case methods and teacher change: Shifting authority to build autonomy.* Paper presented at the annual meeting of the American Educational Research Association, Atlanta, GA.

Bereiter, C., & Scardamalia, M. (1987). An attainable version of high literacy: Approaches teaching higher-order skills in reading and writing. *Curriculum Inquiry, 17*(1), 9–29.

Borko, H. (1991). The integration of content and pedagogy in teaching. In A. L. Gardner & K. F. Cochran (Eds.), *Critical issues in reforming elementary teacher preparation in mathematics and science. Conference proceedings* (pp. 25–45). Greeley, CO: University of Northern Colorado. (ERIC Document Reproduction No. ED 359176)

Carter, K. (1988). Conveying classroom knowledge through cases: A proposal for framing mentor/novice conversations about teaching. *Theory into Practice, 27,* 214–222.

Clark, C., & Lampert, M. (1986). The study of teacher thinking: Implications for teacher education. *Journal of Teacher Education, 37*(5), 27–31.

Cooper, J. A., & McNergney, R. F. (1995). Introduction: The value of cases in teacher education. In J. A. Cooper (Ed.), *Teachers' problem solving a casebook of award-winning teaching cases.* Boston: Allyn & Bacon.

Doyle, W. (1986, March). *The world is everything that is the case: Developing case methods for teacher education.* Paper presented to the Annual Meeting of the American Educational Research Association, San Francisco.

Driver, R., Asoko, H., Leach, J., Mortimer, E., & Scott, P. (1994). Constructing scientific knowledge in the classroom. *Educational Researcher, 23*(7), 5–12.

Elbaz, F. (1991). Research on teachers' knowledge: The evolution of a discourse. *Journal of Curriculum Studies, 23,* 1–19.

Feiman-Nemser, S., & Buchmann, M. (1986). Pitfalls of experience in teacher preparation. In J. Raths & L. Katz (Eds). *Advances in teacher education* (Vol. 2, pp. 61–73). Norwood, NJ: Ablex.

Flick, L. B. (1995). Navigating in a sea of ideas: Teacher and students negotiate a course toward mutual relevance. *Journal of Research in Science Teaching, 32,* 1065–1082.

Griffith, P., & Laframboise, K. L. (1997). The structures and patterns of case method talk: What our students taught us. *Action in Teacher Education, 18* (4), 10–22.

Grossman, P. L. (1992). Teaching and learning with cases. In J. H. Shulman (Ed.), *Case methods in teacher education* (pp. 227–239). New York: Teachers College Press.

Harrington, H. L. (1995). Fostering reasoned decisions: Case-based pedagogy and the professional development of teachers. *Teaching and Teacher Education, 11,* 203–214.

Harrington, H. L., Quinn-Lerring, K., & Hodson, L. (1996). Written case analyses and critical reflection. *Teaching and Teacher Education, 12*(1), 25–37.

Kagan, D. M. (1993). Contexts for the use of classroom cases. *American Educational Research Journal, 30,* 703–723.

Kagan, D. M., & Tippins, D. J. (1993). Classroom cases as gauges of professional growth. In M. O'Hair & S. Odell (Eds.), *Teacher education yearbook 1: Diversity and teaching* (pp. 98–110). New York: Harcourt Brace Jovanovich and the Association of Teacher Educators.

Knirk, F. G. (1991). Case materials: Research and practice. *Performance Improvement Quarterly, 4*(1), 73–81.

Koballa, T. R., & Tippins, D. J. (Eds.) (2000). *Cases in middle and secondary science education.* Upper Saddle River, NJ: Merrill.

Kowalski, T. J., Weaver, R. A., & Henson, K. T. (1994). *Case studies of beginning teachers.* New York: Longman.

Lundeberg, M., Levin, B. B., & Harrington, H. L. (1999). *Who learns what from cases and how: The research base for teaching and learning with cases.* Mahwah, NJ: Lawrence Erlbaum Associates.

McNergney, R., Herbert, J., & Ford, R. (1994). Cooperation and competition in cases-based education. *Journal of Teacher Education, 45*(5), 339–345.

Merseth, K. K. (1991). *The case for cases in teacher education.* Washington, DC: American Association for Higher Education and American Association of Colleges for Teacher Education.

Miller, B., & Kantrov, I. (1998). *A guide to facilitating cases in education.* Portsmouth, NH: Heinemann.

National Research Council. (1996). *National science education standards.* Washington, DC: National Research Council.

Naumes, W., & Naumes, M. J. (1999). *The art and craft of case writing.* Thousand Oaks, CA: Sage Publications.

Nichols, S., Tippins, D., & Wieseman, K. (1997). A "toolkit" for developing critically reflective science teachers. *Journal of Science Teacher Education, 8*(2), 77–106.

Phillips, D. C. (1995). The good, the bad, and the ugly: The many faces of constructivism. *Educational Researcher, 24,* 5–12.

Redman, G. L. (1999). *Teaching in today's classrooms: Cases from elementary education.* Upper Saddle River, NJ: Merrill.

Richardson, V., & Kile, S. (1992, April). *The use of videocases in teacher education.* Paper presented at the annual meeting of the American Educational Research Association, San Francisco.

Schon, D. A. (1983). *The reflective practitioner.* New York: Basic Books.

Schon, D. A. (1987). *Educating the reflective practitioner.* San Francisco: Jossey-Bass.

Shulman, J. H. (Ed.). (1992). *Case methods in teacher education.* New York: Teachers College Press.

Shulman, L. (1992). Toward a pedagogy of cases. In J. Shulman (Ed.), *Case methods in teacher education* (pp. 1–30). New York: Teachers College Press.

Silverman, R., Welty, W. M., & Lyon, S. (1994). *Classroom management cases for teacher problem solving.* New York: McGraw-Hill.

Smyth, J. (1992). Teachers' work and the politics of reflection. *American Educational Research Journal, 29,* 267–300.

Tobin, K., Kahle, J. B., & Fraser, B. J. (1990). *Windows into science classrooms: Problems associated with high level cognitive learning in science.* London: Falmer.

Weiss, I. S. (1987). *Report of the 1985–86 National Survey of Science and Mathematics Education.* National Science Foundation, SPE-8317070. Washington, DC: U.S. Government Printing Office.

Zeichner, K., & Tabachnik, R. (1991). Reflections on reflective teaching. In R. Tabachnik & K. Zeichner (Eds.), *Issues and practices in inquiry-oriented teacher education* (pp. 1–21). London: Falmer Press.

2

Children as Scientists in the Elementary Classroom

Many young children today are growing up in a manner that isolates them from opportunities to explore and be involved in their world. Science education at the early childhood level means finding ways to help children make sense of what is happening in the world around them. It is difficult to imagine the world through the eyes of a child. As research suggests, a young child's perception of the world and his or her way of learning differ considerably from those of older children (Wilson, 1994, p. 7). Nevertheless, most science teachers recognize that young children have a marvelous propensity for selecting, interpreting, and organizing information to make sense of their world in unique ways. A critical role for science teachers is to guide students in their struggle for understanding by creating environments that encourage sense making and exploration of their world. The type of early childhood science learning that we envision is one that encourages students to ask questions and prepares them to deal with ambiguities. And as the *National Science Education Standards* (1996) suggest, it takes place in an environment premised on the belief that learning is something that students do, not something that is done to them (p. 2). This does not mean, however, that doing activities becomes the goal of science teaching and learning or that vicarious experience with science, in and of itself, adequately supports meaningful science learning. As the cases in this chapter illustrate, teachers are more than conduits through which information may pass; they play an essential role in cultivating a vision of classrooms where young children can be scientists.

The three cases in this chapter explore dilemmas that early childhood science educators face in their efforts to create meaningful science learning environments. In the first case, "Inquiry: To Do or Not to Do?," Anita Roychoudhury explores novice teacher Sandra Montgomery's attempt to teach science by inquiry in a school where this kind of teaching is neither understood nor valued. Carla Zembal-Saul recognizes that teachers and students can be researchers together. Her case, "Insects and Scientific Problem-Solving Go Together," tells the story of Amanda and her experiences in Bug Camp and how these experiences transform Amanda's teaching practice and lead her to seek ways to help students become good problem solvers. This chapter concludes with Denise Mewborne's case, "How Full Is Full?," which reflects on the role of questioning in helping young children to explore firsthand scientific and mathematical relationships among phenomena.

■   C A S E   2 . 1   ■

Inquiry: To Do or Not to Do?

Anita Roychoudhury

■ *Sandra Montgomery is a new teacher at a high-poverty urban school who has been assigned to plan the science lessons for all the classes taught by members of her fourth grade team. She believes in teaching by inquiry, but the predominant mode of teaching among veteran teachers at her school involves giving information to students through direct instructional methods. The difference between what Sandra believes is good science teaching and what is practiced and advocated by the veteran teachers creates a dilemma for her. Should she adopt the school culture and try to fit in, or should she teach in her own way and deal with the conflicts that accompany being a misfit? Sandra is the pseudonym for one of Anita's former university students, who continues to consult with her about science teaching and learning. This open case is followed by a response written by Carolyn Wallace, a science educator who teaches elementary science methods courses and conducts research on inquiry teaching.*

The students who attend Gordon Elementary School come from a neighborhood where drugs, crime, and physical and other kinds of abuse are part of the daily life of children. All students take part in the free lunch and breakfast programs of the school. The reading and mathematical abilities of a large group of students are below grade level. Many students drop out after they finish sixth grade.

Teachers at Gordon Elementary work in grade-level teams. They plan their lessons and assessment measures together and attempt to make various decisions cooperatively. Sandra Montgomery and Bridget Pass are two first-year teachers teamed with fifteen-year veteran Joyce Lott. Mrs. Lott has taught at Gordon for her entire teaching career and takes great pride in her teaching as well as her classroom management skills. She has assumed responsibility for guiding the young teachers in the practical methods of teaching these low-ability students, often touting her past experience and her master's degree.

Mrs. Lott asked Sandra to take charge of planning the physical science lessons on motion, force, gravity, and energy for the team because of Sandra's strong science background. On agreeing to do so, Sandra was reminded by Mrs. Lott of the importance of planning the lessons to follow the district curriculum. Adherence to the curriculum was deemed necessary because students often move from one school to another within the district.

Sandra believes that students should learn by doing. She does not want her students to follow recipe-type steps in science or any other subject. She wants them to explore, think about certain concepts, and come up with their own explanations. Her plans include some questions to guide large-group discussions at the end of the activities so that students learn the science concepts at the core of the lessons.

Consistent with the plans she developed for her team, Sandra proceeded to teach her fourth graders about motion by inquiry. Her objectives were to have students explore the motion of wind-up cars, study what makes a car move, and speculate on what makes it stop. Sandra organized her students in groups of four with each person assigned a role. They had worked in similar groups on simple measurement tasks before, following definite protocols. But for this activity, Sandra gave the students only two open-ended questions: (1) What do you think makes the car move? (2) What do you think makes the car stop?

About fifteen minutes into the lesson, Sandra observed that most of the class was playing with the cars, and only a few students were writing down their observations. At this point, she realized that a little more guidance was needed, and she began to circulate from group to group. A few students who had written down a response to the first question asked Sandra whether they were right. She insisted that they need not worry about the correct response right now; just writing down their thoughts was enough. After she said this to a group of students near the door of her classroom, she heard Mrs. Lott's soft voice behind her: "These kids don't know what to do with such open-ended questions. You have to ask them something concrete." Mrs. Lott apologized for interrupting and explained that she had come to give Sandra a memo from the principal and could not help but offer the suggestion.

During the team meeting after school that day, Mrs. Lott told Sandra that the group work that she had observed during this lesson was too chaotic. In her opinion, the students at Gordon Elementary did not have any leadership qualities and were therefore unable to work together. If they had to work in groups, then there should be very specific protocols like the one she had designed for the measurement activities. Students need to have step-by-step instruction, particularly for complex concepts in physical science, Mrs. Lott insisted.

After listening intently for several minutes, Sandra finally spoke: "I think that if they do these kind of activities regularly, then they will learn to construct reasons of their own, and later they can learn scientific explanations by comparing their observations with their reasoning."

"Yes, but look how much time it took to teach them that they must do something to move the car and that friction stopped the car," countered Mrs. Lott. "You could show it to them, explain what was happening, then have them do worksheets and practice vocabulary. These students need to practice writing a lot."

"But they will not learn science that way," explained Sandra forcefully. "They need to make their own observations and write them down. It is invaluable!"

"Sandra, that all sounds very good, but don't forget, we have so many topics to cover to get them ready for the proficiency exam. You need to budget your time to cover all the topics in the curriculum. These are the topics tested on the exam, you know. Besides, these children don't need to inquire deeply about these or other science topics. They won't go to college. Think about their family backgrounds! What you are trying might work in middle-class and rich schools, but not here at Gordon. Trust me, I've been teaching here for a long time. I know what works!"

On her drive home that afternoon, Sandra reflected on her conversation with Mrs. Lott and what had happened earlier during her science lesson. She was pleased that the students were engaged with the materials but disappointed that only a few seemed to be writing down answers and thinking deeply about the forces that move and stop the cars. She thought about how important it is to teach children to work in groups and to record their observations and inferences. She knew that this would not happen quickly or easily. Sandra also realized that from an outsider's perspective the classroom might have appeared chaotic. Students were talking loudly and lying all over the floor, and some were even arguing about who should wind up the cars. She knew that this type of student behavior did not fit the image of teaching shared by Mrs. Lott and other veteran teachers at the school. Sandra understood that order and discipline are of utmost importance at Gordon Elementary. Chaos in a classroom is interpreted as the teacher's inability to manage students' learning. Sandra's thoughts also focused on her teaching team. On the basis of their recent discussions, she knew that Bridget was also feeling stifled by Mrs. Lott. She wondered why their teaching team was called "team," since they had to follow Mrs. Lott's suggestions, even if they seemed flawed. As Sandra turned in to her driveway and parked her car, she found herself with questions in need of answers: Is it best to teach science by inquiry or as show-and-tell followed by giving students the correct answers and practicing vocabulary? Is it okay to ignore Mrs. Lott's suggestions? How will ignoring Mrs. Lott's suggestions affect our relationship and my relationship with other veteran teachers in the school?

FOR REFLECTION AND DISCUSSION

1. What is your definition of inquiry teaching? What elements of your definition are found in Sandra's lesson? What elements of your definition would you suggest she incorporate?

2. What are some beliefs about disadvantaged learners that seem to affect Mrs. Lott's advice about how to teach children at Gordon Elementary School?

3. How might Sandra resolve the tension she is feeling between Mrs. Lott's mandate to cover the prescribed curriculum using direct instructional methods and her belief in the strength of inquiry teaching to ensure meaningful student learning?

4. Veteran teachers at Sandra's school use student noise and movement to make judgments about student learning. What other factors might a classroom observer use to gauge the effectiveness of a teacher's science lesson?

5. Grade-level teaming in which teachers work together to plan the curriculum for a group of students is a common practice in many elementary schools. What recommendations might Sandra and Bridget make to Mrs. Lott to improve the functioning of their grade-level team?

■ COMMENTARY

Inquiry Is Not for the Faint of Heart

Carolyn Wallace

Sandra is facing a double dilemma. Not only is she struggling with the issue of how to teach science to her students, but she is also faced with confronting Mrs. Lott, a more experienced and powerful teacher in the school. As a university science educator interested in facilitating inquiry in classrooms, I can empathize with Sandra, because I've had similar experiences. I recently taught an inquiry lesson on dissolving solids in liquids to a group of students from a low socioeconomic area. I wanted the students to design their own experiments to determine how various factors, such as heat and amount of solvent, affect dissolving rates. Although the students were for the most part engaged with the lesson and practiced several laboratory skills, I'm not sure how much they learned about the concepts at the heart of the lesson. Many outcomes of the lesson were unexpected. For example, the most memorable learning for one student occurred when she learned how to use the second hand on her watch!

Because inquiry is open-ended, not only the lesson outcomes, but also the agenda of the class and the behavior of the students are unpredictable. This is a very challenging situation for any teacher, particularly if the students have not had many opportunities for independent learning either at home or in previous school experiences. Teachers like Sandra who want to use inquiry approaches will face uncertainty about both classroom management and the level at which students are constructing conceptual understandings from the experiences. Some of this uncertainty is due to the opposing nature of two important elements of learning science by inquiry: freedom and privileging. To capture the spirit of inquiry, teachers must allow their students freedom to ask questions, make a range of observations, try out interpretations, and experiment with materials. Yet scientific ideas have been constructed throughout history within a complex web of social consensus, so some ideas, observations, and skills are privileged over others. Children's naive views may be reasonable, but they are not all scientifically correct, and learning science involves coming to understand the scientific concepts and explanations that are most useful for understanding the natural world. The tension between freedom to think on one's own and coming to understand the privileged ideas of others can be a major roadblock in teaching and learning science by inquiry.

Some educators have noted that it is particularly important to use direct instructional methods to teach concepts and skills to students who do not have the resources to learn them on their own. For example, the children of groups that are traditionally underrepresented in science often come from cultures in which the white European interpretation of science is not valued or discussed. These children need to know what is expected of them to succeed in the culture of school science, and they must be provided with opportunities to learn the privileged skills, such as observation and prediction, that are necessary to function in that culture. This point of view contrasts with that of educators who emphasize open-ended, hands-on exploration for children and the significance of physical and social interaction in constructing scientific understandings.

I suggest to Sandra that she provide a wide range of approaches to science instruction for her students. For example, she could design several open-ended lessons, with materials such as a sandbox, a water table, and moving toys and ramps, in which students are free to play with the materials and investigate on their own. Using these materials, they will be able to develop physical and social knowledge through experiences. During these open-ended lessons, Sandra could challenge the children to pose their own questions and try to solve them without being held strictly accountable for the "right science answer."

In parallel to open-ended activities, Sandra could design several teacher-directed activities to focus on the cognitive and social skills that the students will need to engage meaningfully in science inquiry. For example, she could teach them how to work in cooperative groups, how to discuss science ideas with each other, how to make scientific drawings and written observations, how to be a careful observer, and how to pose useful scientific questions, while using some of the materials and ideas from the motion unit. My belief is that she should not worry about linking the open-ended activities with the teacher-directed activities at first but allow the students opportunities to build skills in both arenas simultaneously. After a few weeks of practice, she can begin to bring the two types of instruction closer together so that students become accustomed to using their skills to answer questions in an open-ended investigative environment. Once students begin to think scientifically, I believe Sandra will find it less problematic and time consuming to teach specific science concepts through inquiry.

What should Sandra do about her problem with Mrs. Lott? I believe that Sandra needs to assert her own teaching beliefs, or she may never be happy with herself as an elementary teacher. Sandra will need to muster all her people skills to confront Mrs. Lott and convince her that time is needed to teach the children the skills that they need to learn science. Sandra should inform Mrs. Lott that she will plan the science curriculum to include as many of the district objectives as possible but that she will not sacrifice meaningful learning just to give lip service to the objectives. Sandra's stance will require ingenuity and courage, but I believe that her students are worth it.

■ **C A S E   2 . 2** ■

Insects and Scientific Problem Solving Go Together

Carla Zembal-Saul

■ *In this open case, Carla tells the story of Amanda, a beginning fourth grade teacher who discovers the natural curiosity of the children in her class when she introduces a unit on insects.*

As students explore a variety of creatures, they begin to make detailed observations and ask interesting questions about insects. Although her unit includes many hands-on activities, Amanda recognizes that something is missing. For her students to pursue their original questions about insects, they will need to develop problem-solving skills. As she considers the kinds of skills her students need and the ways in which she might assist them in developing such skills, Amanda draws on an experience she had during her teacher preparation program in which elementary children designed and conducted research projects using insects. The case is presented in Amanda's voice and is followed by commentary from Robert W. Matthews, an entomologist with a wealth of experience in guiding teachers and children in the investigation of insects.

Being new to teaching, I was a little anxious about my first science unit, which I recently introduced to my fourth graders. I spent several weeks before the introductory lesson playing up the topic of the unit with my students: insects! Therefore, it was not surprising that students began bringing specimens to class—some living, some pinned. Anna brought her praying mantis in an aquarium; Joey brought his butterfly and moth collection; Meghan brought a Tupperware container filled with damp leaves, dirt, and roly polys. Given the growing collection of insects, I decided to begin the first lesson with an observation period that focused on student specimens as well as our class mascots, a pair of hissing cockroaches. The children were thoroughly engrossed. As they squealed with excitement, I began recording their observations and questions on the board.

"Look! I found a whole bunch of roly polys under a rock. I wonder why they hang out there?"

"It tickles when the cockroach walks on my hand. Hey! It can hang on when I hold it upside down!"

"The moths look *fuzzier* than the butterflies—their colors are more boring, too."

"Check it out! The little praying mantis is white, but the big one is green. Do you think it's an albino?"

"Wait! Roly polys can't be insects—they have more than six legs."

This went on for well over our allotted time for science. With very little direction from me, some children gathered around the computer and started to do an Internet search on insects. A few others carefully examined insect books that I had gathered at a resource table in the back of the room. Yet another group was involved in a heated debate over whether roly polys were indeed insects. I watched in amazement. The students' natural curiosity was certainly aroused by insects. They were making detailed and astute observations that led to thoughtful and intriguing questions. My amazement shifted to dismay as I realized that I ran a terrible risk of stifling this excitement with my well-organized unit modified from the district curriculum guide. Although it included many hands-on activities, worksheets, and demonstrations, my unit was missing something. At this juncture, what my students really needed was to develop sciencing skills that would support them in pursuing their wonderings about insects. How was I ever going to help them with that?

This question took me back to an experience I had in my teacher preparation program. I took elementary science methods over the summer. Because public schools were not in session, the associated field placements were nontraditional. On the first day of class, it was announced that we would be mentoring elementary children (8–12 years old) attending Bug Camp for Kids and Advanced Bug Camp, two week-long day camps hosted by Penn State's Department of

Entomology. Initially, I was horrified. I didn't know much about bugs, aside from the fact that I didn't want to spend my summer with them. My anxieties had peaked by the time Bug Camp for Kids began; however, I was surprised to learn that the kids didn't share my perspective. They were excited about insects and not the least bit afraid of handling them. By the end of the week, I was actually starting to appreciate six-legged critters and was gaining confidence as I learned more about them. I even held an Australian walking stick and ate a chocolate-covered cricket!

I was feeling pretty good about my summer science experience until I learned that the focus of Advanced Bug Camp was to support elementary students in conducting original research with insects. How was I going to help kids do this when I had never experienced it myself? I guess the staff must have considered this, too, because prospective elementary teachers like me were paired with entomology graduate students. Interestingly, during the ice-breaker activity at the orientation session, it became apparent that the graduate students were as concerned about working with children as we future teachers were about doing science. One of my peers eased the tension with a phrase that became our credo for the summer: "Don't squash the kids, and we won't squash the bugs!"

To help mentors—both entomology graduate students and education majors—gain a better understanding of the kinds of abilities students would need to develop to conduct their research projects, the bug camp staff engaged us in an activity using paper airplanes (Cothron, Giese, & Rezba, 1993) that addressed the basic concepts of experimental design: developing a hypothesis, identifying variables, establishing controls, and conducting repeated trials. I had memorized the definitions of these terms at some point, but my recollection was more than a little hazy. The activity clarified a number of issues for me and helped me to understand what these concepts look like in action. Was I ready to help kids do this, though?

I arrived at Advanced Bug Camp still feeling unsure of my capacity to support children's scientific inquiry in any meaningful way. Seeing the kids and how excited they were to be there eased some of my anxieties. We all introduced ourselves by sharing a question we had about insects based on an observation we had made. We were halfway through the introductions before it hit me that we were starting already. This was the essence of doing science: It's as much about the questions as it is the answers.

After touring several research labs and interacting with a number of entomologists, we organized into research groups (two children, one entomology graduate student or staff member, and two prospective elementary teachers per group) and got down to the business of crafting researchable questions. The two girls in my group had become very interested in biological control of crop pests, specifically parasitic wasps, during the lab tours. In particular, they wanted to know how the wasps knew to target particular pests when laying their eggs. It took some work, but our graduate student mentor, Erin, helped them to refine their idea into a testable question: "Does the wasp *Cotesia congregata* have a favorite host?" The girls were ready to proceed by placing three caterpillars of different species into a container with several wasps. Erin asked, "How will we know the wasps didn't just oviposit [deposit eggs] into the first caterpillar they encountered?" Through a series of guiding questions, Erin helped the girls realize that for their test to be fair and meaningful, they would need to set up separate containers, each having the same number of wasps and caterpillars of a given species. In addition, they would have to observe for equal amounts of time and repeat their trials the same number of times for each.

The girls decided on three different species of caterpillars: the tobacco hornworm, tobacco budworm, and cabbage looper. Next, we helped them set up twelve containers with equal

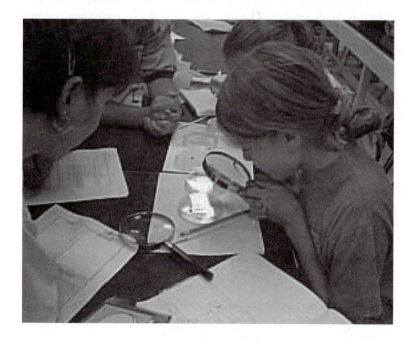

numbers of wasps in each. Using four of each species of caterpillar, we placed one in each container and made observations for ten minutes per container to determine whether and how often the wasps would oviposit. In other words, four trials were conducted for each species of caterpillar. The results were dramatic. In three out of four trials, the wasps oviposited in the tobacco hornworms. None of the other caterpillars were touched by the wasps.

The girls were very excited about their findings, which were fairly conclusive. However, their results had generated even more questions. Clearly, the wasps preferred the tobacco hornworms, but how did the wasps locate them, especially in a large crop? Were the wasps using their vision or sense of smell? Again, with a little support from Erin, the girls designed an experiment in which they developed three treatments: painting the wasps' eyes black (no vision); removing the antennae (no smell), and painting the eyes and removing the antennae (no vision or smell). At this point, one of the girls suggested that we include some wasps that had not undergone any of the treatments so that we could make comparisons. Erin agreed and said that this was a very important aspect of experimental design: Always include a control group. The girls conducted four trials (ten minute observation periods) for each of the treatments and the control. Across all of the trials, only the control wasps oviposited; therefore, the girls concluded that the wasps needed both their sense of vision and their sense of smell to locate tobacco hornworms. However, they did admit that the stress of the treatments might have influenced their findings.

The majority of our time in Advanced Bug Camp was spent working in our research groups; however, each day ended in a round table discussion in the Entomology Department conference room. During this time, teams reported on their progress. The final afternoon culminated with research talks in which teams presented their questions, hypotheses, methods, findings, and conclusions. Time for whole group discussion was provided, and each group was encouraged to end its presentation by sharing new questions that arose from their research. I remember being so proud of my team and feeling such a sense of accomplishment. I had been somewhat skeptical all along about the capabilities of elementary children to engage in such an ambitious project. What an underestimate! This was science; and with the proper scaffolding and skill development, kids could do it.

Why had it taken me so long to return to this experience? Unfortunately, it had been all too easy to slip back into a more traditional mode, making excuses for why a bug camp approach would never work in a classroom setting. "One teacher could never facilitate such a project with an entire class of students." "Children need more structure; they have never done anything like this before and they don't have the necessary skills." "The curriculum is too packed with actual science content to spend time on problem-solving and sciencing." "The kids at Advanced Bug Camp opted to be there. Most children don't have the necessary abilities or interests."

Watching the children in my fourth grade class, I knew that there was the potential to create a community of young scientists; in fact, they were already well started on their own. The responsibility for fully realizing this potential was mine. The task at hand: translating my bug camp experience into classroom practice. The ultimate aim: helping children to develop the problem-solving skills necessary to pursue their science-related questions.

FOR REFLECTION AND DISCUSSION

1. Through her Bug Camp experiences and observing her fourth graders, Amanda came to value problem solving and the processes of science as much as content. What role do you think problem solving plays in elementary science education?

2. Which Bug Camp activities might Amanda modify for use in her own classroom to support the development of children's problem-solving skills? What might those modifications look like?

3. In Advanced Bug Camp, the children were supported by a number of adults—scientists and teachers. As the only adult in her fourth grade classroom, what strategies might Amanda use to facilitate small group research projects?

4. At the end of her story, Amanda summarizes some of the excuses she generated that made it easier to dismiss a problem-solving approach in the classroom and return to an activity-based curriculum. How would you respond to each of these points?

■ COMMENTARY

When It Is New to You Both

Robert W. Matthews

Amanda writes, "The student's natural curiosity was certainly aroused by insects." How true! How often I have observed the same. At the same time, Amanda's reaction—"How was I ever going to help them?"—is one that all teachers confront at various times in their careers. Part of Amanda's dilemma stems from a feeling of being unprepared, and this feeling is often justified. A survey of seventh grade life science teachers in Georgia (Koballa et al., 1997) revealed that most received no more than one to two weeks of instruction on insects or arthropods, usually as part of a comprehensive unit surveying invertebrate diversity and classification. Fewer than 5 percent had undertaken any formal university-level coursework in entomology. This dearth of subject-matter training is not unique to the case of insects, of course. It could equally apply to geology, botany, or microbiology. Given the many subject areas for which elementary teachers must prepare, their preparation in science is inadequate for the challenges they will face in the real world of the classroom. Most of us find ourselves learning right along with our students, but as time goes on and we gain confidence in our abilities, this idea becomes progressively less threatening to us.

In the case of insects, a second factor also is often at work. As the largest and most diverse group of animals, insects evoke varied emotions, but "uncomfortable" would be a fair descriptor of the feelings of many teachers. Amanda's venture at the Bug Camp was a critical period in her development as a teacher. Like ducklings that imprint to form a lifelong attachment to whatever stimulus is presented during their first forty-eight hours of existence, Amanda had an experience that indelibly changed her expectations relating to insects and, more important, to how science is learned and should be taught.

In my experience, new teachers tend to be very reluctant to stray from their assigned curriculum and lesson plans. Even seasoned teachers are often hesitant to try new approaches. The usual excuses for such conservatism in classroom instruction all rear their heads in Amanda's story. All too often, these excuses make it easy for the teacher to rationalize stick-in-the mud behavior. However, because of her pivotal experience at Bug Camp, Amanda willingly sets aside her initial squeamishness about insects and is eager to try something new with her students, right from the start.

Amanda's remark "the essence of doing science: It's as much about the questions as it is the answers" is extremely perceptive. The overwhelming consensus of science educators is that exploratory activities with an element of inquiry succeed best in capturing interest, stimulating thinking, and developing scientific attributes that a real scientist uses. Lacking the resources and personnel of Bug Camp, how can Amanda create and facilitate a science experience for her students that will be true to this ideal?

As Amanda seems on the verge of realizing, a teacher doesn't need to be an expert on this diverse assemblage to use insects effectively in the classroom. However, she will probably find it easiest to start with one or more of the half-dozen widely available species for which background information is readily obtained (Matthews et al., 1997).

She can have the students work in small groups and begin by listing the insects or arthropods that they have questions about or are interested in. From their initial lists, Amanda can guide them to consider which bugs on their lists are readily available and safe. They will soon exclude black widow spiders and exotic walking sticks but will realize that arthropods such as roly polys, hissing roaches, mealworms, and crickets might be good experimental subjects—safe to handle and easily maintained in the classroom. Let each group vote for their favorite insect on the list and reach a consensus as to what their research subject organism will be. Alternatively, Amanda might have the entire class work on the same organism, but each group could research a different experimental question.

To formulate their research questions, I would suggest that Amanda guide her students with an approach adapted from Cothron et al. (1993). This powerful four-step technique works extremely well with any student problem solving, regardless of the specific area of investigation. To begin, Amanda can assign each group the task of brainstorming the question "What does your insect do?" The list will be long, and when each group shares its list with others, the lists will grow longer still. For example, a list of what crickets do would include crawl, fly, chirp, hop, eat, fight, and dig, and this is only a beginning.

Next, she can ask students to consider what things could be changed that might affect something that their chosen insect does. For example, for cricket hopping, they might come up with the idea of changing the substrate. Would standing on sand, glass, metal, paper, or gravel affect how far a cricket can jump?

Many fanciful ideas may arise during this session. That's fine, for it leads to the next question. Ask the children what materials are readily available for them to use that relate to each of the things their insect does and things that can be changed. Obviously, an electron microscope would not be on such a list. The availability of materials is a realistic constraint not only for classroom teachers, but for working scientists as well. (Later, after the particular research questions have been clarified, Amanda can send the honed list home to involve parents in gathering necessary materials, a potentially daunting task for a teacher to do alone.)

Now that her students have identified an experimental organism, a behavior of interest, and appropriate materials for the investigation, Amanda can encourage her students to consider a final important two-part question: "What things about this behavior can be measured, and how can we do it?" In this example, it is cricket jump distance, which suggests marked lines and rulers. However, an important part of learning science is realizing that the same general experimental question can be approached and quantified in many different ways. Some teachers have successfully used a single insect species and general research question and still have had students simultaneously conducting a dozen original experiments, simply because each group chose to measure something in a slightly different way (see Matthews et al., 1996, for ideas).

As part of this final consideration, Amanda should ask her students, "How many measurements or repeated trials will show whether there is a difference or not?" This last aspect is critical to the success of a science investigation. Something must always be quantified, and a single trial is never adequate to account for natural variation. However, students should be helped to realize that "how much is enough" is a judgment call.

In the process of asking these questions, Amanda's students will necessarily confront such problems as having more than one manipulated variable and controlling for extraneous factors that could influence the outcome of their experiments. Gathering numerical data naturally leads to consideration of how to best present it. Thus, science projects naturally and inevitably reinforce skills in mathematics and graphing. Having the students keep journals of their projects will help to develop communication and critical thinking skills.

As the teacher, Amanda will need to provide guidance at critical junctures to help the children consider potential pitfalls and clarify their thinking. However, these exploratory student efforts do not have to absorb all of Amanda's energy and time. By reflecting the issues and concerns that arise back to the students to discuss and resolve, Amanda can successfully foster an attitude of problem solving in her students.

In the end, student experiments need not be complex or require sophisticated equipment to be meaningful and authentic science experiences. Amanda saw how the Bug Camp children were guided to ask questions that became a springboard to investigation. The first experimental results generated a flurry of additional questions, and soon the kids were doing science: planning and conducting experiments, controlling variables, replicating, communicating. A similar approach can be highly successful in her classroom—and in yours.

■ **CASE 2.3** ■

How Full Is Full?

Denise S. Mewborne

■ *Fifth grade teacher Carmen Thompson was trying to incorporate more open-ended questions into her lessons by asking children questions that had more than one correct answer and questions that allowed students to explain their thinking. As Carmen implemented these new questioning techniques, she began to see that the children had more to contribute to the class than she had previously assumed. However, she also came to realize that asking good questions was only one piece of the classroom communication conundrum. Carmen Thompson is a composite of teachers with whom Denise has worked in recent years. A response from Rachel E. Foster, an experienced teacher and science education doctoral student, follows this open case.*

"Oh no! It's going to overflow!" shrieked Nicole.

"Nah, not yet. Be careful; don't touch the table," said Patrick calmly as he added another drop of water to the cup.

"Add one more, Patrick," said Ivonne. "This is it! There it goes! It finally overflowed. How many drops was that?"

"Eighty-three," reported Doug.

"Wow! I didn't think it would take so many," said Ivonne.

Just as they finished their experiment, Carmen Thompson called her class of fifth graders together to discuss their findings. The lesson for the day was intended to integrate science and mathematics by having students investigate the number of drops of water it would take to overflow a plastic medicine cup filled to the brim with water from a beaker. The science objectives of the lesson included helping students to develop an understanding of surface tension and having students identify variables that would affect the results of the experiment. The mathematics objectives of the lesson included helping students apply their developing knowledge of measures of central tendency: mean, median, and mode.

Carmen Thompson's class of twenty-four students included children with a range of understandings of the science and mathematics content and a range of communication skills. During this school year, the teachers in Carmen's school had been focusing on engaging all students in activities and in class discussions. The teachers had participated in professional development workshops, had read articles, and had been visiting each other's classes in an effort to find effective ways of involving all students in learning. A significant focus of the professional development workshops was on the use of questioning strategies.

Carmen had been trying to ask her children questions that had more than one correct answer and questions that encouraged them to explain their thinking. As she implemented these new questioning techniques, she saw that children had more to contribute to the class than ever before. They had lots of ideas about the content and were able to make connections to other topics they had been studying.

However, Carmen also came to realize that asking good questions brought other, unanticipated challenges into sharper focus. When students are invited to share their ideas, the teacher must listen carefully to what they are saying and think quickly about ways to respond to their contributions. Responding in ways that are respectful and encouraging was harder than Carmen initially expected. The other unanticipated challenge was getting the students to listen to each other. The students were used to the teacher being the authority in the classroom and were not accustomed to listening to their peers. They were also sometimes impatient with their peers who were less articulate, and they occasionally ridiculed each other. Carmen was comforted to discover that her fellow teachers were struggling with many of the same issues, but no one seemed to have a ready solution.

"Let's look at your initial predictions of how many drops of water it would take to overflow the cup and the actual results. Who can say something about these numbers?" asked Carmen. On the basis of her prior experience with this investigation, she had expected the students to have minimal understanding of surface tension and to intuitively assume that the cup would overflow quickly. By posing the open-ended question, she was hoping to elicit students' developing conceptions about surface tension.

"We were way off!" said Lou Ann.

Carmen was hoping for a more thorough response, so she asked a probing follow-up question: "What do you mean by that? Can you give me some examples using the data?"

"Ummm, well, I don't know how to explain it exactly. Like, if you look at my guess, I guessed it would only take 5 drops to overflow it, but it took 74. So I was way off. And most people were just like me, way off," explained Lou Ann.

"Who thinks they understand the point Lou Ann is making?" asked Carmen. About half of the class raised their hands. "Who has another way of explaining what Lou Ann noticed in the data?"

"The numbers in the predictions are small, and the numbers in the actual results are big," offered Jacob.

"What mathematical idea could we use to help us describe these data?" Carmen asked.

"The range?" Nathan posited, tentatively.

"OK," said Carmen hesitantly. This was not the answer she was looking for, but she decided to pursue it to see what Nathan was thinking. "What is the range for the predictions and the range for the actual results? And how does that help us?"

"The range for the predications is 1 to 15. Oops! No, I didn't see the 25 in there. The range is 2 to 25. And the range for the actual results is 72 to 98. Well, I guess the range isn't much different. The range of the predictions only covers 23 numbers, and the range for the actual results covers 26 numbers. It's not that much different."

"But it shows that our initial guesses were way lower than the results," offered Megan.

"What is another way we could use numbers to characterize or describe our predictions?" probed Carmen. "Think of something we've been studying lately in math."

"Oh, those average things! Like the mean, median, and mode!" said Michael.

This was the answer Carmen had been waiting for. She was tempted to direct Michael to the mean and skip any chance for an extended discussion of median and mode, but she decided to take the time to allow the students to explore which statistic would make the most sense in this case. After about five minutes of discussion on the three statistics, the class settled on the idea that the mean would be a useful way to represent the collection of predictions and the collection of actual results.

At this point, Carmen realized that only about one-fourth of the class was participating in the discussion. She started to call on Kayla to answer a question, but she hesitated. Kayla was very shy and had frozen in the past when called on to answer a question for which she had not volunteered. Carmen was also concerned that some students were not paying attention because they were not being involved in the discussion. So she made an on-the-spot decision to engage students in some small group discussion about the investigation.

"With the members of your group, I want you to discuss how you came up with your predictions. Why did you think it would take so few drops to overflow the cup? And then talk about why you think it took so many more drops than you expected. Try to visualize what happened to the water in the cup as you added more drops," directed Carmen.

After about five minutes of small group discussion, Carmen pulled the class back together. The children shared the reasons behind their initial predictions. These reasons centered primarily on the idea that the cup was already filled as full as they thought it could go, so they thought that adding only a small amount of water would overflow the cup. Several students gave nearly identical answers, making Carmen wonder whether the students were even listening to what others were saying. She didn't want to discourage the children's contributions by noting that their ideas were not novel, but the discussion didn't seem to be going anywhere because no one was adding anything new. So she moved the discussion to what happened when the drops were added to the cup.

"What did you notice about the surface or top of the water as you continued to add more drops?" asked Carmen.

"It seemed to swell up," noted Marcus.

"It got round on top," commented Jan.

"It was like a bubble. It kept getting bigger and bigger like a bubble does," said Matthew, using his hands to demonstrate how the surface was changing.

"You could see it jiggling sometimes. I thought it was going to overflow about ten times, but it didn't. The surface got all wiggly, but then it got still and didn't overflow," observed Todd.

"What things, or variables, seemed to affect how much the surface wiggled?" probed Carmen.

"When Matthew bumped the table!" said Todd.

"When we dropped the drops from way high up instead of down low."

"If you accidentally touched the eye dropper on the top of the water."

"If you made great big drops or little drops."

"Which one caused the problem—the big drops or the little drops?" asked Carmen, probing a child to give a more complete answer.

"The big ones."

"Why do you think the water got round on top like a bubble instead of overflowing?" asked Carmen.

"I think it's like the magnets we used. The water is magnetic, so it sticks together instead of spilling."

Joshua was definitely on the right track, but Carmen wasn't sure whether or not surface tension had anything to do with magnetism. She didn't really understand the scientific explanation of surface tension; she just knew that surface tension was the reason the water didn't overflow as easily as expected. Intuitively, it seemed plausible that surface tension could be related to magnetism, however. Perhaps there was some connection between magnetism and molecules bonding together. At the very least, it might be a reasonable analogy if not a correct scientific link. Because she was unsure about Joshua's assertion, she hesitated to either validate or reject his statement.

Before Carmen had a chance to respond, Frank blurted out, "That's stupid! Water isn't magnetic. If you put a magnet in water, you won't pick up anything."

"Frank!" Carmen reprimanded him with a stern look. "Joshua is entitled to say what he thinks. We're just exploring what might have happened to the water. Well, we need to move on to language arts, so we'll continue this discussion tomorrow."

FOR REFLECTION AND DISCUSSION

1. How can Carmen involve more students in the discussion without making shy students, like Kayla, feel put on the spot?

2. What should the teacher do when a student gives a response and the teacher is not sure whether the response is scientifically correct?

3. When a student gives an unexpected response, like the one offered by Joshua, how do you decide whether to pursue the response or to redirect the question to the response you were expecting?

4. Asking children to explain their thinking is time consuming. How might a teacher balance the need to cover material with the desire to elicit thinking?

5. How do you help children learn to listen respectfully to each other? How might you respond when a child ridicules the answer of a peer or when children become impatient with a peer who is less articulate?

■ COMMENTARY

Say What?

Rachel E. Foster

Having participated in professional development courses that made questioning strategies a significant focus, Carmen was well prepared to begin learning how to use them in her classroom. Experience is the best teacher, so her classroom became a learning environment for both her and her students. She asked her students to explain their answers, and she began to notice that asking open-ended questions led to greater student contributions to class than she had originally assumed. She also noticed that her students became able to make connections to other topics that they had been studying.

Carmen learned to ask probing questions that encouraged her students to think, such as "What do you mean by that?" or "Who else has another way of explaining?" She allowed incorrect or unexpected answers to see where the students' thoughts were going and whether their problem with understanding could be resolved through discussion and additional probing questions. She allowed class discussion to veer slightly from the day's objective to see where it might lead them, even though her initial impulse was to refocus immediately. Carmen also became aware of the students that were not participating in the discussion and came up with a creative way to include them without singling out students like Kayla who might be too shy to participate. Small group discussions minimize the anxiety that many students feel when asked to participate in a class discussion. Small groups can engage all students while creating a safe learning environment. In this way, shy students can contribute to the small group, and then their more vocal classmates can share what the group discussed.

Asking effective open-ended questions is probably the most difficult and beneficial thing that a teacher will ever do as part of the learning environment. It is a learned skill and cannot be learned without an enormous amount of practice with students and an equal amount of patience. And because the students that we work with are so complex, strategies that work in one situation might not work in another. In my opinion, knowing your students is the key to effective questioning. Knowledge of who your students are and how they interact with each other and with you will alert you to their understanding of the topic being studied, by the answers that they give.

What is an effective open-ended question, and how do you ask it? Good question! An effective open-ended question is one that elicits a response from students that builds on the topic of study, leads it in another interesting and informative direction, or simply readdresses the previous knowledge that the students have built. Effective open-ended questions challenge your students to think and to build on their existing knowledge and have meaningful discussions regarding their answers. Effective open-ended questions do not have one right answer. As the teacher, you have to decide whether the answers to your questions are taking you in a direction that builds on the topic of study or your students need to be redirected. You are restricted by your curriculum and by time. You are not free to allow the answers and the class discussion that they generate to lead the class into topics that take the students too far away from that day's topic of study. Ideally, we could let our students exhaust their answering and class discussion in any way that it takes them, but this isn't an ideal world, and we have to know how to focus our students on the topic they are studying. My suggestion is that you start with an organized list of questions to lead your discussion. Approaching your open-ended questions as a script that must be followed is a prescription for failure, but using those prepared questions as a way to focus both yourself and the group, as well as to refocus the discussions when they go astray, is a vital part of successfully asking open-ended questions.

So how do you respond to student answers to ensure that students feel comfortable answering your questions in class and feel encouraged to answer in the future? Responding to student answers to your questions is a delicate task and by far the hardest part of making open-ended questions effective. Your responses must be respectful and encouraging. If you expect to build an environment that fosters thinking, you cannot praise one student for answering the way that you expected them to and not praise another for answering in an equally correct but unexpected way. In fact, students tend to quickly become aware of how you respond to their answers. Students may become unwilling to participate in discussions if they feel that their contributions are not valued. Your responses can shut down a productive line of thinking. Your role can have a huge impact on whether or not your class can learn to think using open-ended questions. Be open to your students' ideas. If an answer is "way off," do what Carmen did and ask more questions of the student to gauge why they thought what they did. If an answer is just what you are looking for, do not forget that the other students may also have something valuable to contribute, so ask for other ideas. If a student's response goes beyond your knowledge of the subject, as happened to Carmen with the idea of magnetism and surface tension, suggest that your students try to find out something more about it that night or tell them that you are not sure of magnetism's effect on surface tension but will look for information on it tonight. Discussions that arise from open-ended questions may produce statements that you are not sure about; let the students take responsibility for investigating the question, but your knowledge of the topic is crucial for guidance. You might even want to begin class the following day with an experiment that addresses their statement/answer.

Asking open-ended questions is an effective way of questioning. It encourages participation by the entire class, teaches the students to think, engages the students' creative minds, and allows for different paths of discussion that enrich the topic being studied that day. Effective questioning requires the teacher to be organized, to listen carefully to all student responses, and to think and respond quickly. Carmen did have difficulty with this new questioning strategy but was relieved to find out that others struggled with the same things. The problem remains that there is no ready solution for the difficulties that Carmen and her colleagues face. But if you know your students and are willing to learn how to effectively question and respond to their questions in ways that encourage participation and thinking, asking open-ended questions can and will enrich the learning environment for both you and your students.

References

Cothron, J. J., Giese, R. N., & Rezba, R. J. (1993). *Students and research: Practical strategies for science class-rooms and competitions.* Dubuque, IA: Kendall/Hunt.

Koballa, T. R., Pyle, E. J., Matthews, R. W., Flage, L., & Ranger, S. (1997). *Wowbugs: Materials development and classroom implementation of a novel organism.* (ERIC Document Reproduction Service No. ED 403 147)

Matthews, R. W., Flage, L. R., & Matthews, J. R. (1997). Insects as teaching tools in primary and secondary education. *Annual Review of Entomology, 42,* 269–289.

Matthews, R. W., Koballa, T., Flage, L., & Pyle, E. (1996). *WOWBugs: New life for life science.* Athens, GA: Riverview.

National Research Council (NRC). (1996). *National science education standards.* Washington, DC: National Academy Press.

Wilson, R. (1994). Pairing early childhood education and environmental education. In R. A. Wilson (Ed.), *Environmental education at the early childhood level* (p. 7). Troy, OH: North American Association for Environmental Education.

Resources to Consider

Chaille, C., & Britain, L. (1991). *The young child as scientist: A constructivist approach to early childhood education.* New York: HarperCollins.

This book presents a vision of what elementary science teaching and learning might look like from a constructivist perspective.

Howe, A. C., & Nichols, S. E. (2001). *Case studies in elementary science: Learning from teachers.* Upper Saddle River, NJ: Merrill/Prentice Hall.

This handbook is a collection of teacher-authored case studies that explore issues and challenges in elementary science teaching and learning.

Matthews, R. W., Koballa, T., Flage, L., & Pyle, E. (1996). *WOWBugs: New life for life science.* Athens, GA: Riverview.

Children can learn a great deal about animal behavior through working with insects such as the WOW-Bug. This volume contains information about WOWBug behavior and its life cycle as well as dozens of investigations.

Metz, K. E. (1998). Scientific inquiry within reach of young children. In B. J. Fraser & K. G. Tobin (Eds.), *International handbook of science education* (pp. 81–96). Dordrecht, The Netherlands: Kluwer Academic Publishers.

Metz critiques literature related to developing skills of scientific inquiry in young children. She examines some of the limitations of traditional Piagetian theory and discusses the importance of collaborative work in fostering inquiry communities.

Saul, W., Reardon, J., Schmidt, A., Pearce, C., Blackwood, D., & Bid, M. D. (1993). *Science workshop: A whole language approach.* Portsmouth, NH: Heinemann.

In this book, four elementary teachers share their thoughts and perspectives on involving children in science through a whole language approach.

3

Organizing Meaningful Science Learning Environments

Current theories of intelligence as a multidimensional phenomenon emphasize the many ways in which students know, understand, perceive, learn, and process information as they make sense of their world. Howard Gardner (1993) contends that all humans possess musical, spatial, bodily-kinesthetic, intrapersonal, interpersonal, and maybe many more forms of intelligence. These intelligences interact and build on one another throughout one's life (Kincheloe, Steinberg, & Tippins, 1999). Consequently, it is essential that teachers develop the capacity to organize meaningful science learning environments that can uncover the hidden talents of all students. Bransford, Brown, and Cocking (1999) describe four perspectives that are useful in thinking about the design of environments that enhance and deepen the science learning of students: learner-centered environments, knowledge-centered environments, assessment-centered environments, and community-centered environments.

The learner-centered environment is consistent with instructional practices that emphasize sensitivity to students' prior experiences, beliefs, knowledge, skills, and habits of mind. It is an environment in which students are empowered to use their everyday language to talk about science. In their case "Who's Teaching Whom?," Brad Lewis and Nancy Wagner narrate the story of Jim Edmonds, a fourth grade teacher who comes to realize that the development of a student-centered learning environment requires rethinking the traditional roles of teachers and students. Knowledge-centered learning environments also take into account students' prior knowledge; however, in the knowledge-centered learning environment, greater emphasis is placed on particular kinds of information and activities that are essential to the development of scientific understanding. The knowledge-centered learning environment is compatible with the development of National Science Education Standards that emphasize that "knowledge is produced in the classroom through the interaction of student experience with information derived from the disciplines" (Kincheloe et al., 1999, p. 179). The assessment-centered learning environment is a natural outgrowth of learning that takes place at the intersection of student experience and disciplinary knowledge. In this environment, the focus is on the design of appropriate modes of assessing what students know about science, rather than what they don't know. In this sense, assessment can be viewed as an extension of the learning process that can and should become part of the daily classroom routine. The more recent attention given to social dimensions of science teaching and learning reflects the underlying premise of the community-centered learning environment. In this context, the classroom or school can be viewed as a minicommunity that is characterized by opportunities for learners to build common understandings through group processes and connections to the world outside the classroom. In her case "To Group or Not to Group," Melissa Warden explores the value of cooperative group learning through the eyes of Maggie, a first-year teacher in an inner-city school.

The four perspectives on meaningful science learning environments described above are not mutually exclusive. Rather, there is a need for student-, knowledge-, assessment-, and community-oriented environments to be collectively designed in ways that support both students and teachers in their quest to derive meaning from the world around them. In the final case in this chapter, "A Dilemma in Which Time Matters," Nate Carnes wonders how he might go about designing a meaningful learning environment for elementary science in the face of perceived time constraints.

━━━━━━━━━━━━━━━━━━━━━━━ ■ C A S E   3 . 1 ■ ━━━━━━━━━━━━━━━━━━━━━━

Who's Teaching Whom?

Bradford F. Lewis and Nancy Wagner

■ *One change among many advocated by recent science education reform is the creation of communities of learners. However, the vision of a community of learners is not always shared by school administration, teachers, parents, and even students. One barrier to the creation of communities of learners might be the traditional expectation that teachers are content experts and knowledge bearers and students are not. This open case is based on a set of experiences that Brad and Nancy have had with student expertise and how it can lead to changes in the traditional roles for teacher and student. In this account, fourth grade teacher Jim Edmonds is confronted by a student whose physical science expertise exceeds his own. Jim's dilemma, one that is shared by his class of students, concerns the need to rethink and make adjustments to their roles as they move toward becoming a community of science learners.*

This week is certain to be the most trying of my two-year teaching career. Here I am, a beginning elementary school teacher with a bachelor's degree in fine arts, and I am expected to design and teach a month-long unit on simple machines. But I know very little about science and even less about simple machines. What's worse, I doubt that Stephen Hawking himself could teach for an entire month about simple machines.

In the final moments of my prep time, I reassure myself by recounting the extent to which I have prepared for this unit. "Calm down, Jim. You've aligned your objectives with the *National Science Education Standards,* and state standards, and district standards, and the principal's personal preference standards. You've reviewed several middle school science texts. You've worked practice problems. You have several exciting hands-on activities. You even have a stack of simple machine worksheets and puzzles. Besides, they're only in the fourth grade. How bad could it be?" Friday is the day to worry about. That's the day the principal, Mrs. Jones, will attend to evaluate my newly designed unit.

The afternoon bell rang, and students poured in from recess. As usual, there was an air of excitement. Lunchtime sugar and recess play always made this time of day a bit tough. From his seat, Darren Todd Rosen began speaking feverishly at me.

"Mr. Edmonds, guess what we saw at recess? We saw a Harley-Davidson FLSTF Fat-Boy! It was sooooo coooeeel. It was black and gray, and it had silver trim, and . . . "

"Darren, that's very interesting. But now it's time to focus on science."

Unable to restrain his passion, Darren continued, "But Mr. Edmonds, you should have seen it. It was . . . "

"Darren, that's enough. Sit down and be quiet."

Darren is my toughest student. No, that's too mild, and it's not accurate. Darren is a behavioral nightmare. This is my second year with him, and I have yet to find a way to reach him. He is a major distraction to the other students. Darren somehow manages to create pockets of rabblerousers out of students who would otherwise be angels. I think a lot of his problem is that he doesn't get much attention from his parents at home. Both parents work full time (his father has two jobs), so they probably don't spend much time with him. His younger brother has already had run-ins with the police. I have really tried to work with him, but to no avail. Little can be done when there is no family support.

"Today we will begin with the K-W-L chart. Who would like to act as the recorder?" Several students raise their hands. Darren became a bit more animated than the rest and nearly fell out of his seat. "Amy, thank you for volunteering." (I sometimes ignore Darren to avoid disruption.)

As Amy walked by, Darren leaned over and whispered loudly, "Dirty nose, brown noser."

"DARREN! That's enough!" He often says hurtful things to the other students, especially the bright students. It is very discouraging to those students and to me. At times, I find myself not liking Darren, and it is very disconcerting.

"OK. Today we are going to talk about simple machines. What can you tell me about simple machines? What do we know?" Darren began wagging his hand frantically. After a substantial pause, John raised his hand. "Yes, John?"

"Computers are machines, and they make our lives easier."

"Mr. Edmonds," Darren blurted, "pulleys are simple machines, and my dad used one to move an engine. He's really strong."

"Darren, raise your hand."

Darren sank into his seat, peered out of the corner of his eyes at John, and mumbled, "What's so simple about computers?"

"Yes? Kelly. What do you want to tell us about simple machines?"

"Simple machines make it easier to do things. Like a ramp. When we helped my aunt move to a new house, we used a ramp to wheel heavy boxes because it was easier than carrying them up the stairs."

"OK. Great, Kelly!"

"Mr. Edmonds! Mr. Edmonds! Please call on me!"

His exaggerated enthusiasm upset the other students. "Yes, Darren?"

"Mr. Edmonds," Darren said with an extremely rapid cadence such that I barely caught what he was saying. "Wheels are simple machines. They move big things long distances in a short period of time. Like trucks that move furniture . . . and cars . . . and choppers."

"OK. Thank you, Darren."

"Wait a minute. I'm not finished." He continued, "The bigger the wheel is, the more helpful it is. A wheel can be big in two ways. It can be wide or fat, or it can be tall. Either way, you need big wheels to do big jobs."

"Thank you."

"Wait a minute, wait a minute."

"Darren, that is enough!"

His excited tone diminished. "But gears . . . "

As several students stared at Darren, who now wore a look of dejection, Marcelius spoke up and broke the tension. "Mr. Edmonds, cars and trucks have engines. Is an engine a simple machine?"

"I'm not sure about that, Marcelius. That's a very good question."

Darren took over. "No, Marcelius. An engine is much too complicated to be a simple machine. In fact, there are so many different types of engines that it doesn't really make sense to speak of an engine because they're all different. You have to be specific. And most engines contain all of the simple machines. Like in my dad's car. It has a 2.5-liter, sixteen-valve, four-cylinder torque system engine. And it transfers the power generated by the explosions in the cylinders to the crank shaft and then to the transmission to power the car. It also has gear sets connected to a set of belts . . . "

"Darren, please. That is enough. You are not the teacher of this class." As I interrupted his gabble, I noticed that students were staring at Darren in confusion.

Kelly then looked at Darren and back at me. "Mr. Edmonds, is that right, what he's saying about engines?"

The entire class then looked at me—and waited. I began to feel very uneasy, and I made certain to pause, preparing myself to speak in a very thoughtful tone.

Darren then commented smartly. "Sure it is. I know a lot about engines. My dad fixes them all the time, and I help. I know all about simple machines too, because they . . . "

Finally, exhausted by the distraction that was Darren and uneasy because of my inability to speak knowledgeably about engines, I lost my thoughtful demeanor and erupted, "Darren! Do you want to teach the class?"

Darren's face beamed with excitement at the invitation. "Yes! I can teach about engines and simple machines in car and bike engines!" Without hesitation, Darren came to the front of the room. Astonished by what had transpired so quickly, others in the class stared at me with puzzlement and awe. Then Darren began to speak. For nearly ten minutes, he held the class in rapt attention, myself included. He spoke in a way that even a fourth grader could understand, which was perfect for me. I learned so much. Darren described pulleys, incline planes, the wheel and axle, levers, and the wedge and their use and occurrence in and around cars and bikes.

"Tomorrow I'll have my dad drive me to school so we can bring my dirt bike. I also have an old engine that I took apart, and I can show everyone the different parts."

Darren continued thundering away, like an odd cross between a physics professor and a garage mechanic in miniature. Never had his classmates seemed to like him this much, nor had he ever treated them with as much respect as in these few minutes.

Suddenly, the bell rang, rousing the entire class as we sat engrossed in this novel lecture. I thanked Darren, who proceeded, smiling, to his seat. Marcelius then raised his hand.

"Yes, Marcelius?"

"Are you going to let Darren teach class tomorrow?"

FOR REFLECTION AND DISCUSSION

1. Considering Darren's behavioral problems and his history of antagonizing fellow students, should he be permitted to continue his presentation?

2. If Darren is not permitted to continue with his presentation, how should Mr. Edmonds deal with Darren's knowledge and his desire to share it?

3. If Darren is permitted to present, are there guidelines that the teacher will need to develop for Darren? For other students in similar situations?

4. What should be done if other students want to share their knowledge of this topic and other topics in the future?

5. If Mr. Edmonds does allow Darren to speak for another day, how might that affect his Friday evaluation by Mrs. Jones? Is it worth the risk?

6. What are some ways in which teachers can recognize and draw on students' expertise to teach science?

7. Why might a teacher fail to recognize students' expertise?

■ **COMMENTARY**

Rare and Well Done: Teaching in the Other World

Dana L. Zeidler

"Who's Teaching Whom?" presents a wonderful snippet of a day in the life of Mr. Edmonds' class while he stands at the crossroads of a teachable moment. The tension he faces arises when his role as teacher as director squares off with an alternative role consisting of teacher as facilitator and colearner. The tension is very real. The traditional paradigm of the teaching profession requires that Mr. Edmonds never relinquish control of his class—that he stick to a well-developed lesson plan with precise objectives specified ahead of time. This compels him to stay the course, not to deviate from the "game plan." There is no time for unplanned interruptions that interfere with the main objectives and are likely to lead the lesson astray.

Fortunately, Mr. Edmonds (quite accidentally and out of frustration) allowed an alternative path to be traveled. The moment he relinquished control of the lesson to his student Darren, an alternative reality came into existence. In this alternative reality, a different world snaps to the forefront of Mr. Edmonds's consciousness. In such a world, there are possibilities for teaching and learning that were not formerly part of Mr. Edmonds's traditional paradigm. In such a world, teachers dare to enter into a community of learners where students are afforded the opportunity to take responsibility for their own learning, and the roles between teachers and students sometimes become blurred. It is only after the traditional roles become blurred that a new vision of science instruction becomes clearer. The distinction between traditional and contemporary recommended practices in science education is evident in current national reform documents such as the *National Science Education Standards* (National Resource Council, 1996) and the *Benchmarks for Science Literacy* (American Association for the Advancement of Science, 1993) as well as many state-level initiatives. Consistent with teaching practices that are aligned with constructivist philosophy and learning theory, current thinking in science education reflects a shift from the teacher imparting knowledge to students, with communication mainly one way, to the teacher as a facilitator of learning with students acting both as learners and, in some circumstances, as teachers too. When this occurs, networks of student teachers and learners may spring into existence, and it is quite possible that the teacher sometimes begins acting as a colearner as well. This is a view of teaching turned on its head. For a very traditional teacher it is, indeed, an inverse world.

It is difficult for some teachers to yield control of their class. There is safety in sticking to your script, ticking off your objectives one by one. However, once you are willing to leave your safety zone, opportunities will present themselves that allow for the construction of meaningful knowledge on the part of the students. For some teachers, these opportunities will seem like threats to their position and status as head of the class. For others, such opportunities will be viewed and understood as teachable moments.

The idea of recognizing teachable moments is not spanking new. Good teachers who are in tune with their students recognize when to seize the moment. In fact, Eleanor Duckworth wrote about them in an article entitled "The Having of Wonderful Ideas" (a story worth reading) many years ago. Duckworth (1972) cited the example of a boy named Hank who was learning about electric circuits with flashlight batteries, bulbs, and wires. Hank was a typical, energetic fifth grader who surprised his teacher when he went far beyond her expectations in reasoning and testing out various conditions related to electric circuits. Duckworth understood the having of wonderful ideas to be the *sine qua non* of intellectual development. She also made it clear that the having of wonderful ideas depended on occasions for having them. In other words, Hank's teacher had to recognize a teachable moment and allow Hank, in his personal exploration, to deviate from the expected objectives of that lesson and take ownership of his own learning. The idea of teachable moments might not be new, but the consistent practice of creating opportunities for student-centered learning is a vision that requires focus, unwavering flexibility, and a commitment to foster scientific habits of mind such as curiosity, skepticism, and critical thinking.

The authors of "Who's Teaching Whom?" raise some very good questions to consider at the end of their story. It is difficult, if not impossible, to pretend to understand Darren's behavioral problems without walking the walk in the teacher's classroom. Context is everything. We cannot presume to have a tacit knowledge of Mr. Edmonds's students and classroom environment. But we can recognize that if our students truly come first, then it is worth the risk, even during the teacher's own evaluation, to allow the students to explore their hidden talents. Perhaps Mrs. Jones, the principal, would need to understand the justification for his approach. Perhaps she already understands what it takes to achieve a true community of learners. One thing I am certain of: Mr. Edmonds's respect for the children will not be an issue.

While riding a public bus to class in Syracuse, New York, I once saw a poem mixed in with the advertisements above the windows. Every month, a new poem would go up as part of an effort to bring the public in touch with the arts. One poem struck me in a peculiar way, and after seeing it day after day, I committed it to memory. It read like this:

Antimatter by Russell Edson

On the other side of the mirror there's an inverse world,
where the insane go sane; where bones climb out of the
earth and recede to the first slime of love.

And in the evening the sun is just rising.

Lovers cry because they are a day younger, and soon
childhood robs them of their pleasure.

In such a world there is much sadness
which, of course, is joy . . .

I do imagine an inverse world of sorts in education—one that turns our traditional vision of teachers on its head, in which the hidden talents of children are realized, in which teachers and administrators recognize the necessity of creating multiple opportunities for teachable moments. In such a world, revealing the hidden talents of children would not be rare, and the joint construction of social and scientific knowledge is well done.

■ **CASE 3.2** ■

To Group or Not to Group

Melissa A. Warden

■ *Maggie is an enthusiastic and highly motivated first-year teacher in an inner-city school. Her determination to make science personally meaningful for her third grade students spurs her to commit considerable time and resources to setting up and using cooperative groups to carry out scientific investigations. The early success that she sees these groups achieve is later tempered by the knowledge that not all students in every group are benefiting from the shared experience. Maggie wonders how her decision, based on sound and professionally advocated classroom-based research, could have led to such undesirable and unexpected ends. Maggie is a composite of beginning elementary teachers with whom Melissa has worked. Commentary about Maggie's dilemma is provided by Kathy Cabe Trundle, a science educator and advocate for group learning.*

Maggie O'Conner was completing her first year as a third grade teacher in an urban school located in a large Midwestern city. Her students were primarily African Americans who came to her with little or no school science experience. Because Maggie had finished her teaching degree with a concentration in science, she was anxious to make science learning a priority in her classroom and brought with her many highly recommended teaching strategies for developing in her students the science habits of mind that the *National Science Education Standards* suggest are crucial to doing science in ways which parallel the work of scientists. Prominent in Maggie's plan to make her classroom a place where children pose questions and investigate the world around them was her desire to establish cooperative learning groups.

Maggie's enthusiasm for the use of cooperative learning remained undaunted even in the face of skepticism early in the school year when she casually mentioned her idea to another third grade teacher, who replied, "Oh, honey. I tried that stuff my first year, too, and believe me, it's just not worth the effort! These children are much too wild to handle that kind of responsibility. You'll spend most of your time repeating the same thing over and over as each separate group needs your attention. And that's not to mention all those materials that will need to be handed out; and the noise, and the kids out of their seats that will absolutely drive you wild. No, you'd be much better off to just do a demonstration at the front of the room and have each child draw a picture or write a report about what happened. Believe me, it will save you lots of time and aggravation."

Maggie thought about this advice and weighed it against everything she had read and been told about the positive outcomes that resulted when children worked together to complete a task. She remembered reading in her college textbooks and in the research literature that co-operative learning would allow students to co-construct deeper and more powerful understandings than they could individually construct alone. Whether they were cooperating by dividing a complex task into smaller parts or were collaborating on a single solution through brainstorming and consensus, it was clear to Maggie that the children would be learning more communication skills and generating more science ideas in these ways than they would via the traditional teacher-centered model, in which the students merely listened and only she explained. However, Maggie did heed her colleague's warning about the potential management problems associated with giving up (to the children) some of her classroom control.

Before implementing her idea, Maggie spent considerable time talking to the students about how real scientists go about doing their work. She told them that they would become scientists when they began to ask "how" and "why" questions about the world around them. She told them that they would work in laboratory teams to investigate these questions by performing observations and keeping records of what they observed. They would measure, weigh, mix, time, describe, and compare various objects and processes and would construct explanations (or answers to their questions) based on all the evidence the team had collected. For the team to work more effectively, each student would be given a specific role to play during each investigation. Maggie divided the children into working groups based on academic strengths and on personality traits so that every team comprised a heterogeneous mix. She made colorful wall charts to describe the various team roles and to remind the children of their associated duties. She made laminated badges that the children would wear to identify themselves as Chief Investigator, Materials Manager, Maintenance Supervisor, or Data Keeper and then asked the PTO for help in securing safety goggles and mock lab coats for each child so that the image of a real scientist doing real science would be maintained. Maggie even had the children practice moving their desks into various configurations and then back into straight rows so that the time spent in performing this task would eventually be reduced. When she thought she had sufficiently prepared her students to handle their new responsibilities, Maggie held her breath and set the plan in motion.

The first week was, of course, still a little rough. Children needed to be reminded of where to pick up materials, how to clean and store items after use, whose job title went with what set of duties, and how to use their inside voices when holding group discussions. Generally though, Maggie was satisfied that they would all eventually overcome such preliminary hurdles. By the third week, Maggie was getting more time to observe the intergroup and intragroup dynamics. Although she was very pleased with the quality of the work that was being done (the detailed nature of both written and oral descriptions, the accuracy of mathematical computations, the meaning making across groups when results were different), she did begin to get the feeling that not everyone on every team was reaping the same rewards.

As she moved around the room and listened to conversations, Maggie noticed that the contributions of girls were sometimes being marginalized by the male members of the group, the girls' ideas not being as readily accepted as those of the boys. In one instance, when a female Chief Investigator led her team to a faulty conclusion, there were loud cries of "We were wrong because we listened to Nina. That just proves that girls can't do science!" Maggie also began to realize that certain students with stronger personalities or higher perceived status seemed to dominate group decisions, whether they necessarily had the best ideas or not. Such domination tended to silence shier students, who preferred to go along rather than risk embarrassment or humiliation as the lone dissenter.

As if these isolated problems weren't serious enough, during the fourth and fifth weeks, Maggie discovered to her dismay that the previously high quality of the work that the majority of the groups had been producing was now beginning, here and there, to deteriorate. On close inspection, it appeared that in one or two groups, data collection was being fudged, and conclusions were being drawn from nonsupportive evidence. As she began to panic, Maggie wondered whether the increased camaraderie that was being fostered as the teams began to feel more at ease with each other was resulting in collaboration that was both unproductive and faulty. A myriad of frantic questions came immediately to her mind. Had she so misunderstood the concept of cooperative learning that her students were now the victims of her good but naive intentions? Was there something inherent in urban children that made cooperative grouping the wrong teaching strategy? And most important, how in the world could she turn it all around?

FOR REFLECTION AND DISCUSSION

1. What are the advantages of using cooperative work groups to promote science learning? What kind of classroom environment can it foster? How are the traditional roles of teacher and student altered when cooperative learning is used?

2. What are some of the disadvantages of using cooperative work groups to promote science learning? Can you think of other problems that might arise as a result of involving children in group work? How can such problems be minimized or eliminated?

3. Do you think the potential advantages of cooperative learning outweigh the potential disadvantages? Why or why not? Would you encourage Maggie to continue with her original plan, modify her original plan, or scrap the plan entirely?

4. How do you explain the apparent mismatch between the classroom-based research Maggie learned in her college courses and the reality of her classroom practice? What does this tell you about being a wise consumer of education research?

■ C O M M E N T A R Y

Building on a Cooperative Learning Foundation

Kathy Cabe Trundle

Maggie's efforts to use cooperative learning as a teaching strategy are commendable. Her decision to use cooperative learning to teach science is consistent with constructivist learning ideas, principles of teaching and learning presented in the *National Science Education Standards* (National Research Council, 1996), and current educational research. The demands and stresses of Maggie's first year make her initial successes with cooperative learning even more remarkable. However, it appears that she is doubting her decision to use cooperative learning in her teaching. I encourage her not to abandon this instructional strategy. Maggie's situation clearly indicates that if certain dynamics are ignored, group work may hinder or detract from learning. Therefore, I suggest that Maggie build on the solid foundation she laid for cooperative learning through three strategies: addressing students' individual learning styles, implementing homogenous gender grouping, and holding students individually accountable for their work in cooperative groups.

Although cooperative learning can be an effective strategy for some students, not all students learn successfully in a group arrangement. In addition to determining whether their students are auditory, visual, or kinesthetic learners, teachers also must determine whether students are independent or social learners. A learning styles inventory, such as the one in Philip Turner's (1993) book *Helping Teachers Teach,* may help Maggie to assess and address her students' individual learning styles.

Maggie accurately identified another likely hindrance to her students' overall success with cooperative learning. She noticed that "the contributions of girls were sometimes being marginalized." Cooperative learning is particularly important for girls. Much research attention has been directed toward factors that influence girls' negative perceptions of science, low science achievement, lack of interest in science-related careers, high levels of science anxiety, and low enrollment in science classes (Baker & Leary, 1995; Kahle, 1984; Kahle & Lakes, 1983; Lee & Burkam, 1996). Cooperative learning, a socially interactive learning strategy, provides one method to help female students succeed in science. Maggie used academic performance and personality traits as criteria to establish heterogeneous groups. Although some researchers (Oakes, Ormseth, & Camp, 1994; Slavin, 1990) agree with this strategy and suggest heterogeneous grouping by ethnicity, gender, or an ability, other studies (Light, 1990) suggest that a student who is the only female in a group is likely to participate less. I suggest that Maggie also consider using same gender-groups as opportunities for females to participate and succeed.

Finally, I encourage Maggie to revise her plan for student assessment. When the team is assessed as a whole, individual students are not being held accountable for their learning. Consequently, the quality of students' work may decline over time. For cooperative groups to be successful, students must have a group reward and individual accountability (Slavin, 1984). The group must be held accountable for learning and collaborating with other team members. Maggie could add an individual student assessment component to her cooperative learning model by giving individual tests or quizzes to each student or randomly selecting work from one student to represent the entire group.

Cooperative learning offers multiple benefits to students, and Maggie has already tackled the most challenging aspects of having students work in groups: logistics and management. The suggestions offered here provide opportunities for Maggie and her students to overcome the setbacks they experienced and to move forward with learning in a collaborative environment.

A Dilemma in Which Time Matters

G. Nathan Carnes

■ *This open case describes a dilemma that Nate faced in his attempt to implement a teaching approach that was new to him and closely aligned with a constructivist theory of teaching and learning. After completing a year-long intensive professional development experience, he planned to implement a more student-centered approach to science teaching and learning. Specifically, Nate sought to increase the degree to which his students were actively involved in their science lessons. In doing so, he encountered a challenge with time management. The class period seemed much shorter than usual, and there was less time to teach. The case is followed by commentary from Melody Brown, a science teacher educator with strong beliefs about making optimal use of science class time.*

Now in my third year, I teach in a large urban school district near a major Midwestern university. With a daily average attendance that exceeds 48,000, it is one of the largest school districts in the state. Approximately 780 of these students attend the magnet school where I teach. My teaching responsibilities include fifth grade science instruction for three different classes. The colleagues on my grade-level team are grateful for my willingness to teach this subject. Most of them are terrified of science and do not feel qualified to teach it. As a graduate of this school system, I am grateful to be able to give back to my community. In addition, my teacher preparation program gave me opportunities to earn an elementary education degree with an emphasis in general science education.

Despite my academic background, I felt a need to add depth to my science knowledge and develop a more diverse repertoire of teaching skills, so I attended an intense year-long professional development program designed for elementary and middle school science teachers. Throughout this experience, I became familiar with our state's science standards, which promote innovative instructional practices and alternative assessment techniques. The instructors from the College of Arts and Sciences and from the College of Education placed me and my teacher colleagues in small cooperative groups to complete a variety of modules designed to deepen our science content knowledge. In doing so, they refrained from the use of lectures and other teacher-centered practices, choosing to provide hands-on activities in which we addressed our prior knowledge and understanding of science concepts. At the end of each activity, the instructors used a variety of questions to assess our understandings. We often completed essay tests at the end of each module. These kinds of activities and assignments gave me a sense of accomplishment and challenged me to meet the science needs of all of my students. The small group instructional method that my professors demonstrated provided more opportunities for active student involvement. If it worked with me and my colleagues, maybe it would work with fifth graders.

I returned to my fifth grade classroom with the determination to increase the number of activities and lessons in which my students would be actively involved, decreasing the amount of time spent on lectures and teacher demonstrations. A physical science unit on matter was the starting point for designing lessons that incorporated many of the student-centered strategies I had experienced the past year. My school district's curricular guidelines required students to describe the properties of matter. In place of my traditional lecture, I planned a series of activities in which my students would discuss their definitions of matter, classify substances that they thought were matter, and conduct investigations with various substances. My revised plans required my fifth graders to work collaboratively in assigned groups of four or five students. As indicated in the instruction packet given to them, each student group would meet with me to share questions, findings, ideas, and models. When they were not meeting with me, the groups would complete the activities autonomously.

The following week, I prepared to teach my new lesson with mixed emotions. I visualized my students buzzing with excitement, as they engaged in thoughtful discussions and practical experiences. At the same time, I wondered how my students would react to the new lesson format. Would my reluctant students abandon their apathetic attitudes and see learning in a new light? What if the students just went through the motions in completing the activities? How long would it take for my students to complete these activities? Would there be sufficient time for me to visit each group?

I pressed through this swirl of questions, concealing my inner feelings during my usual opening ritual. I announced that the students were going to complete the day's lesson in small groups and instructed them to follow the directions printed on the stapled packet that they had just received. The students looked at me blankly but seemed to understand my expectations.

As my fifth graders began to work in small groups, I walked around the room, monitoring their progress and joining in their discussions. One group was debating whether or not gaseous substances contain matter. I joined their discussion without invitation.

Chris: You can inhale oxygen. So it's something.

Pat: Yeah. You can inhale it, but it doesn't fill up the room.

Me: But does it have volume?

Pat: Yeah.

Me: Does it take up space?

Pat: It doesn't fill up the room.

Me: But does it take up space?

Pat: Yeah.

Chris: Yesss! That's what I said! It does take up space.

Bo: But you can't measure it with a ruler.

Me: Well, just because it doesn't have a definite . . . [I gestured boundaries with my hands], it doesn't mean that it occupies no space.

Chris: That's what I said. Gas takes up space.

Pat: You didn't say it had volume.

Chris: Yeah, but I still said it takes up space.

The discussion continued among the group as I left them to check on the rest of the class. They were still involved in a heated discussion when I returned several minutes later. I presented a situation for them to consider.

> *Me:* Let's think about this. What if I blew up this balloon and put it on the balance up there (gesturing in the direction of an equal arm balance atop a wooden cabinet)? Let's say that I took another balloon with the same amount of air. If I popped one and left the other filled with air, what do you think would happen?
>
> *Pat:* One side would go down.
>
> *Me:* So, does it have matter?

Despite my intervention in the discussion, the discussion among the students continued for another fifteen minutes.

On the one hand, I was encouraged to see that my students really were getting involved in their own learning. However, a glance at the classroom clock cast a shadow on my feelings of accomplishment. It was 10:08; only seven minutes were left before the students had to leave for their next class. There was barely time to clean up or review the homework assignment for tonight! My students had far exceeded the time set aside for the first activity, actively discussing their views on what constituted matter, yet there was much more material to cover. Should I have limited their discussions? How will I judge the meaningfulness and timeworthiness of these discussions? It seemed impossible to teach this way all the time, as did my professional development instructors. How could I possibly cover all of the required science topics at this pace? After all, my reputation would be on the line if my students performed poorly on school and state tests.

FOR REFLECTION AND DISCUSSION

1. For most elementary teachers, the time devoted to science teaching and learning is limited. In what ways could Nate resolve his difficulty with the lack of instructional time?

2. How much time should Nate allow his students to deliberate on questions such as "Does air takes up space?"

3. For this lesson, should Nate revert back to a lecture/teacher demonstration format or continue to allow small group investigations? Provide a rationale for your answer.

4. To actively involve your students in timeworthy activities, what do you need to know about your students? About the content that you are teaching? About yourself as a teacher and a learner?

5. How can elementary teachers balance the tension between designing highly structured lessons and ones that are open ended?

■ COMMENTARY

The Time Bind

Melody L. Brown

The dilemma that Nate faced in his science classroom is an all too common one. Teachers often come back from professional development workshops with much enthusiasm and many great ideas for their science class. However, they quickly discover that many of the activities and experiences are too time-consuming and may be unrealistic for the time allotted in a typical classroom schedule. Although Nate had good intentions and was excited about the prospects of a less traditional science learning experience, several issues complicated his lesson. There are many advantages to student-centered instruction and cooperative learning activities, but adequate planning and organization are essential for promoting a successful learning environment.

In this particular case, it would have been much more effective if Nate had provided more specific instructions and guidelines at the beginning of the lesson. First, Nate should have explained the purpose and objective of the lesson, as well as exactly what students were expected to accomplish. Even though Nate disseminated an instruction packet with the expectation that students were capable of working autonomously, it was obvious that students were not exactly clear about how they were supposed to proceed with the exercise. Nate mentioned that students stared at him blankly after receiving the instructions, which should definitely have raised a red flag. Blank stares from students often result in their wasting time trying to figure out exactly what they are supposed to be doing in laboratory activities. It is imperative that at the beginning of a lesson, teachers explicitly state the purpose of the lesson as well as what students are expected to have accomplished by the close of the lesson.

Second, Nate should have given the students more direction and a time frame for the exercise. He should have also planned on completing one activity, rather than the series of activities he mentioned. Although his intent was to increase the amount of activity and decrease traditional lecture time, it is obvious that students were overwhelmed by the lesson. In this case, as the saying goes, "less is more." For example, he could have explained to students that they would be divided into groups and work collaboratively. He could have also designated various tasks for each student within the group to be responsible for completing. This would have encouraged students to work more cooperatively toward completing the assignment as a whole. Nate could also have allotted students a specific time frame for discussing their definitions of matter, classifying substances, and actually conducting the investigations. In addition, Nate could have been prepared for another exercise, in case time permitted. I say this because it is important for a teacher to recognize that the dynamics of each class may be different. In some instances, one class may complete the activity faster than another, and a backup activity could have been planned in the event that one of his classes took less time to complete the lesson. Furthermore, Nate should have left ten minutes or so at the end of the lesson to bring students back together for a brief, large group discussion of the exercise. This is often helpful in assessing what students actually learned from the assignment.

Additionally, it is important to recognize that students often need guidance when working in small groups. Although Nate circulated throughout the classroom and attempted to monitor students' progress, it seemed as though the questions he asked only confused students more. Nate failed to redirect the small group discussion, and his input only caused students to bring up more questions that were not clearly answered. When this happens in the classroom, students are more likely to become frustrated and disenfranchised, and they may simply give up on the assignment and consider it meaningless. The upper elementary grades are often considered critical to student's participation in the science pipeline, and it is important that students feel that questions are not just encouraged but clearly answered.

Finally, I am glad that Nate encouraged collaboration in his science classroom. However, it is important to realize that there is an art to using the cooperative approach. It is critical that teachers structure student interactions and assign small groups that maximize student achievement (Trowbridge & Bybee, 1996). Just placing students into small groups and giving them an assignment does not ensure that all students will learn the material or that time and effort in cooperative groups will be well spent. Although Nate was encouraged by his students' discourse during the lesson, he should have limited their discussion time.

During collaborative work, it is essential to monitor and intervene in both a constructive and productive manner. Trowbridge and Bybee's (1996) cooperative learning model (p. 209) provides the following guidelines for monitoring and intervening:

1. *Monitor students work.* Once the students begin work, your task is to observe the various groups and help solve any problems that emerge.
2. *Provide task assistance.* As needed, you might wish to clarify the assignment, introduce concepts, review material, model a skill, answer questions, and redirect discussions.
3. *Teaching collaborative skills.* Because collaboration is new, it may be important to intervene in groups and help them learn the skills of collaboration.
4. *Provide closure for the lesson.* At the end of the lesson, it may be important for you to intervene and bring closure. Summarize what has been presented, review concepts and skills, and reinforce their work.

It is clear that Nate started off on the right track and actually followed some of Trowbridge and Bybee's (1996) tenets for effective monitoring and intervening. However, he should have taken a more active role by guiding and limiting the small group discussions. In the future, more guidance, structure, and instruction before the activity, as well as more clarification and direction throughout the laboratory, would make his collaborative lessons much more effective and time-efficient. This in turn can prevent running into what I like to call the time bind, or running out of time without providing some lesson closure designed to assess what students actually learned from their experiences.

References

American Association for the Advancement of Science. (1993). *Benchmarks for science literacy.* New York: Oxford University Press.

Baker, D., & Leary, R. (1995). Letting girls speak out about science. *Journal of Research in Science Teaching, 32*(1), 3–27.

Bransford, J. D., Brown, A. L., & Cocking, R. R. (1999). The design of learning environments. In J. D. Bransford, A. L. Brown, & R. R. Cocking (Eds.), *How people learn: Brain, mind, experience and school* (pp. 119–142). Washington, DC: National Academy Press.

Duckworth, E. (1972). The having of wonderful ideas. *Harvard Educational Review, 42*(2), 217–231.

Gardner, H. (1993). *Multiple intelligences: The theory in practice.* New York: Basic Books.

Kahle, J. B. (1984). *Girls in school/Women in science: A synopsis.* Paper presented at the Annual Women's Studies Conference, Greeley, CO.

Kahle, J. B., & Lakes, M. K. (1983). The myth of equality in science classrooms. *Journal of Research in Science Teaching, 20*(2), 131–140.

Kincheloe, J. L., Steinberg, S. R., & Tippins, D. J. (1999). *The stigma of genius: Einstein, consciousness, and education.* New York: Peter Lang.

Lee, V. E., & Burkam, D. T. (1996). Gender differences in middle grades science achievement: Subject domain, ability level, and course emphasis. *Science Education, 80*(6), 613–650.

Light, R. (1990). *Explorations with students and faculty about teaching, learning and student life.* Cambridge, MA: Harvard University Press.

National Research Council. (1996). *National science education standards.* New York: Oxford University Press.

Oakes, J., Ormseth, R. B., & Camp, P. (1994). *Multiple inequalities: The effect of race, social class, and tracking to students' opportunities to learn mathematics and science.* Santa Monica, CA: RAND Corporation.

Slavin, R. E. (1984). Students motivating students to excel: Cooperative incentives, cooperative tasks, and student achievement. *The Elementary School Journal, 85*(1), 53–63.

Slavin, R. E. (1990). *Cooperative learning, theory, research, and practice.* Englewood Cliffs, NJ: Prentice Hall.

Trowbridge, L. W., & Bybee, R. W. (1996). *Teaching secondary school science: Strategies for developing scientific literacy* (6th ed.). Englewood Cliffs, NJ: Prentice Hall.

Turner, P. (1993). *Helping teachers teach.* Englewood, CO: Libraries Unlimited.

Resources to Consider

Atkinsons, S., & Fleer, M. (1995). *Science with reason.* Portsmouth, NH: Heinemann.

> The stories in this book are narrated by elementary teachers who have striven to make science a meaningful activity for children by encouraging them to ask their own questions, study what interests them, and solve their own problems. The teacher-authors provide examples of how they integrate living processes, materials and their properties, and scientific investigations into students' learning.

Fraser, B. J., & Wubbels, T. (1995). Classroom learning environments. In B. J. Fraser & H. J. Walberg (Eds.), *Improving science education* (pp. 117–144). Chicago, IL: National Society for the Study of Education.

> This chapter provides on overview of research in the field of classroom environment with particular emphases on the learning environments of science classrooms.

Lazarowitz, R., & Hertz-Lazarowitz, R. (1998). Cooperative learning in the science curriculum. In B. J. Fraser & K. G. Tobin (Eds.), *International handbook of science education* (pp. 449–469). Dordrecht, The Netherlands: Kluwer Academic Publishers.

> This chapter provides an overview of cooperative learning methods and review of research on cooperative learning in science education.

Scott, J. (1993). (Ed.). *Science and language links: Classroom implications.* Portsmouth, NH: Heinemann.

> The chapters in this book examine the role that language plays in science learning. The authors provide suggestions, ideas, and approaches for using language to support young children's learning in science.

Creating a Culture for Learning Science in the Elementary Classroom

Just as teaching is a holistic, complex activity, so is learning. It is not always possible to determine why learning does or does not take place. However, it is widely recognized that the learning environment plays an important role in the science teaching–learning process in the elementary classroom. The classroom environment consists of two main aspects: (1) the physical appearance and layout and (2) the nature of social interaction that occurs among the members of the class. Traditionally, the science–teaching–learning environment was defined by physical space, the teacher's arrangement of furniture, displays, science materials within the space, the size and shape of the classroom, and adequate storage (Loughlin & Suina, 1982). More recently, this view of the teaching–learning environment has been expanded to include the social-emotional climate. Perhaps the most encompassing of all the teacher's responsibilities is to provide a positive classroom learning environment that is supportive, invites students into the classroom, and communicates that they are valued as individuals and that they will learn. In addition, elementary students need to feel safe and secure and believe that you as their teacher care for each of them individually. Elementary students also need learning tasks that they understand and value and that are interesting and challenging for them (Kauchak & Eggen, 1998).

When teachers create a culture for learning science based on constructivist principles, they are ensuring that their students are active in solving problems, practicing learning strategies, making choices, and developing understandings of important ideas. These learning approaches involve complex, challenging learning environments, social negotiation, and shared responsibility as part of learning; multiple representations of content; and student-centered instruction. Creating a learning climate that makes minimal use of rote memorization encourages in students an excitement about learning and a thrill in discovering how the world works. When designing learning environments to support the construction of knowledge by young children, teachers should create opportunities for children to develop their abilities while retaining curiosity and zest for learning. The goal of understanding, not just memorizing, in science has to be established early. This type of child-centered teaching–learning environment is consistent with the National Association for the Education of Young Children's (1996) guidelines that highlight the importance of developmentally appropriate practice. This instructional approach places the child at the center of the curriculum and recognizes young children's unique characteristics. Whether the focus is on the physical setting, arrangement of learning materials, or patterns of social interaction and support, teachers have much to consider when attempting to create a culture for learning science in elementary classrooms.

The four cases in this chapter emphasize different aspects of the science learning environment in elementary classrooms. In the first case, "Who Said Child's Play Isn't Important?," Dee Russell observes a prekindergarten classroom and a fifth grade classroom where students are engaged in blowing soap bubbles through straws. She wrestles with questions about the relationship between children's work and play and the teacher's responsibility for fostering children's intellectual growth. The second case, "The Tension of Being on the Cutting Edge," by Judith McGonigal, identifies and describes the tensions that surface in a public school when a first grade teacher engages in an innovative inquiry-based science program with her students and their parents as co-researchers. This case highlights how social interaction and support from the principal and teaching colleagues are central to a healthy learning environment. In the third case, "Truss Troubles," Thomas Dana and Joseph Taylor describe a sixth grade teacher's demonstration and discussion that are intended to help her students understand the presence of tension in the beams of a structure when they are not ready for this type of learning experience. In the final case in this chapter, "Do I Listen to My Students? Or Do I Cover the Mandated Curriculum?," Patricia Cincotta and Elizabeth Pate describe a teacher's frustrating experience of wanting to seize a teachable moment while faced with a perceived need to cover the mandated science curriculum.

■ C A S E 4 . 1 ■

Who Said Child's Play Isn't Important?

Dee Russell

■ *Helena's observation of a fifth grade class leads her to question Harold, a prekindergarten teacher, about what she had observed in his class only days before. Children in both classrooms were blowing soap bubbles through drinking straws, but the connections that the teachers were willing to help the children make between their playful explorations and subsequent intellectual discoveries were markedly different. Harold's explanation for the activities of his prekindergarten students left Helena wrestling with questions about the relationship between children's work and play and the teacher's responsibility for fostering children's intellectual growth. The characters in this open case are composites of people with whom Dee has worked. The case is followed by a response by Sharon Parsons, a science teacher educator whose research interests include children's play.*

Helena found that one of the pleasures associated with her job in the teacher education department of a small college were her regular visits to public school classrooms to observe science lessons at various grade levels. Today, having driven to a school in a town just north of where her college is located, she was watching a class of fifth graders blowing through straws at tables covered with soapy liquid.

"I want them to have a chance to play with the soap and the straws today before they work through some investigations making bubbles tomorrow," Julie Chancellor, the classroom teacher, explained. "The children take such pleasure in seeing how big a bubble they can blow, how many they can make at one time, and how the bubbles move across the table. They really aren't ready to observe carefully until they have had a chance to experience what making bubbles is all about. But tomorrow, I think they will be able to make some observations about surface tension. At least, I am hoping that will be the case."

Helena stood quietly near a wall and watched the children. Julie's room differed from most fifth grade classrooms she had visited. There were no desks, just six big tables, each with four chairs. Julie seemed to like to keep her children working in small groups, no matter what the subject. On the basis of Helena's observations, she presumed that Julie highly valued social interaction. Today the grouping allowed for lots of sharing among the children. She saw one boy chase a bubble across the width of his table. His neighbor tried to do the same thing, and without a word being exchanged, they were soon both blowing bubbles in a kind of race. The two students who were sitting across the table were cheering them on.

As Helena left the fifth grade room, she remembered something she had seen in a prekindergarten class on an adjacent hall. The classroom she had observed the week before was filled with shelves on which sat trays and baskets, all filled with attractive, interesting materials. She had watched children choose a tray or basket, carry them to tables or to small carpet squares, and play with quiet pleasure. Helena enjoyed the feeling of ordered activity in the classroom and recalled being told by the teacher, Harold Glass, that the prekindergarten program in this school was modeled on the principles of Montessori education. Compared to other preschool classes she had visited, in this one, Helena had not witnessed children being herded from one group activity to another or teachers barking orders at recalcitrant four-year-olds. She remembered being impressed by the calm sense of purpose and structure in the room.

"Play" was the word she had used when she had first watched the children, but Harold had corrected her: "Children *work* with the materials here. All of these materials are prepared in such a way that the child will learn something by using them in specific ways. That child with number rods"—he had pointed to a girl who had a series of ten rods of varying lengths and painted with stripes of red and blue—"is building a sense of number as she arranges the rods by length and as she counts the various sections."

Helena had seen shelves filled with bowls, pitchers, and glasses. Children had poured beans, rice, and colored water from one container to another. She had watched one boy carry a tray with a bowl, a small plastic squeeze bottle, and pitcher to a table. He had chosen a paper-covered straw from a metal vase, placed it on the tray next to the bowl, then filled the pitcher with water from the faucet, carried the pitcher slowly back to the table, poured the water into the bowl, added three drops of liquid soap from the small squeeze bottle, and removed the paper from the straw. After all of this, he had concentrated on blowing slowly and steadily through the straw into the bowl until clouds of soapsuds rose above the edge of the bowl.

Today, having watched the fifth graders blow bubbles, Helena wondered about the prekindergarten boy blowing bubbles. Hadn't he been playing, just like the fifth graders? What purposeful "work" could Harold possibly intend for prekindergarten children to be doing through such an activity?

Helena quietly opened the door into the prekindergarten room. Again she was struck by the activity throughout the room. Everywhere she looked were children. Again she saw a child (a boy today) laying out the red and blue rods on a mat. At a nearby table, a girl was picking rocks out of a basket and grouping them into categories. Another girl was striking bells with a little mallet and listening intently to the soft, clear tones. Harold's assistant was sitting near two girls who were using wooden letters to spell words associated with colorful pictures lying in a row across a table. Helena caught Harold's eye as he looked up from a clipboard on which he had been writing.

"Good morning," he said as Helena maneuvered her way across the room, avoiding children, tables, chairs, and mats. "May I help you with something?"

"Yes, you can," Helena replied. "I was watching some fifth graders get ready for some science investigations with bubbles tomorrow, and I remembered seeing something here that I was curious about." She glanced around the room until she saw a boy seated at a table, leaning over a bowl, blowing through a straw into a mound of bubbles. "There," she pointed to the child. "Why have you included that in your room?"

Harold smiled. "Blowing through a straw is a wonderful means of learning to control one's breathing. It helps to develop breath control for speaking and, I suppose, even singing."

"But children don't choose it for that reason. I see children in restaurants blowing bubbles into their soft drinks. Surely, children choose to do that because they want to play with a straw and bubbles?"

"Certainly," Harold said, "that may be the point of interest that they find in that activity. But we often provide materials that have multiple purposes. When they trace geometric shapes and color them in with colored pencils, they enjoy the colorful pictures they create. But, indirectly, they are learning to hold a pencil so that they can write with greater precision later."

"But what about the bubbles themselves?" Helena asked. "Aren't children able to learn something about the nature of bubbles, about surface tension, and the consistent shape a bubble forms? Isn't there some cognitive dimension as well to that activity?"

"Sure, there is," Harold said. "Providing such experiences with bubbles now lays the foundation for future understanding of scientific principles."

"But why not help the child develop some understanding now? Could you not ask questions that direct the child's attention to some of the qualities of the bubbles? Why not encourage the child to do some more with the bubbles to investigate some of the bubble's properties?"

"We design materials for specific purposes," Harold replied. "I suppose I could put together some other activities that would help children explore those properties."

"But why put together more materials? Why not ask questions about what they are doing right now? Why not talk to them? Why not make suggestions?"

Harold smiled. "One of the characteristics of a Montessori classroom is that we work through the materials as much as we can. We observe children as carefully as we are able, and when we see a need for some further development, we devise an activity that will facilitate that development. We want children to learn from their environment."

Helena realized why today's observations had begun to disturb her. She had always assumed that teachers of preschool children had a deep affection for the attachments and interests that children developed through play, yet, today, she had heard a fifth grade teacher articulate the close connection between free, playful exploration and the subsequent ability to investigate purposefully and to formulate some generalizations abstracted from those investigations. Harold, concentrating on the world of preschoolers, seemed to resist making a direct connection between a child's play and subsequent intellectual discovery. It seemed that the intellectual purpose was all his; he seemed unwilling to draw the child more deeply into his own intelligent understanding of the world.

FOR REFLECTION AND DISCUSSION

1. What is the relationship between play, that seemingly purposeless activity in which children seem to delight for the activity's sake, and more purposeful investigations? What is the basis for your response?

2. Harold describes a learning environment for young children based on his understanding of the teachings of Maria Montessori. What do you consider the strengthens and limitations of this learning environment?

3. Helena admires the way that Harold has constructed the physical environment in his classroom to facilitate science exploration but thinks that it lacks the dimension of social interaction. She believes that a teacher who asks questions and models actions is a very important dimension of the science learning environment. Do you agree with Helena? Explain your response.

4. What is the ideal role for an adult in helping young children develop their understandings of science? Is your ideal more closely aligned with the beliefs of Harold or Helena?

■ **C O M M E N T A R Y**

Both Play and Work Can Lead to Learning

Sharon Parsons

There are a number of critical questions that emerge from this case. In reading the case, you probably noted some of the following:

1. What is play versus work?
2. What teaching style best facilitates student learning?
3. What type of student grouping (independent student work versus cooperative groups) is best for student learning?
4. What is the teacher's role in creating the learning environment?

In reviewing the above list, at first it appears that question 1 is most prominently highlighted in the case, with questions 2–4 being secondary. However, on a second reading of the case, I see "difference in teaching style" as the central issue of the case because it encompasses all of these other instructional issues. When we consider the description of Harold and Julie's teaching presented in the case, we immediately sense a difference in educational philosophies that is influencing their classroom actions. This difference is clearly demonstrated in their interpretations of the role of play in learning. It leads me to think again about question 1 and to ask other related questions: What is play versus work? When does learning stop being play and become work? Does it matter? Far too many educators view work as learning and play as not learning. "Play" is obviously a term that can have different interpretations. In this case, Harold associates play with activity without purpose. In contrast, Julie views play as part of the exploration essential for learning. Their different interpretations of play influence their classroom actions and bring into focus the instructional dilemma with which Helena wrestles.

This case requires Helena to make decisions about potential solutions to her instructional dilemma. However, no one solution is immediately obvious. A successful solution therefore requires Helena to exercise good professional judgment to work successfully with teachers like Julie and Harold. Both Julie's and Harold's viewpoints are valid, so this will require her to conference with both of them to work out a solution. A workable solution is often a mixture of several instructional approaches or a compromise that reflects a position somewhere in the middle. It is important to identify the main scientific concepts to be developed at the prekindergarten and fifth grade levels. Some scientific concepts such as surface tension of bubbles lend themselves to the use of one method over another. In classes like Julie's, play can be quite useful for introducing a lesson or for generating questions to investigate. She might need to strive for a balance between cooperative learning through social interaction and independent/individual learning. To create a successful learning environment, it is often important for teachers to be attentive to a variety of student learning styles. Helena might need to hold her judgment about what play is and ask the teachers to focus on ways to engage all their students to achieve the desired learning outcomes. She will need to convince teachers like Harold and Julie that the role of the teacher is important for facilitating instruction, guiding through questioning, challenging students' naive ideas, and engaging them in problem solving.

Harold's interpretation of Montessori principles of teaching has both strengths and limitations. The strengths include his focus on student-centered learning, which allows for the emergence of student multiple intelligences and independence. Among the limitations are his limited control over learning during activity, his inability to capitalize on teachable moments, and the lack of interaction between students. Julie might need to examine her use of free exploration in the learning process. She might need to consider the use of questioning within the context of guided versus open-ended inquiry. Helena might find it helpful to share with these teachers some of the education literature on student learning styles, different learning cycles, and use of questioning in guided versus open-ended inquiry. A lot is known about inquiry-based learning that can be helpful to both teachers.

Helena should also be cautious about recommending the use of a specific solution. Alternative instructional methods should be recommended as guidelines, not as the only way of teaching. When working with teachers with varying teaching styles, classroom visitation may be important in creating a learning environment in which teachers learn from each other. There are lots of variables to consider, in addition to the ages of the students, when choosing an instructional approach. By recommending an eclectic instructional approach, Helena might be successful in convincing Harold that his preferred method of instruction might limit opportunities for student interaction. Similarly, Helena might be more successful in convincing Julie that free exploration might not provide enough structure for some students.

"What is the role of the teacher in the classroom?" If we consider this question, then we will most likely note that it is the teacher's responsibility for creating a successful learning environment. In creating a successful learning environment, the use of different teaching styles is important. One lesson that could be taken from this case is to not jump to hasty conclusions about either Harold's or Julie's teaching. If we assume that Julie's teaching style is better and that we want Harold to become more like Julie, then we run the risk of alienating Harold by asking him to change his teaching style. We also run the risk of Julie not learning about the importance of structure in student learning and the role of questioning in inquiry-based learning if we advocate the she adopt Harold's teaching style. Although science concepts related to a topic such as bubbles can be learned at different ages, they can also be developed in different ways. Because both teachers appear to be successful at engaging students, then we might wish to focus on why both teaching approaches are successful rather than critiquing Harold's definition of play. Teachers need to be open to a variety of teaching methods so that student learning is not limited. We should not let teaching semantics get in the way of student learning. Teaching should be based on students' needs, with the teacher guiding students to deeper understanding. Students will rise to the teacher's expectations, and expectations often lead to higher achievement.

■ C A S E 4 . 2 ■

The Tension of Being on the Cutting Edge

Judith A. McGonigal

■ *This is an autobiographical case that describes how a classroom teacher, with students and parents as co-researchers, discovered how to implement self-selected science inquiries in first grade. The case identifies and describes the tensions that surface in a public school setting when a teacher engages in innovative practice. The case is followed by commentary from Kenneth G. Tobin, a science educator who strongly supports science instructional reform efforts that lead to the development of learning communities.*

With the publication and dissemination of the *National Science Education Standards,* my small, suburban school district in New Jersey became aware of the need to expand and reshape the science learning opportunities it provided elementary students. In an attempt to improve the science skills and teaching competencies of elementary teachers, this school district provided all primary grade teachers the opportunity to participate in a sixty-hour science education course. This training prepared elementary teachers to use a constructivist, inquiry-based science program in which students and teachers together used recyclable materials to investigate and to co-construct a shared understanding of science concepts.

This in-service course provided me with my first exposure to science inquiry and ignited within me the desire to explore and learn more about the potentials of supporting inquiry in the elementary science classroom. I petitioned and received permission and financial support from my school district to participate in several other science education courses. As a result, I became very comfortable with the idea of carrying out science investigations with my students as co-researchers. Most other teachers in my school district found this constructivist, inquiry-based curriculum too unstructured, open-ended, and difficult to implement in their elementary classrooms. They requested that this approach not be adopted as the official district science curriculum.

In response to the teachers' concerns, my school district decided to conduct a one-year field test of several other science programs that provided not only manuals with careful instructions for students and teachers to follow, but also kits with all the materials needed to complete each prescribed grade-specific science investigation.

While several of these science kit programs were being piloted and evaluated for adoption, I asked my principal whether I could informally research in my first grade classroom how to implement student-selected individual science inquiries. I had been challenged by the director of the summer science inquiry institute, which I had just completed, to mentor a few first graders through a self-selected science inquiry during the school year. My principal's response was that for the first few months of the school year, I should pilot only the mandated weather and plant science units, just like the other two first grade teachers in the building. Because these two teachers had newly been appointed to first grade, he wanted parents to view all the first grade programs as similar until the parents had gained confidence in the new teachers. Although I orally agreed to implement only the two science pilot units initially, I walked out of the principal's office hoping to find a crack that would allow me to investigate with my first graders how to do self-selected science inquiry. The crack appeared near the end of September when a first grader, Arthur, brought a baseball to school that he had opened at home to see what was inside of it. The next day, I gave him a golf ball to take home and explore. Soon his classmates and the school janitor were bringing Arthur, now known as the ball expert, various kinds of softballs, tennis balls, rubber balls, and even a cricket ball to open.

As Arthur, his parents, and his younger brother carried out their ball investigations at home, they began to keep a science notebook about their inquiry to keep me updated about their discoveries. Not only did they examine the inside of the balls, but after reading an article from a science education journal that I had given them, they also began carrying out fair tests to explore how high each ball would bounce when rolled off a table. They measured and recorded the circumference and weight of each ball. They even explored how the texture of a ball influenced the way it rolled on the floor or traveled in the air.

At the end of November, I invited Arthur to present to the class his findings in an organized account, using a whiteboard to display his balls. I assumed that this six-year-old would speak for a few minutes. Instead, his report lasted twenty minutes, and his first grade class extended his presentation by probing him with specific questions about his investigation. I had discovered, with the help of my students and Arthur's family, a successful way to carry out individual self-selected science inquiries by using the home and family as a science community of learners to support a child's individual questions about a phenomenon that exists in the everyday world.

In December, feeling totally constrained by the structured lessons in the plant and weather science kits that I was field testing, I decided that it was time to ask each student to carry out an individual science inquiry at home. Arthur's mother wrote directions for the students and their families to use as a guide. Within two days, all twenty first-graders had self-selected a different topic to investigate at home. These topics included clocks, crayons, crystals, feathers, fungus, flowers, frogs, human hair, mealworms, structures, and symmetry. As these young scientists became experts who later taught their peers and their teacher about their science topic, family members became co-learners in science with their first grader. Families also began sharing resources with each other to support the various investigations.

In March, each child selected a day to showcase the results of his or her science inquiry. Early in the morning, on their designated day, the first grader and family members arrived at school to set up all the materials that they had gathered and explored together at home. In the afternoon, each first grader spent at least twenty minutes showing and describing evidence of what had been learned and how it had been learned. These self-selected science inquiry presentations generated a first grade science curriculum that gave six- and seven-year-old students the opportunity to authentically participate in doing and sharing science. After all the presentations were completed, all evidence of science exploration and learning was displayed in the classroom at a Science Inquiry Conference, in which each student guided his or her family and reported to parents and grandparents what each peer had investigated and discovered.

In May, I invited the parents of the first graders to come together to reflect and celebrate what they had done together as families in a learning community of coresearchers of science and science education. It was my intent at that meeting to publicly recognize each family for how they had supported my professional inquiry and the science learning of the first graders in this classroom. At the evening meeting, however, the parents were not interested in celebrating success: rather, they wanted to find a way to continue as a community of co-learners together. They suggested that each family select a social science problem in the community to research. Because the school year was drawing to an end, they wondered whether students could be allowed to stay together as a class for second grade and continue as co-learners and co-researchers.

I pondered the possibility of working with these students as second graders, especially since a second grade teacher was retiring. Several parents of students in the other two first grade classrooms interrupted my contemplation of the possibilities. These parents began to complain to the school principal that he should not have allowed one class to engage in something that was significantly different from what the other first grades in his school were experiencing or learning. These parents valued "equity" and believed that every student had the right to be provided the same educational experience.

Simultaneously, the second grade teachers voiced their belief in the importance of a schoolwide standardized delivery system of the science curriculum at each grade level. The second grade teachers requested that the first graders who had explored self-selected science inquiry be evenly dispersed next year among the three second grade classes. They also suggested that I consider teaching second grade with them only if I were willing to deliver the science curriculum in a way that did not deviate significantly from how they would implement the newly adopted science kit program.

The principal told me that he believed that there was no one right way to teach science. Because I had mentored the families through dialogue journals and had visited the homes of the students as they were carrying out their science investigations, my principal said that my innovative model had increased my class size to include all family members of my students. Therefore, teachers could not be required to duplicate this model of science inquiry unless their student class population was reduced to seven or eight children.

The district science supervisor was unaware of this discussion because he was preparing for his retirement, which he had announced four months after the constructivist, inquiry-based curriculum had not been adopted by the district because it was not a "teacher-friendly" program. In retrospect, the science supervisor now believes that perhaps he had tried to move the district elementary teachers too quickly to a new paradigm of science teaching. After his retirement, the school district eliminated his position and selected a classroom teacher at each school to facilitate the coordination and implementation of the district's new elementary science program.

Without public support from my principal, I was too scared to challenge the system alone, and so I did not request to co-learn and co-research with these children and their families for another school year. Although I was amazed at how much science first graders could learn by investigating their own self-selected topics with the participation of their families and classmates, I was not sure whether I could duplicate the results with another group of children unless I had administrative support and continued professional mentoring. The parents of my first graders wanted me to join them as they went to the district superintendent's office to request that our inquiry community be maintained and perhaps even extended to all the second graders in our school for the coming year.

But I was unwilling to publicly question or challenge my teaching peers and principal, so I did not support my parents' attempt to reframe the primary science curriculum in our school. I was unwilling to risk failure as I tried to expand the implementation of self-selected science inquiries. I said that an open-ended, student-directed science curriculum had to be the self-selected vision of teachers and the administration. It could not be a curriculum imposed on educators by a school district or by a small group of parents. Not willing to create additional havoc for those parents who wanted an equal educational experience for all, I internalized their beliefs. I questioned whether self-selected science inquiry should be the experience of just a few students who would eventually have to be absorbed into more traditional elementary classrooms with a standardized science curriculum.

The following school year, I could not face again the perils of being on the cutting edge, as an innovator who co-researches science theory and practice with my students and their families. I decided not to continue creating tension for my principal, the parents of students in other classrooms, my teaching peers, and myself. I chose not to search for another crack that would allow me to explore the innovative outer edge of elementary science teaching and learning practices. After fifteen years of experiencing the joys and tensions of being an innovative educator, I left classroom teaching.

FOR REFLECTION AND DISCUSSION

1. What are the characteristics of a teacher-friendly science program?

2. How can a teacher best accommodate both the requirements of a standardized curriculum and the needs and interests of individual students?

3. How should an innovative teacher respond to peer pressure to conform to a mandated curriculum?

4. Should students, parents, and teachers function as co-researchers of effective educational practices?

5. How should educators respond to the parents who demand educational equity for all students in a school?

6. How could parents and this teacher have worked better with the administration to move the elementary school science curriculum to a constructivist, inquiry-driven program that more teachers valued?

7. What should a teacher do when he or she discovers an effective innovative science teaching practice that no other teacher or administrator on the school staff will try or support?

■ COMMENTARY

Helping Students Realize Their Potential

Kenneth G. Tobin

I attended a national meeting where students from McGonigal's grade 1 class presented with their parents about their science investigations. Not only that, but the principal and superintendent were in attendance at the same meeting and were well aware of the impressive levels of student understanding and parent participation and the unbridled enthusiasm of the participants and those who heard what was accomplished for the manner in which inquiry was practiced in this first grade class. That students were capable of even more than is required in the *National Science Education Standards* and that parents could get so involved without taking over their students' projects are astonishing. But it happened, and ample supporting testimony is available in the words of not only the teacher-researcher, but also students, parents, principal, superintendent, science supervisor, and colleague teachers. So what went wrong?

This case exemplifies the social aspects of doing. In most respects, McGonigal is anything but a typical elementary teacher. For example, when I first met her, she was dragging a suitcase filled with artifacts collected from years of research in classrooms. I have not met many teachers who are quite so focused in undertaking research in their own classroom or so intent in learning from what they have done. However, in several other regards, McGonigal is typical of elementary teachers I have met. First, despite her accomplishments as a teacher of elementary science, she lacked confidence in her ability to be an effective science teacher. Before teaching science as is described in the case, she had a fifteen-year history of avoidance. Second, although she was willing to search for cracks in the system through which she could maneuver to benefit the learning of her students, she was hesitant to take on the system even when she knew she was right. When powerful others acted politically, McGonigal fell into line or retreated.

Probably because of her intensive grounding in language arts, McGonigal embraced constructivist ways of thinking about learning and her roles as a teacher. Accordingly, even though science inquiry was a mystery to her, she understood that the way to proceed in enacting a science curriculum involved eliciting questions from students and making it possible for them to follow their own instincts. She also knew that the path toward meaningful learning involved support from the home. Her instincts were grounded in her graduate studies as a doctoral student in language arts (before she became a doctoral student in science education some years later). Even though she did not know exactly what to do to enact an inquiry-oriented science program, she knew that the solutions were not associated with greater teacher structure and the use of science kits. Even when her colleagues sought the safety of science kits, McGonigal knew that this was not in the best interests of her students. She was prepared to take risks and make it possible for her students to realize the elusive goal of learning through inquiry.

The one-size-fits-all approach to science standards that is incorporated in national reports that call for reform, such as the *National Science Education Standards* and *Science for all Americans* (National Research Council, 1996), are reflected in the principal's idea that there should be a standard way of teaching science throughout the first grade. Given his lead, it is small wonder that the teachers should insist that if McGonigal were to teach in the second grade, she would have to fall into line with their approach to the teaching of science. Why the call for standardization? At one level, it is understandable that teachers would not want to look bad. "Get a life," they might think as they watched McGonigal devote her entire being to the education of her students. Why should they spend their weekends and out-of-school hours working with parents in homes and on field trips? Because they had witnessed the enthusiasm of students and parents for what McGonigal was prepared to do, it is not surprising that they would not want someone working so hard and effectively at their elbows if the pressure would be on them to perform similarly. Likewise, it is possible that the principal did not want pressure from parents to get other, less experienced teachers involved as McGonigal was doing. Not only that, the school had a history of parents getting involved to the detriment of the education of students whose parents could not or would not get as involved in their children's education.

Cases like this make me wonder about the purposes of education. Do schools exist for the comfort of teachers and principals, or do we really take seriously the education of the students? Calls for the reform of science education have had in mind curricula much like what McGonigal has described. We are rarely privileged to experience such a curriculum. Perhaps we are therefore entitled to get angry when we read about or experience cases such as this.

Rather than curtailing the energy and resolve of teachers like McGonigal and pushing them from the classroom, we should be providing incentives for them to continue and extend their work so that others can learn from them and perform in a like manner. As a teacher-researcher, McGonigal is a rare jewel who, through her dedication, talent, and vision, is able to make a difference in the lives of her students and then, through her efforts as a teacher educator, provide a model for us all to emulate.

We do not have to do what McGonigal has done, but we all can learn lessons from what she has done, make sense of it in our own ways, and then act according to the resources we can bring to the task. Rather than feeling that we must lose our lives to education, each of us can decide, within the resources we can give, how to adapt our teaching and enacted curricula so that our students can realize their potential, especially as it relates to doing science. We all might look forward to the day when McGonigal reenters the elementary schools of the world, not in any physical sense but through the images that her research and her stories of success build in each of us and the extent to which her voice is with us when we listen to the voices of our students and allow them to find answers to their own questions.

■ **C A S E 4 . 3** ■

Truss Troubles

Thomas M. Dana and Joseph A. Taylor

■ *Many concepts in physical science are abstract and involve specialized use of language and graphical representations. One such concept that is becoming visible in contemporary elementary curricula is the presence of tension or compression in the beams of a structure. Unlike a rope or a cable, tension or compression in a solid beam cannot always be directly observed. As a result, students often struggle with the task of analyzing a structure such as a truss to determine the type of force (tension or compression) that is present in each beam because they need to imagine what might be happening in a picture or figure. This case describes students' difficulties in learning these concepts and asks us to consider ways of making concepts such as tension and compression more developmentally appropriate for students to learn. Maria, the central character in the case, is a composite of teachers with whom Thomas and Joseph have worked. The case is followed by commentary from the authors that describes how Maria resolves the dilemma.*

Maria Chavez, a teacher at Pinewood Elementary School, is teaching a series of lessons on bridges and structures to her sixth grade class for the first time as part of a unit on design technology. One of her expectations is that students will be able to conduct a truss analysis to determine the kinds of forces that are at work in structures. Maria decides to begin with a demonstration/discussion to help students understand how tension and compression can arise in a beam. She provides the illustrations and explanations shown in Figure 4.1. Maria then shows students a diagram of a simple truss bridge (see Figure 4.2) and distributes copies of the truss model to each student. She asks her students to work in pairs and use their knowledge of tension and compression to determine which beams (A–G) are in tension and which are in compression.

As the students discuss with each other what is happening in the truss, Maria notices that one group of students—Devon, Holly, and Tony—is struggling with ways of describing what might be happening. She had thought that these students understood her initial explanations of tension and compression when they were first introduced and is now surprised that they are having trouble identifying the type of force present in some of the beams in the figure. Maria approaches the group in an attempt to facilitate their thinking:

> *Maria:*   What do you think is happening with beam C?
>
> *Devon:*   It's in tension . . . I think.

"Compression occurs when two forces push inward on each end of a beam."

"Tension occurs when two forces pull outward on each end of a beam."

FIGURE 4.1

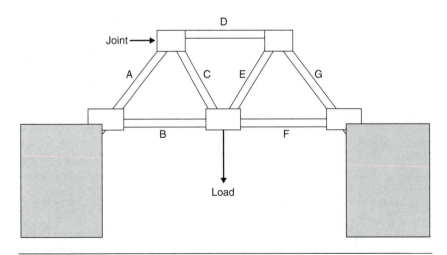

FIGURE 4.2

Maria: You are unsure. What are your reasons?

Holly: Well, it's tension if it stretches, but how do we know if it's stretching in this picture?

Maria: Let's try to see if we can visualize the forces on beam C. Wouldn't the load pulling down on the truss pull outward on the bottom end of beam C?

Devon: Yes, but what is pulling on the other end?

Holly: There is no load on the other end, right?

Maria: Well, the joint in the top left corner is pulling outward on the other end of beam C.

Holly: How do we know it is doing that?

Maria: Hmmm. Just as the load pulls on the bottom of beam C, beam C pulls on that joint. If beam C pulls on the joint, then the joint pulls back on the beam.

Tony: I'm confused. Why will the joint pull back?

Maria: Well, there is a law in science that says that for every force, there is an equal and opposite reaction force. Let me draw a picture of the equal and opposite forces involved. [Maria draws the diagram in Figure 4.3 for the students.]

Maria: See, the force on top represents the joint pulling out on the beam.

Tony: But what about the arrows pointing in? Won't those forces compress the beam?

Maria: Well … They are just reaction forces. Those forces are not acting on the beam.

Holly: But they are forces, right? Why don't they count? I don't get it.

Devon: Now I am really confused.

Looking around the room, Maria realizes that it's not just this student group who is confused. Many students have gotten off task, and no one seems to have analyzed the truss in the way she expected. Feeling frustrated, Maria does not know what to do next.

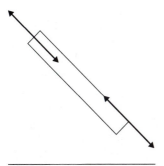

FIGURE 4.3

FOR DISCUSSION AND REFLECTION

1. What conceptual difficulties are the students having?
2. Why do you think the students are having these conceptual difficulties?
3. If you were the teacher, what would you do now?
4. What do you think about teaching abstract concepts such as tension and compression in this manner?
5. What are some alternative approaches to teaching this concept that might be more developmentally appropriate?
6. Look into instructional uses of everyday toys to teach concepts about structures. Web sites for LEGOS (http://www.lego.com) and K'NEX (http://www.knex.com) have some suggestions. What might be some ways in which Maria can make the concepts of tension and compression more visible to students for their inquiry into structures?

■COMMENTARY

Here's What Maria Did

Thomas M. Dana and Joseph A. Taylor

After reflecting on the class discussion of tension and compression, Maria concluded that the students' conceptual difficulties were probably in part due to the fact that they could not see any evidence of a tensile force on beam C. In addition, Maria suspected that the students had seldom or never observed an inanimate object (such as a joint) exerting a force. Maria also recognized that the diagram of beam C was confusing to students because the forces on the beam were not clearly distinguished from the other forces.

To make the presence of tension or compression observable, Maria subsequently decided to construct six truss models using LEGO pieces. In each model, one of the six beams was replaced by a string (see Figure 4.4). Maria decided to use string because she knew that it behaves in very observable ways when under tension or compression.

The next day, Maria introduced her students to the LEGO truss models, as she carefully applied a load to each model and instructed the students to observe the behavior of the string. By determining whether the string in each model became taut or slackened, the students were able to determine the type of force on each beam of the truss rather easily. Although Maria could have used a force probe and data collection software to measure the tension or compression in each beam, she ultimately decided not to utilize this option, since exactly how the force probe measures force would not be obvious to her students. As Maria developed and revised her instructional plans using the LEGO models, she remembered to focus clearly on her objective: to make the forces more observable for her students.

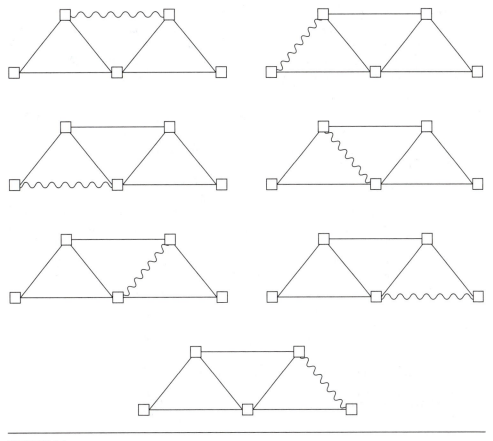

FIGURE 4.4

CASE 4.4

Do I Listen to My Students? Or Do I Cover the Mandated Curriculum?

Patricia Cincotta and P. Elizabeth Pate

■ *This is a narrative account of a videotape presentation compiled by fourth grade students after completing an environmental science project. The student narrators vary throughout the presentation. Each bracketed statement reflects a different still shot captured on the videotape. The videotape is followed by the thoughts of Patricia, a fourth grade teacher who wants to seize a teachable moment but wonders whether she can cover the mandated science curriculum. This closed case is based on an actual experience that Patricia encountered in fostering a student-centered science curriculum. Patricia, the teacher of the students in the videotape, collaborates with Elizabeth, a middle school educator at the nearby university. The case is followed by commentaries from Kathy Thompson and Grace Lyon, both of whom have used learning experiences that students perceive as meaningful and relevant to cover mandated curriculum.*

[View of two fourth grade boys frowning as they point to a large orange mesh fence in front of trees.] "One day when we were outside, we noticed a big orange fence. [The boys in unison say, "Humph! "] We were so sad because we thought all the trees next door were being cut down by the building company man."

[View of the fourth grade trailer.] "Mrs. C. suggested we write letters to the company." [Behind the trailer, you can see the orange mesh fence and trees.]

[Background shot of students sitting in their classroom. Foreground shot showing two men at front of class.] "Two very nice men from the company came to our class and explained what they were doing."

"We had lots of questions for the men." [Students with hands raised for questioning.]

[Men pointing to colorful map.] "They explained to us how they made a tree protection plan. They said a tree protection plan had to be drawn from a bird's eye view."

"Next we all looked down at our desk to see what a bird's eye view was." [Students standing at desks looking down to get a bird's eye view.]

[Men speaking to class.] "The men were very careful to explain their plan so we could understand."

"While the men talked, we all took notes." [Students taking notes in journals.]

[Landscape drawing.] "One of the men showed us the map of the company property. If you look closely, you can see a big lake. [Pointing to the lake.] They're going to keep that and most of the trees."

"Then they showed us a drawing of their tree protection plan." [Smaller drawing of property site.] "A tree protection plan is required by the county and explains where all the trees will be. A landscape architect needs to draw this plan."

"Here is when they showed us where their property ends. See that green? [Pointing to green areas on smaller drawing.] That's their land. See the part that isn't colored? [Pointing to land surrounding company property.] Our school is in that surrounding land."

"They had hired an arborist to tell them the best ways to save the trees and have space for their company too. [Men holding up pictures of large trees.] An arborist is a tree expert."

[Pointing to tree protection plan drawing.] "From the map, it looks like they are going to save as many trees as possible and have a nice company."

[Students and men shaking hands.] "We are happy to learn that some companies do care about the environment."

[Students standing in front of orange mesh fence and trees.] "We are all earth savers. You could be too. Just notice what is going on around your environment and write letters if you are not happy."

[Picture of whole class yelling] "Kids can have power! "

I have always taken my students very seriously. I treat them with respect, as I am aware that their concerns and interests are very real to them. In many ways, they are wiser than many of the adults around them. Their ideas are usually better too. So when we were out on the playground one afternoon, I listened as they pointed out the property beyond our school's boundary line. There was a new orange fence, and we could see bulldozers moving back and forth knocking trees down. This sight made the children very angry. They were further appalled when I told them a company was building a national headquarters on that spot. They were very worried about the trees dying and the animals losing their homes.

Children should not feel powerless. There had to be something they could do to express their feelings. I was facing a dilemma, however. Our county has specific science objectives for each grade level, and taking the time to address the children's needs would likely be perceived as taking too much time away from the required fourth grade science curriculum. It seemed that there was little enough time to cover everything as it was. Should I listen to my students and seize the opportunity? Or should I follow the mandated curriculum sequence for science?

I began to look at the science objectives to see what we might cover if we took the time to investigate this environmental issue. Surely we could find a way to learn science and make a difference in our community. Over the next several days, I got little sleep as I wrestled with this dilemma of meaningful learning. Finally, I gathered my courage and took the plunge. I invited my students to collaborate with me in designing and carrying out a series of activities and investigations that would enable us to learn more about the habitat and ecology of the nearby lot. It was not long before the children's frustration was channeled into an actual campaign. They wrote polite business letters to the company, expressing their concerns about the land clearing and its effect on the environment.

While listening to the children's comments as they investigated the effects of tree cutting, I realized that none of us were familiar with the environmental protection laws of our county. We invited representatives from the company to visit our class. They brought a landscape architect. He explained that there were laws, however flawed, that protected the trees of our county. This was an enormous relief to the children, whose vivid imaginations had conjured up images of the company randomly cutting down as many trees as they wanted. The landscape architect explained to students about county tree protection plans. The students learned how to draw a "tree protection plan" of their own using the calculations taught to them by the landscape architect.

During the course of this project, my students also learned about erosion, water drainage, the relationship between landscape and the needs of local animals, plant and animal species, public relations, letter writing, organization, teamwork, videotape technology, occupations, laws, public responsibility, landscape design, map reading, empowerment, and much more. In the future, will I listen to my students or will I follow the mandated science curriculum sequence? I believe I'll do both!

FOR REFLECTION AND DISCUSSION

1. What kinds of decisions must a teacher make when thinking about covering mandated curriculum in a nontraditional manner?

2. Once the decision has been made to seize a teachable situation, what strategies can a teacher use to keep track of the wide variety of curriculum that is covered?

3. In the project described in this case, what kinds of assessments would be appropriate and why?

■ **C O M M E N T A R Y**

Real-World Learning Can Lead to Student Empowerment

Kathy Thompson

A critical problem for students involves applying knowledge learned in school to problems and situations around them. Many of my students read and write quite well but lack experience in applying these skills to science in meaningful ways. Meanwhile, other students see science as having little relevance to their lives in school and therefore lack the motivation necessary to experience academic success. As a result, students' thinking and problem-solving skills and their abilities to apply them are impeded.

How can we engage such diverse students in science learning? How can educators encourage students to make connections between school and the rest of the world? The answer lies in the degree to which students see a real link between what they learn in school and what happens in their lives and in their futures. These connections empower students to take on the challenges of success and to make a difference in their communities.

Students in my classroom have experienced empowerment in various ways. I will discuss two of these approaches.

Kids With Powers (KWiPS) is one of the most exciting approaches to learning that I (in collaboration with a colleague) have used in my classroom. KWiPS is a student problem-solving approach in which students identify science challenges within their school and community and explore possible solutions to the problems they encounter. Using the KWiPS approach, students initially engage in brainstorming to identify science problems in our school and community that they believe are important. Students, working in teams, then select one of the most pressing issues and begin to develop a plan for conducting background research.

Over the past four years, my students have selected a wide range of science issues to study using the KWiPS approach. The nutritional value of cafeteria food, restroom sanitation, schoolyard erosion, and peer pressure in relation to substance abuse are just a few of the issues they have explored in depth. Preliminary student research includes such activities as observing, developing surveys, interviewing, conducting laboratory investigations, and documenting data. After the data have been collected, students analyze what they have learned and develop feasible goals and action plans. My goal is for students to generate and evaluate possible solutions to the issues they have explored; this may include the development of more surveys, interviews with school and district personnel, or videotaped observations. Throughout the process, we conduct miniconferences, at which groups share their success and failures and classmates offer suggestions.

The KWiPS approach to science learning has been met with much enthusiasm and has garnered great success. For example, the Cafeteria Group met with school and district food services personnel to make eating in the school's cafeteria more appealing and valuable in terms of nutrition. The group's efforts resulted in new food items being offered and the addition of self-serve items to the lunch menu. One of the group's favorite activities was serving as taste testers for potential new food items. The Peer Pressure Group investigated the problem

"How can we change peers' attitudes toward substance abuse?" As a result of their real-world problem solving, they created "Get to Know You" activities carried out during lunch. Last year, the Restroom Sanitation group was successful in getting door locks installed, and hot water quickly followed. After learning about the impact of trampling on the schoolyard habitat, the School Grounds Group planted grass in the commons area that had been made bare by student traffic. The group met with district personnel for groundskeeping assistance, solicited funds, and enlisted parent volunteers. This group could not contain their excitement in class after a trip to a local home improvement store to purchase the necessary planting materials.

Another approach to empowering students in my science classroom has been through the Community Context Curriculum Project (CCCP), a collaborative project involving the area Chamber of Commerce and its member businesses, industries, and agencies. The desired goal of this project is confidence—a belief of trust and faith in oneself, the school, and the community. With confidence comes self-reliance. Self-reliance stresses self-trust, manifested in action with implied independence and self-sufficiency, all necessary traits of successful middle school students. The path to these ends is student empowerment.

Students participating in the CCCP were empowered in their science learning through a variety of activities. Through the CCCP, students engaged in real-world activities such as learning how to use and construct maps of our county or learning about the impact of local businesses, industries, and agencies in our community. They integrated mathematics and science knowledge as they mapped out routes to different workplace settings in the community. They also learned how to write business letters as they contacted each workplace to arrange meeting times. Students learned interviewing techniques and etiquette and had the opportunity to apply their knowledge as they interviewed store and factory managers, business owners, and presidents of companies. One of the main goals of the CCCP was to allow students to make connections between school science and the workplace. Through their experiences, which included on-site visits to factories, small businesses, and local agencies, students learned what science and academic skills are pertinent to various workplace contexts. Students were amazed at how often math, language, and science were used in these workplaces. Students spent time exploring the elements of the workplace ethic and how it might affect future employment, and they discussed its importance with the employers of the workplaces they toured.

For most of my students, prior knowledge of the workplace consisted of information about their parents' place of employment. For many of them, the CCCP was also the first exposure to a variety of career choices. Students began to realize that life did not end after school and that better-skilled and better-educated employees reap the benefits of good jobs. After touring a local rubber plant, Shavoris exclaimed, "I want to work here! "

Is it really important for students to feel a sense of empowerment? Just ask Anthony, who rushed up to me in the hallway saying excitedly, "Did you see our grass? It's finally growing!" Yes, indeed, the grass *was* finally growing, after a full year of being tended. By his own admission, Anthony, a child angered by the divorce of his parents, did not care much for school, much less a class in science, but through KWiPS, he became not only a more confident student but also a more confident person. Then ask Katie, an enthusiastic but cynical young girl who quickly saw through the gimmicks teachers often used to motivate students. She visited my class to share with my current students her experiences with hands-on science involvement in the school. Her group, Bored Science Students, identified ways to make school more interesting for their classmates. After sharing the successes and difficulties of learning about teaching and learning styles and how these affect individual students, one student asked Katie about her favorite part of KWiPS. With absolutely no prompting, she declared, "Knowing that students *can* make a difference. It's not just teachers and adults who can make things happen. Students can too." She laughed as she continued, "In fact, we learned that sometimes kids can get things accomplished better than adults can!"

For students to be successful members of a science learning community and our larger society, it is imperative that they experience empowerment. This is important not only in the science classroom, but also throughout students' lifelong educational experiences. In my experience, this empowerment occurs when students are engaged in real-world problem solving and activities.

Decisions, Teachable Moments, and the Curriculum

Grace Lyon

Teaching is a constant process of decision making. Indeed, becoming comfortable with decision making is essential to becoming comfortable with the role of the teacher. The teacher's decisions are seldom of the concrete (and low-level) variety. They concern where, along a continuum between extremes, to establish their stance toward learning. The dilemma that arises in this case is where, between the teachable moment presented by the students and the sequence and pace of the mandated curriculum, these teachers will establish their stance.

The considerations of the teachable moment concept are far-ranging, including the affective domain and several constructivist concerns. The teachable moment hinges on a provoking event that gives rise to questions, opinions, and feelings. Therefore, the affective domain is a consideration. Relevance and the ownership of learning are constructivist considerations that coincide closely with the concept of the teachable moment. From this perspective, a science curriculum that is relevant to the students' own real-life experiences can provide a scaffold for learning and can assist students in integrating prior knowledge with new learning. Allowing students to control the vehicle by which content is communicated empowers them to take responsibility for their own learning. Cincotta and Pate express concern about the anger and worry of their students that coincides with this aspect of the teachable moment. They also acknowledge the power issues that the students have with what they see happening in the world around them. It appears that these teachers have good reason to direct their instructional stance toward the teachable moment.

In many elementary schools, the mandated curriculum typically consists of a body of content and concept objectives for science at particular grade levels. Many teachers believe that the knowledge that will be required of students at the next grade level and in standardized testing situations is reflected in the mandated curriculum and cannot be ignored, even in part, without students suffering negative consequences. A lesser but still real concern for many teachers is the professional consequence in relation to issues of accountability. However, curriculum mandates generally are about *what* to teach rather than about *how* to teach. How to teach science, as well as other subjects, is generally considered to be the purview of the teacher.

Furthermore, all curriculum objectives require a vehicle for communication. So the decision for teachers like Cincotta and Pate becomes one of how to choose those curriculum objectives that can be addressed in the teachable moment.

A final consideration in this case is pace. Although Cincotta and Pate do not address this issue explicitly in their case, it is a central part of every curriculum decision that teachers make. There must be a fit between the proportion of curriculum covered and time spent. Many teachers and administrators view this issue as the acid test, believing that a vehicle for teaching must have an acceptable efficiency or be discarded in favor of more efficient methods. This has been the death knell for many pet projects as curriculum mandates have tightened. It is not necessarily a bad thing. The choices can be hard; that is why the expertise of the professional teacher is required. If it was easy, all those nonprofessionals who think they could teach really could.

References

Kauchak, D. P., & Eggen, P. D. (1998). *Learning and teaching: Research-based methods.* Boston: Allyn & Bacon.

Loughlin, C. E., & Suina, J. H. (1982). *The learning environment.* New York: Teachers College Press.

National Association for the Education of Young Children. (1996). NAEYC position statement: Responding to linguistic and cultural diversity: Recommendations for effective early childhood education. *Young Children, 52*(4), 4–9.

National Research Council. (1996). *National science education standards.* Washington, DC: National Academy Press.

Resources to Consider

Bell, J. L. (1993). *Soap science.* Reading, MA: Addison-Wesley.
    This book includes guidelines for thirty-six activities and experiments that can be used to engage young children in an exploration of soap and bubbles.

CIESE Online Classroom Projects [On-line]. Available at: http://k12science.ati.stevens-tech.edu/currichome.html.
    Collaborative projects represent a form of innovative practice in science teaching that continues to grow in popularity. This award-winning site provides links to a number of on-line science projects in which teachers and their student can participate. The project organizers are scientists or teachers and their classes, and several of the projects involve collecting real-time data. Links to the *National Science Education Standards* accompany a brief description of each project.

Duckworth, E. (1987). *The having of wonderful ideas and other essays on teaching and learning.* New York: Teachers College Press.
    This collection of essays highlights the significant role children's ideas can play in the learning of science and other subjects.

Paley, V. G. (1992). *You can't say, you can't play.* Cambridge, MA: Harvard University Press.
    This book examines the social worlds of young children in a kindergarten classroom. It includes stories from the perspectives of kindergarten students that shed light on activities such as play and some of the moral dimensions of schooling.

Steinberg, S. R., & Kincheloe, J. L. (Eds.). (1998). *Students as researchers: Creating classrooms that matter.* Bristol, PA: Falmer Press, Taylor & Francis.
    This book examines the importance of engaging and empowering students as researchers. It is premised on the idea that students are knowledgeable instructors who, through the process of inquiry, can create learning and curricula. Instructional ideas for involving students in research are included throughout the chapters.

5

Diverse Science Learners in the Elementary Classroom

In the current era of science education reform, schools are challenged to reinvent themselves in ways that embrace diversity and incorporate the cultural knowledge that all students bring to school into the curriculum. Science educators agree that this is not an easy task, as classrooms in recent years have become complex microcosms of cultural diversity. Between 1980 and 1992, the percentage of Latinos in the United States increased by more than 65 percent and that of Asians by 123.5 percent. English had become a second language to more than 14 percent of the nation's population (U.S. Bureau of the Census, 1993). Those percentages have undoubtedly increased since then.

The growing racial and cultural diversity of the student population creates both challenges and opportunities for science teachers. On the one hand, science teachers in today's classrooms search for ways to understand and respect students' individual cultures and beliefs. At the same time, they struggle with how to best help all students arrive at common science understandings. Many studies illustrate the importance of recognizing and building on the cultural experiences that students bring with them to school. All students, particularly second-language science learners, need opportunities to develop a language for talking about scientific ideas and chances to formulate and explore questions about their own world. However, for many teachers, how they might best accomplish the task of meeting the needs of an increasingly diverse student population remains elusive.

The four cases in this chapter highlight a variety of dilemmas encountered as elementary teachers address the science learning needs of their students. In "Who Eats the Mango?," Janice Koch narrates the story of Kim, a student teacher whose attempt to nurture third grade students' understanding of diversity seems to backfire. Lorie Hammond and Diana Charmbury, in their case "How Do You Grow Rice?," struggle to build a science and language program that connects with the life experiences of immigrant children from Southeast Asia. Their case illustrates how understandings of community and parent involvement in science education are collaboratively developed though the creation of a nutrition unit and a Iu Mien cultural garden. In the case "I Do Not Understand," Julie Luft describes the frustrations of her attempt to involve a second-language science learner in an inquiry-based investigation. Ellen van den Berg's case, "Constructivism: Time for a Reality Check?," sheds light on the dilemmas of teaching elementary science in Dutch classrooms. Her case illustrates the tensions that characterize the constructivist practices advocated in current science education reforms and the reality of Dutch elementary classrooms.

The demographic and social changes reflected in today's classrooms parallel recent increases in both fertility and migration trends (Pallas, Natriello, & McDill, 1995). If these trends continue, the science classrooms of tomorrow will look distinctly different. Whereas modern educational wisdom sought to melt individual differences by making us all the same, postmodern science education cherishes difference and seeks to value excluded voices and understandings in the classroom. There is a growing recognition among science teachers that diversity presents an exciting opportunity. It has the potential to serve as invaluable knowledge in creating the science learning communities of tomorrow—communities that genuinely reflect the values of harmony and understanding.

■ **C A S E   5 . 1** ■

Who Eats the Mango?

Janice Koch

■ *In this open case, my student teacher, Kim, develops a science lesson with our third grade students that explores the properties of edible plant parts. The students have been instructed to bring a fruit and a vegetable to class. The students come from a largely white, middle-class suburban area that is just beginning to experience some diversity from recent Central American immigration. Wanting to expose students to the plants grown and eaten in diverse cultures, this gifted novice teacher brings in many different kinds of fruits and vegetables. Anticipating that our students will be excited and curious to learn about these unusual fruits and vegetables, she is surprised and disturbed when they reject learning about these plant parts because they are "strange" and "weird." She is not sure how to handle the students' reactions and wonders what went wrong. The story is told in Janice's voice as she observed Kim's lesson. Commentary following the case is provided by Pamela Fraser-Abder, a science teacher educator with much experience working with teachers in the design of science learning experiences that acknowledge and build on students' diverse cultural backgrounds.*

It is late fall, and I am observing my student teacher Kim as she develops a lesson on fruits and vegetables with our third grade students in an affluent, predominantly white suburban neighborhood in the Northeast. In this particular classroom, the students have been studying, examining, classifying, and planting seeds for several days They have made germination bags and have manipulated variables to determine the optimal conditions for seed growth. They have also explored the seeds of the deciduous and coniferous trees outside their school building. The science table in the corner of this sunny classroom is covered with different samples of seeds in various stages. There are different bean seeds in labeled dishes, some pumpkin seeds germinating in moist plastic bags, and lima bean plants at later stages that have been placed in pots of soil. There are many types of acorns, and "polly-noses" of maple trees with their seeds at their ends. Several types of pine cones are on display. It feels as though this science table has a direct connection to these students' local environment.

As a science teacher educator, I encourage the preservice teachers with whom I work to help their children make connections between their science experiences and everyday life. I also challenge my students to engage elementary children in diverse learning experiences that encourage the children's own understanding of diversity. Therefore, when Kim planned her lesson on fruits and vegetables as part of this seed-to-plant unit, I encouraged her to seek out fruits and vegetables that are not commonly grown, cooked, or eaten locally. This activity supports my belief that science curriculum can serve as a mirror and a window, a metaphor adapted from Emily Style (1988).

The children were instructed to bring in one fruit and one vegetable to explore in class. Kim explained that they were going to examine parts of plants that we eat. It was apparent that the children were very excited about the assignment. When they entered the classroom, they rushed to their tables. Then each child had an opportunity to describe the plant parts he or she had brought to share with the class. The array of fruits and vegetables included apples; pears; bananas; oranges; tomatoes; grapes; cucumbers; acorn squash; celery; lettuce; green, yellow, and red bell peppers; and cauliflower. The students used plastic knives to examine their specimens carefully, and Kim challenged them to determine which of these plant parts had seeds. Working in small groups, the children made two piles of edible plant parts: those with seeds and those without seeds. Kim coached them as they struggled to determine whether the dots inside the banana were actually seeds. "What do you think?" asked Kim. "If they aren't seeds, then what could they be?"

The pile of fruits was growing at each table with plant parts that the students were used to referring to as "fruits." The fruit pile included the peppers, cucumbers, tomatoes, and squash, in addition to the more conventional fruits—the apples, pears, bananas, and oranges. "If the plant parts have seeds," announced Kim, "do you know what scientists call them?" The children shouted out, "Fruits!" and then started giggling that a tomato cannot be a fruit. Kim went on to explain that scientifically, the plant parts with seeds are called fruits. She then asked the students to describe the vegetable pile. "What part of the plant is the celery? The lettuce? The carrot, the cauliflower?" The students began to identify the stem for the celery, the leaf for the lettuce, the root for the carrot, and the flower of the plant for the cauliflower florets. They learned that these different plant parts are collectively called vegetables. Confident in this new-found knowledge, Ramon said to Kim, "I can't wait to tell my parents that the tomato is really a fruit."

At this point in the lesson, Kim introduced some new and different plant parts and challenged the students to identify them as fruits or vegetables. Kim had brought persimmon, avocado, mango, papaya, fennel, and collard greens. She showed these edible plant parts to the students and asked for group volunteers to explore these new and strange-looking specimens. "Oooh," Keith shouted as he touched the rough surface of the persimmon, "this feels gross." Ignoring Keith's comment, Kim encouraged groups to examine the unusual plant parts. She held up a papaya, then a mango, then the fennel—no volunteers! Kim began to panic as she realized that her students did not want to explore strange and unfamiliar plant parts.

Struggling with the curriculum as window into other worlds, Kim was disappointed by the students' reluctance to extend their initial discoveries. She wanted the students to classify the unusual plant parts as either a fruit or a vegetable and then to examine these plants and learn where they are grown and eaten. Frustrated, Kim held up a large mango. "Let's look at this plant part," she said. The students watched as she sliced the dark-green-skinned fruit in half and revealed a soft, juicy, yellow-orange pulp. Making a mess, Kim separated the juicy pulp until a flat, broad seed was revealed. The sound effects during this exploration revealed the students' disgust for this new fruit, which not one student was willing to taste. "Who eats a mango?" asked Kim. "Where do you think it grows?"

There were no answers, and Kim's desire to expose the students to plant parts from other cultures was thwarted by a class who experienced "different" as threatening or "disgusting."

FOR REFLECTION AND DISCUSSION

1. What could Kim have done before the lesson to anticipate her students' reactions to the unfamiliar plant parts?

2. What strategies might Kim have tried to engage her students in dissecting the strange plant parts?

3. Would students have been more willing to examine the mango and other unfamiliar plant parts had Kim involved them in planning for the lesson? Provide support for your answer.

4. How can elementary teachers prepare for making the science learning experiences of their students more culturally diverse?

■COMMENTARY

Plugging Cultural Holes

Pamela Fraser-Abder

With the increasing diversity in our schools, many teacher education programs are encouraging their teachers to use their science experiences as an avenue for introducing cultural diversity. Kim's attempt to use this activity as a mirror and a window is laudable but required more planning and better contextualization. In this case, the exposure to fruits and vegetables from a different culture causes these third graders to reject the instruction and ultimately miss the opportunity to experience cultural diversity. Their behavior was both unnerving and unsettling to this new teacher. Kim missed the opportunity to use this activity as an avenue for letting her students better understand the fruits and vegetables they eat and for looking through their "window" at fruits and vegetables used in another culture. What appeared to be a well-planned lesson had many cultural holes that the teacher overlooked.

Although the community in which Kim teaches had experienced a recent influx of Central American immigrants, that does not mean that the Caucasian children in this class had been exposed to Central American culture and foods. Kim automatically assumed that the children would make the connection that these "new and strange" fruits and vegetables are part of the same classification scheme as the more "familiar" ones. She did not expand on her description of what fruits and vegetables could be; therefore, it should have come as no surprise that the children categorically rejected the mangoes. No attempt was made to compare the new fruits and vegetables with the familiar fruits and vegetables; instead, they were presented as different from the rest, and to third graders, this did not represent an open door to discovery. As a result, the Central American foods that Kim shared were identified as "strange" and "gross." If Kim herself had been aware of the variety of mangoes, she might also have selected a mango that was less messy when cut, thereby eliminating the initial messy appearance. The class needed a more structured and aesthetically pleasing procedure for examining and comparing the fruits and vegetables.

As Meir and Nelson-Barber (1990, p. 7) state, "Without clear definitions of the common knowledge base and sets of experiences, misinterpretations occur." The hole of the existing schema can be plugged in a variety of ways.

The students in Kim's classroom did not see the mango as part of their existing schematic representations of fruits partly because Kim did not set up a common knowledge base for them. Kim's students were, instead, tightly constrained by their own limited definitions. To establish this conceptual base, Kim could have shown students pictures of mango trees to introduce the idea that these fruits do not grow any differently than common fruits, such as apples. She could have also provided pictures of the mango for comparison with other fruits. These new ideas would have slowly expanded her students' existing understandings of the concept "fruit." After establishing this common base, Kim could then have asked her students how these new understandings about fruits fit with their previous ideas.

Moreover, Kim could have used a high-quality piece of literature to introduce an "Around the World" game, giving each student an opportunity to explore an exotic place in Central America. This game could have been integrated into a social studies or language arts lesson with activities such as reading, journaling, and reporting. The initial reading could have revolved around the culture and customs of the country or been centered on a story that refers to local fruits and vegetables. Students could have made a brief presentation to the rest of the class about the fruits and vegetables used in their cultural study. If any Central American students were present in the class, they could have been asked to discuss fruits and vegetables most familiar to them; this would have been the perfect opportunity to add cultural diversity to the discussion. The Caucasian students in the class could have transformed their understanding of other cultures from the abstract to the real as they came to understand that a peer in their class (someone "like" them) is a person who eats these fruits and vegetables. Therefore, what began as a tourist approach could have metamorphosed into a mirror and a window for understanding fruits and vegetables that are familiar to different cultures and could have served as a mechanism for using diversity as a context for science teaching.

■ C A S E 5 . 2 ■

How Do You Grow Rice?

Lorie Hammond and Diana Charmbury

■ *This closed case highlights the challenges Diana faced as she taught a nutrition unit that she and her "critical friend," Lorie, developed for third grade students. The challenges associated with teaching the unit center on the fact that most of Diana's students come from Southeast Asia, and almost all are from an Iu Mien clan whose language is spoken by one language aide but not by teachers in the schools. Important questions emerged for both Diana and Lorie as they developed the nutrition unit and engaged the students in learning activities. They wondered how a science and language program could be devised and implemented that builds on children's life experiences. How could the program draw on the knowledge and expertise of the children's parents to embed the science learning experiences in the local Iu Mien community and thus make them meaningful for the children? The case is narrated by Lorie and is followed by commentary from science educators Sharon Nichols and Linda James.*

> *Teacher:*   What is good for you to drink?
> *Student:*   Milk. We should drink milk each day.

Teacher: Do you drink milk?

Student (sheepishly):   No. I don't like it. It makes me sick.

This dialogue, between Diana and an eight-year-old Iu Mien student, illustrates the dilemma Diana faced when presenting a traditional unit on nutrition to a classroom of Southeast Asian and Central Asian refugee children. For this group of mostly lactose-intolerant people, dairy products are generally unfamiliar and unhealthful. Yet standard nutrition units, supported by organizations such as the Dairy Council, construct the food pyramid to include milk and many other foods that diverse children may or may not eat. A talented English and science teacher, Diana used hands-on experiments, visits to the supermarket, and even taste tests to make her unit on nutrition understandable to her English-learning students. However, after teaching Iu Mien and other Southeast Asian and Central Asian students this unit, she began to realize that the foods she was so carefully illustrating with plastic models and colorful charts did not reflect the day-to-day realities of these children's lives.

Diana and I agreed that co-authoring a modified unit on food was a good way to create dialogue about how concepts usually covered in a nutrition unit need to be modified for a multicultural group of young learners. We began to ask ourselves the following questions: What would a Southeast and Central Asian, or international, food pyramid look like? From what sources do our community's families access their foods? Finally, would a school garden project be a good way to blend science and a school community collaboration with traditionally horticultural cultures such as Southeast and Central Asians? These were some of the many questions which guided us as we developed Project Food. (Project Food is a science unit for English learners that developed as a collaboration between Lorie and Diana. It was written and piloted as part of a larger science curriculum project for language minority students, the Bilingual Integrated Curriculum Project, which was committed to making exploratory science accessible to English language learners, teaching language through science, and incorporating community languages and cultures into the science curriculum. Initial curriculum projects involved Spanish-speaking students in classrooms where their teachers were native Spanish speakers.)

Diana and I were also guided by a parallel set of questions about how to teach students inquiry skills through training them to be mini-ethnographers, collecting and analyzing knowledge about their own community. Our premise was that bicultural children need to become conscious of the cultural forces that accost them at home, at school, and in the peer community and to understand that they can make conscious choices about which values they choose to embrace. We hoped that by validating community knowledge in the domain of school science, we would help students to feel reinforced in expressing their home values rather than feeling that they had to answer questions in school terms, by stating that milk is good when in fact it makes them sick.

We began Project Food with an exercise in which children looked at pictures taken from *National Geographic* magazines of families from all over the world eating various foods in various postures. We asked them to talk about what the people were doing and then to tell us what foods were common in their homes. Our Iu Mien–speaking aide assisted by writing words on the board in Iu Mien and in English for foods that children suggested, such as greens (*meange*), peppers (*funv chinc*), and onions (*zouv*). Diana helped the speakers of other languages to sound out the words they wanted to write in English. Our next step was to engage the students in an activity in which they were first asked what they *Know* about the subject, then what they *Want* to learn, and finally, after inquiry activities, to reflect on what they have

Learned. When asked what they *Know* about food, the third grade English as a Second Language (ESL) class gave the following responses:

> Rice is a food.
>
> We eat food.
>
> We like to eat.
>
> We grow seeds.
>
> We water the food.
>
> Water makes it grow.
>
> And sun.
>
> Food helps us to grow.
>
> We put slug medicine on the plants so slugs don't eat our food.
>
> We eat apples. We eat potatoes, fish, oranges, crab, shrimp, rabbits, deer, . . .

Diana and I were stunned to find that when our Iu Mien and other Southeast and Central Asian students were asked to talk about food, they immediately tied the discussion to growing gardens. We knew that their families had garden plots at two public sites near schools and that a garden project might be a natural for their school, but we had no idea how strongly Southeast and Central Asian people associated food with the cycle of gardening that produces it. When asked, "What do you want to learn about food?," the children's responses were as follows:

> How to plant it.
>
> How to eat potatoes [a new food to many].
>
> How to cook.
>
> Where a good place to plant is.
>
> How to pick the plants.
>
> How to plant corn, apple trees, radishes, pumpkins, . . .
>
> Why is corn different colors?
>
> How they grow rice.
>
> How they make bread.
>
> How do we make the corn small enough to make the corn bread?
>
> How do we make juice?

We thought the children's questions were very good ones. One question, "Why is corn different colors?," could yield a rich discussion on genetics. Some questions, such as "how to eat potatoes," were easily answered. Many children thought that they had never eaten potatoes, but when we mentioned "french fries," everyone knew what we meant. Some were surprised that the brown objects in the supermarket could be turned into french fries. From then on, when we mentioned potatoes, the children responded "Burger King" with great assurance. They felt that they now knew about potatoes.

The next step in Project Food was to teach children interviewing skills so that they could begin to collect community knowledge about food. Using the simple question "What did you have for dinner last night?," Diana and I modeled how one person would ask the question and then take notes on the other person's answer. We showed that if you did not know how to write all the words, you could draw a picture of the other person's response. Then we asked our Iu Mien aide and another adult who spoke Iu Mien to demonstrate an interview in the Iu Mien language. We clarified that they would be interviewing family members in their home language. Finally, our children practiced interviewing each other. Each child was paired with another from his or her language group for this activity. We then told the children that they were going to be scientists and that we were going to give them special notebooks in which they would record information about their communities. They were very excited. Their first job was to repeat the interview we just demonstrated and practice: to ask their parents what foods they would eat for dinner that night. (Before doing this project, we sent a letter to parents and had an aide telephone parents who could not read English to inform them that we would be studying community foods and that we were not prying into their home life. The parents responded favorably.)

The day after the children were given the interview assignment, Diana reported that they came early to her class, during recess, because they were so excited to share what they had found out. Whereas the Southeast and Central Asian students had always been "good" and had responded to questions when asked, when Diana began to incorporate their home knowledge into the curriculum, their disposition changed from passive to active. They began to volunteer many more answers in class. Diana also reported a marked change in their attitude toward homework. In the past, she had noticed students throwing their homework in the garbage as they left school. Some students said that they could not read the English on the homework papers and that no one in their family could either, so they didn't know how to do it. When we began the ethnographic homework assignments, students were excited about taking their notebooks home.

A journal entry brought in by one Iu Mien child illustrates the typical Iu Mien diet. Rice, chicken, peppers, cilantro, onion, garlic, and mustard greens form the basis of many dinners, as was reinforced from children's journals and by our language aide. We treated the children's descriptions of their dinners as data and made charts marking how many times certain foods appeared, then graphed these data. Children were able to make generalizations from their own data. Their generalizations included the following:

People eat a lot of rice.

People eat a lot of eggs too.

People eat a lot of fish.

Very few people eat bananas.

People drink water.

Mustard greens and pork are good in soup.

When we asked our children what they had learned from this exercise, we could see that the discussions at home went further than just listing foods. One student said, "I learned what pork is, that it comes from a pig." Another said, "My mom told me fish is good. Blue fish is good; it has a lot of protein." It would be easy for a teacher to think that Southeast and Central Asian parents, who are recent refugees and do not have a written language, would not know about protein. Without hearing this from our students, we would never have known what their parents could contribute because of the language barrier between us. We were surprised that many students were excited about using their home languages to do their homework. We thought that a reinforcement of primary language would be an eventual benefit of an ethnographic project in which children serve as language mediators, but we did not realize that the children would respond immediately to this dimension of the project. When asked what they had learned, one student said, "I learned to write Hmong. My aunt helped me to write." Another said, "I learned to write Iu Mien words by myself."

After recording several dinners, the children participated in an art project in which a favorite dinner was constructed on a paper plate glued onto a construction paper place mat. Students were given styrofoam, tissue paper, felt, and colored paper with which to construct representations of their favorite foods. They did so in great detail, with shaved styrofoam rice emerging as a favorite. Students then had to label the foods they ate and break them down into their original ingredients. This prepared them to think about the basic staple foods that make up the diet of their ethnic group. Our next assignment was to ask students to predict the five most important foods eaten by their families, as well as to think about the origins of these foods. After writing their predictions, students went out to interview their parents to find out whether their responses matched their predictions. In the Iu Mien group, which is made up of new immigrants who continue to cook a traditional diet, predictions and results were very consistent. The five most important foods were generally rice, chicken, mustard greens, chiles, and a variety of fifth responses, including various meats, fish, cilantro, onions, and other vegetables. The data that we collected from children enabled us to teach the food pyramid in cross-cultural terms, comparing American, Iu Mien, and other cultural groups' ways of meeting their basic nutritional needs and then studying the function of proteins, starches, and so on in a standard fashion.

Diana and I were very interested in students' responses about the sources of their foods. When reporting on where they got the five important foods, most families listed at least three sources, including their gardens, the river (fish), fields (mushrooms and herbs), farmers' markets, and Asian stores, in addition to the local supermarket. The ways in which people get food made us realize that immigrant families in our community are resourceful and develop resources collectively. Although school personnel may see them as non-English-speaking families who appear helpless at meetings, they have a very different identity within their own community and have creative ways of moving beyond this community to find resources in the larger world of rivers, farms, and special markets.

As a finale to Project Food, parents from Southeast and Central Asia were invited into the classroom to cook traditional meals. Several parents responded, and Iu Mien parents planned a group cooking day. Diana had originally planned a forty-five-minute block of time for Iu Mien parents to cook stir-fry and rice for each class, but in fact the cooking took about two hours and resulted in a feast for about 100 people. It turned out that the Iu Mien parents decided that this was their opportunity to reward the teachers for all their work by making a dinner for all of them. Diana managed to arrange the children's school schedules so that all of the ESL students and some others could watch the cooking and have a chance to try the food, and teachers were invited to a special after-school party, at which they met Iu Mien parents who had never come to school before.

After Project Food ended, Diana decided to pursue the students' question about how to grow rice, since rice is the staple food of the Southeast and Central Asian students. She created a small unit in which she brought in rice seed and a movie on rice growing donated by the Rice Growers' Association. She also brought in a variety of foods made from rice, such as steamed rice, rice cakes, and rice cereal. Children tasted these foods and commented on how they tasted, smelled, and looked. Diana used the opportunity to expand the children's English vocabulary to include descriptive words such as "crunchy," "sticky," and "soft." The children then planted rice seed in two large oil pans filled with soil and enough water to flood the seed. After watching the video on rice, they drew the stages of rice growth, from sprout to seed, and then predicted how long it would take their rice to sprout. The interest in gardening shared by Southeast Asian and Central Asian children and their parents, illustrated by the cultural data they gathered during Project Food, encouraged Diana and other teachers in the school to establish a school community garden. The next year, her rice lesson expanded into a parent demonstration project in which Iu Mien parents volunteered to grow rice in the school garden, then illustrated the process of harvesting, drying, and cooking the rice. The garden became a living laboratory where Southeast and Central Asian parents could demonstrate how their traditional crops are grown, where teachers could study horticulture and entomology from the point of view of Western science, and where both groups could learn from each other.

FOR REFLECTION AND DISCUSSION

1. How did Diana's traditional unit on nutrition differ from Project Food?
2. What novel teaching and learning strategies did Project Food employ?
3. What inquiry techniques did students learn from gathering and analyzing community data?
4. How did Diana use her science projects to teach English to her students?
5. How did these projects reinforce the students' home languages?
6. What are the possibilities and limitations of Project Food as a model for science teachers in other elementary schools?

■ COMMENTARY

Growing New Science Connections

Sharon E. Nichols and Linda E. James

As we read Lorie and Diana's case, we reflected on our own experiences dealing with cultural diversity in teaching science. We have both taught in elementary schools located in the southeastern region of the United States. In terms of the cultural backgrounds of our own students, we generally describe them as being Caucasian or African American children, raised in rural or city areas, low-income or wealthy backgrounds, and single-parent or "family" homes.

Although our students have presented cultural challenges, we felt that our situations were not nearly as complex as those described in the case. However, we read the case with a sense of anticipation, because we are beginning to see rapid increases in the numbers of non-English-speaking (mostly Hispanic) students in our local schools. We are on the brink of encountering more complex types of cultural dilemmas, such as those described in this case. In our view, this case conveys several important guidelines for creating inclusive science education experiences for all children.

One guideline presented in the case is that science learning needs to be built on the experiences and language of children. This idea not only is appropriate for bilingual instruction, but is applicable to all science teaching—especially when teaching young science learners. It is not unusual to see teachers begin science lessons by introducing science vocabulary words, but this is problematic when children have not had experiences and conversations to develop understandings of their science experience. The approach used by Lorie and Diana modeled using children's everyday language as a beginning point for teaching science concepts. They encouraged students to use their own language to describe objects and phenomena related to the science topics they were teaching. Even when English is the student's primary language, it is important for children to use their everyday language to provide a way for them to communicate how they are seeing and experiencing the world around them.

The case also addressed issues concerning the ways in which social experiences shape children's science learning. Sometimes, we tend to think of social aspects of science teaching in terms of strategies that support social processes of science learning in the classroom (e.g., cooperative learning). This case extended the social realm beyond the classroom to consider that children need to be able to take their science learning into the cultural world of their home community. This reminded us of an interesting article by Glen Aikenhead (1998) in which he describes problems students experience when they cannot cross sociocultural borders between home and school and, as a result, may perceive school science as irrelevant to their life experiences. Lorie and Diana recognized this potential hazard, as the children's home cultures were not represented in the food pyramid they were going to teach. Engaging the children in an ethnographic homework assignment to learn how their parents might relate to the science being taught at school was a wonderful way to develop a more relevant science curriculum about nutrition. An important guideline underlying this approach highlights the importance of creating science learning experiences that connect home and school.

The previous guideline also points to the need for children to see science learning as something they value. When science is simply taught from a textbook, teachers are likely to assume that the knowledge in the book is the "official" content to be learned by the students. The children in Diana's classroom showed how they regarded science content when it was imposed on them without consideration for whether or not they saw it as important or valuable knowledge: They threw it in the trash basket. When the children and their parents were invited to use their knowledge as the foundation for building the Project Food curriculum, their life histories, language, and cultural practices were recognized as important knowledge. Science took on a more legitimate purpose for learning as the students and parents perceived that it would authentically generate knowledge they could use. In essence, the case modeled a more authentic view of how science is practiced by scientists, as they too have particular goals and contexts for conducting scientific inquiry (Helms, 1998).

The case also raised several questions for us as we reflected on the possibilities of using such an approach with our own students. In this case, traditional dietary practices of these Asian groups seemed to support eating healthy foods. Our schools, located in eastern North Carolina, are composed predominantly of African American and Caucasian students who live in low-income, rural homes. If we were to conduct an ethnographic study of nutritional habits of our students, their diets would most likely reflect traditional Southern dietary practices (e.g., frequent eating of fried chicken, vegetables cooked in fatty broth, and cornbread fried in an oil-filled black skillet). How should we respond if the sociocultural practices at home sharply contrast with the science concepts that would be taught in our nutrition unit? It also made us think about finding support for teachers as they try to incorporate children's sociocultural backgrounds in science teaching. In this case, Diana was fortunate to have Lorie as a collaborator in this project. What kinds of support systems are in place for teachers in self-contained classrooms that can lend assistance as they try to understand issues of cultural diversity? Finally, with the increasing emphasis on accountability, to what extent do assessment policies encourage teachers to address cultural diversity in teaching science?

■ **C A S E   5 . 3** ■

I Do Not Understand

Julie A. Luft

■ *This open case reveals how difficult it can be to meet the needs of students whose second language is English. In this case, Weir-Sen, a new student to my class and the country, engages in an investigation that emphasizes the abilities to do scientific inquiry and an understanding of scientific inquiry. Throughout the investigation, I was concerned about Weir-Sen's level of participation in his group and his understanding of science as inquiry. When my concerns were confirmed, I wondered what I should have done differently and, more important, what I should do next. The case is followed by commentaries from Julie and from Nam-Haw Kang, a former teacher in Korea and graduate student in science education with personal experience as a second-language science learner.*

It is the fifth day of sixth grade science, and a new student is standing in front of my desk. It is not uncommon for new students to enroll in Center City Middle School at the beginning of the semester; this year, we just seemed to have more students enrolling than previous years. The diverse student body at our urban school is gradually increasing in size, and it seems that a majority of our new students are bilingual or English as a Second Language (ESL) learners. The location of the school (the center of the city, with good public transportation), an established diverse community, and affordable housing seem to make this area attractive to incoming families. Unfortunately, there are not enough programs for minority-language students in our school, and very few teachers are trained to work with bilingual or ESL students. I am a prime example of this. English is a second language for about three fifths of my students, and I have no ESL training.

I welcomed Weir-Sen to my class and asked whether he liked science. He responded with a quiet "Yes." He continued to stand patiently, with paper and books in hand, while I added him to my student roster. Weir-Sen's papers indicated that he had recently moved from Taiwan and was new to the United States. He watched intently as I wrote his name in my book and as I looked at my seating chart for an empty desk in the class. When I found a location for Weir-Sen, I told him he could have a seat behind Michelle and pointed in the direction of the empty seat. He looked uncomfortable in this new setting as he walked toward his desk. When Weir-Sen was seated, he glanced around the class, then removed a sheet of paper and a pencil from his backpack in preparation for the lesson. At that moment, I wondered how much English he spoke.

When the bell rang, I took attendance and then proceeded to describe the activity. "Over the next few days," I began "we will be completing an investigation in class." I went on to explain that we would be engaging in a scientific inquiry activity in order to begin to learn how to do science and about science. I added that the focus of the study would be characterizing the typical sixth grader at our school and that students would have to work in groups of three or four. Because I barely knew the students, I randomly assigned students to groups, except for Weir-Sen. I assigned him to work with Maria and Jose, two students who had already demonstrated an ability to work cooperatively with other students.

I place this activity at the beginning of the school year for two reasons. First, I want my students to engage in a simple investigation at the beginning of the year that provides an opportunity for them to start to learn about collecting data, analyzing data, drawing conclusions, and sharing their findings. In addition, I want my students to begin to develop fundamental ideas about scientific inquiry. These topics are important to me as a teacher, and I emphasize them throughout the year. Second, this investigation gives the students an opportunity to get to know each other. While the students enjoy talking to their peers, I also need this opportunity to learn about my students and their ability to engage in scientific inquiry.

After the students moved into their groups, I asked each group to discuss and list what they would like to learn about the sixth graders at our school. While the student groups pondered different ideas, I looked around the class to assess the participation of students. Weir-Sen was sitting quietly, listening to the conversation between his two teammates. When it looked as if student groups had formed ideas, I asked for one volunteer from each group to summarize what their group would like to know about Center City Middle School sixth graders. Within a few minutes, a list was generated on the blackboard that included items such as number of pets, favorite movies, favorite athletes, number of siblings, favorite sports, number of hours spent watching TV, number of hours spent sleeping, and shoe sizes. With ten minutes of class remaining, I asked each group to select and write down the five items that would make up their survey. Weir-Sen looked at Maria's and Jose's papers and copied the five items that they selected onto his own paper. Before I knew it, class was over, and the students were gone. I wanted to talk briefly with Weir-Sen about my class, but he left before I had a chance.

The following day, I had planned to have student groups develop their surveys. Most students were not familiar with the concept of a survey, so I shared various examples with different formats. Weir-Sen again looked on as his teammates turned survey topics into survey questions. As I observed Weir-Sen primarily copying his teammates work, it became clear that he was not participating in the group discussion. After class, I made a trip to the main office to locate his student file, as I was concerned about his proficiency in English. His file revealed that his first language was Taiwanese. The results of a test administered by the ESL teacher in my school indicated that Weir-Sen should be able to converse in and comprehend the level of English in my class.

During the next three days, students collected data from other sixth graders, and they practiced graphing the collected descriptive and correlational data. It is always exciting to see students collecting and analyzing data; they are beginning to use appropriate tools and techniques to handle data, and they are developing descriptions and explanations based on evidence—important goals in the state and national science standards. Weir-Sen followed Maria and Jose as they collected data from the other students. When it was his turn to record the answer provided by the student, he listened attentively and wrote the answer down. After all of the student groups had collected their data, the task of transforming data began. Whenever I had the chance, I stopped by Weir-Sen's group to assist them. I was pleased that Maria and Jose, his teammates, were patient and helpful. They frequently explained directions in English, and they involved Weir-Sen in the group by having him tally the responses and add and divide the collected numbers. During the last day, Maria and Jose enlisted Weir-Sen in the task of creating graphs. Weir-Sen was meticulous in measuring the size of the graphs and proportioning the bars of the graph. For the most part, he seemed to be fitting into the group, even though he was quiet and withdrawn at times.

Finally, the day came for students to present their findings. I had required that all students be involved in the presentation and that each presentation have a data table and a graph. I assigned a random order for student groups to discuss their results, and Weir-Sen's group drew the last presentation spot. When it was time for their group presentation, they stood behind the large demonstration table that occupied the front of the classroom. Weir-Sen stood off to the side. Maria went first and shared the questions they had selected. Jose followed and discussed how they had collected and analyzed the data. As the final presenter, Weir-Sen began quietly reporting the topics and numerical results. When he got to the last number, a mispronunciation resulted in laughter among a few students. I quickly quieted the students down and asked whether there were any questions. One student volunteered and asked why their data were at odds with the results from another group. Maria and Jose answered while Weir-Sen quietly stood by.

Following the presentations, I handed out self and team member evaluation forms, three open-ended questions about the typical sixth grader investigation that related to scientific inquiry, and I asked the students to draw themselves during the investigation in my class. Each student, including Weir-Sen, worked diligently on the task. After class, I stopped Weir-Sen before he left. I told him how proud I was of his work in the class and how glad I was to have him in the class, and I said that I knew it was hard moving to a new country. He acknowledged my comments and left for his next class.

At the end of the school day, I looked through the evaluations and drawings that the students had completed. Weir-Sen's work was at the bottom of the stack for sixth grade science. He had assessed his teammates to be helpful but rated himself low on helping the group. His responses pertaining to collecting data, examining data, contributing to the group, and cooperating with teammates were similar. His answers to the open-ended questions were incomplete and difficult to understand. Weir-Sen's drawing, attached to his evaluation, had a picture of him sitting in a desk with tears streaming down his face. Underneath, he had written, "I do not understand." I stopped and wondered what I could have done differently to help him in my class and—more important—what I should do next.

FOR REFLECTION AND DISCUSSION

1. How could Julie have organized the lesson and the class differently to better meet Weir-Sen's needs?

2. How should science lessons be structured to meet the needs of second-language science learners?

3. What should Julie do in subsequent science lessons to assist Weir-Sen?

4. How can a teacher ensure that his or her academic standards are upheld while working with ESL or bilingual students?

5. What or who are resources that can assist science teachers as they work with ESL or bilingual students? What type of information does each resource provide?

■ COMMENTARY

Creating Learning Environments for Bilingual Students

Julie A. Luft

In working with bilingual students, I try to create environments that allow students to form procedural and declarative knowledge while developing language. I try to provide concrete experiences before introducing new vocabulary, I often write two or three words that are associated with the lesson on the board, I have students write or draw daily, I utilize as many hands-on experiences as possible, and I accept non-English responses from students (although I usually have to ask for a translation). Because working in small groups is an essential part of my class and an important place to practice language, I try to place students in groups who have similar language backgrounds. But in the case of Weir-Sen, this was not possible.

I know it is easy to lower my standards for bilingual students. Moll (1992) and others have pointed out that bilingual classrooms have the potential to be intellectually limiting, with an emphasis on very low literacy skills. I want to create an intellectually stimulating environment, and I am trying to do this by constantly examining my instructional goals and the achievement of students. In assessing both, I frequently have to look beyond creating an effective environment that produces desired responses from students. Instead, I have to understand my students and try to create an environment that best meets their needs for learning science, about science, and language. This is not always as easy as it sounds.

Weir-Sen Speaks: Caught between Two Worlds

Nam-Hwa Kang

As an urban schoolteacher, Julie is faced with understanding the world of an immigrant child and creating an environment in which he can succeed in science. Weir-Sen entered her classroom not only speaking a different language, but also separated from a familiar culture, community, and social system. There are no doubt many students like Weir-Sen sitting in our science classrooms today, a reflection of an increasingly diverse student body. Julie clearly understands that the science education of second-language science learners is the responsibility of all teachers, not just those with specialized training to work with bilingual or ESL students. In her attempt to help Weir-Sen participate and succeed in an inquiry-oriented science experience, she used many of the strategies that have been recommended in research on second-language learning. Her cooperative grouping strategies have been shown to be an effective way of learning for second-language students (Menken & Look, 2000). Likewise, she maintained high expectations for Weir-Sen, a strategy that has also been advocated in the teaching of second-language learners (Duran & Dugan, 1997). However, for the most part, Julie focused her efforts on language and might have missed some of the other issues that might have affected Weir-Sen's participation and success in the science classroom.

As an Asian student myself, I will share some thoughts about how Weir-Sen might have experienced education before immigration. Although Asian cultures do not have a common language, values, or beliefs, there are nevertheless some characteristics that are typically shared across these cultures. Asian students are generally less verbal and expressive on social occasions. Under the influence of Confucianism, talking is not valued in Asia; this results in a lack of emphasis on social skills in education. Julie's new student, Weir-Sen, may have had social skills that were quite different from those of his classmates; this in turn may have influenced his interactions with others. Julie assessed these social skills in terms of less participation in group work. Teachers are highly respected throughout Asia, and their orders are strictly followed. In many Asian schools, students must show respect and reverence when they meet teachers in and out of classrooms by bowing to them. Therefore, to an Asian student, teachers' instructions are to be obeyed and never challenged. Because of these cultural and moral norms, Asian students rarely reveal their opinions or abilities voluntarily. Because Weir-Sen was initially educated in the structured and passive learning context that is found in many Asian educational systems, he might have felt uncomfortable presenting his work in front of his peers or critiquing the work of others; these kinds of learning styles are not common in Asia.

What Weir-Sen "does not understand" is likely not *what* he was taught but rather *how* he was taught and what he saw in Julie's classroom. His lack of understanding is not only because of language; he is unfamiliar with the classroom culture, including a teaching style he might not have encountered previously. For many children, the culture of school science differs markedly from their worlds outside of school. Julie's instructional efforts were focused on helping Weir-Sen fit within the structures of her classroom and the culture of school science. This points to a dilemma that is ultimately at the heart of this case: What will Weir-Sen ultimately gain or lose by negotiating borders into the culture of school science?

■ **CASE 5.4** ■

Constructivism: Time for a Reality Check?

Ellen van den Berg

■ *Worldwide, constructivism seems to be accepted as the educational philosophy that underpins thinking about high-quality science teaching. In the reality of daily classroom life, however, it is rather difficult to meet the high standards set by constructivist ideals. This case presents tensions between the ideals of two science curriculum reformers and the implementation of those ideals in a Dutch elementary classroom. The source of inspiration for this case is to be found in a discussion of a videotaped lesson.[1] The case is followed by commentary from Wolff-Michael Roth, a science educator who is deeply interested in student learning.*

To provide a context for interpreting the dilemma central to this case, let me share some basic facts about the Netherlands and the Dutch elementary science curriculum. With a total area of 41,526 square kilometers, the Netherlands is a small European country (see Figure 5.1). Its size is nearly twice that of New Jersey. About 15 million people live in the Netherlands, so the population density is very high. The Netherlands has about 7,000 elementary schools and about 1.6 million elementary students. This implies that Dutch elementary schools (on average 214 students) are smaller than those in the United States. Many elementary students walk to school or go by our national mode of transport: the bicycle. (To counter a common misconception about the Netherlands, it is far more likely to see Dutch children walking in Nikes than wearing wooden shoes.)

ELEMENTARY SCIENCE

Characteristic of the Dutch elementary science curriculum is that a broad conception of science is advocated, including the following main themes:

Living organisms (animals, plants and human body)

Phenomena in nature and technology (such as magnetism force, sound, and light)

---

[1]This lesson was taped in the framework of the MUST (MUltimedia in Science Technology) project. This project aims at designing multimedia cases for the professional development of prospective teachers. The core of every MUST case is an edited videotape of science lessons. This video is supplemented by audiotaped comments on the video, written curriculum information, and context information about the school, the teacher, and the class.

FIGURE 5.1 *Map of the Netherlands*
(Source: http://www.odci.gov/cia/publications/factbook/nl.html)

Materials and objects (such as form and function and technical applications)

Weather and seasons

Environmental education

At the national level, only general core objectives are mandated. Consequently, elementary schools and teachers have considerable freedom to establish their science curricula. In most schools, biology and environmental education dominate the elementary science curriculum. Science does not have a high status in Dutch elementary schools. The time devoted to science is about one and a half hours per week. However, there are large variations among schools. Despite the low status and little time spent on elementary science, the Third International in Mathematics and Science Study (TIMSS) shows that elementary students' science scores in the Netherlands (and also the United States) are above the international average.

The majority of Dutch elementary teachers do not feel comfortable teaching constructivist science lessons. They face the following problems:

Difficulty deviating from a "teaching is telling" style

The complex and time consuming nature of preparing science lessons

Lack of content-specific background knowledge and confidence in subject matter and skills

An unclear view of student learning outcomes related to science instruction

An overloaded curriculum reform agenda on all kinds of subjects and issues

This latter point may be illustrated by the heartfelt cry of an elementary teacher:

Since the new Elementary School Act[2] we end up with all kinds of new subjects on our plate. Artistic subjects such as drama, but also technology education, computers, and cultural movements in society. Then the Ministry comes up with an idea again that special attention should be paid to science education. Or there is a growing body of opinion that the elementary school should concentrate on mathematics and language. With all these different subjects you are forced to be a jack-of-all-trades.

One might argue that implementing a constructivist approach to elementary science is not very realistic. However, it would be rather shortsighted to ignore the rich potential that this approach has for developing children's cognitive, social, and creative skills that can aid in the construction of better understandings of and interactions with the physical world surrounding them.

ELEMENTARY SCIENCE IN IDEALS

Joop Maissan and José Simons are both veteran teacher educators and devote an important part of their professional lives to improving elementary science in the Netherlands. They are well known in the field because of their leading roles in professional organizations and curriculum committees. They are also members of the MUST team. This team consists of science teacher educators, curriculum specialists, and specialists in educational technology. The team members share an excitement for elementary science. Moreover, they are the authors of textbooks both for elementary schools and for teacher education.

Their magnum opus is a recently published textbook for elementary science entitled *Bird's-Eye View (In Vogelvlucht)*. Major characteristics of this textbook series are the following:

It gives equal attention to biology and nonliving nature (physics and chemistry).

Every chapter starts with addressing children's conceptions about the topic at hand.

Hands-on activities are an integral part of all chapters.

---

[2]The new Elementary School Act sets an ambitious reform agenda. New subjects are added to the curriculum (for example, English). New core objectives are formulated for old subjects. For example, the core objectives for history break with a tradition of 100 years in decreasing the attention on national history in favor of a more global orientation. Also, more general reforms are advocated. An important one is that more students with special needs will be served in regular schools.

Joop Maissan   José Simons

These characteristics distinguish *Bird's-Eye View* from other textbooks in the Netherlands. In these textbooks, biology topics outnumber topics on nonliving nature, childrens' conceptions are not systematically addressed, and hands-on activities are mainly incorporated in the teacher guide as extra activities.

It is fair to say that *Bird's-Eye View* adheres to a constructivist vision of teaching and learning. Such a vision implies the following:

Students' conceptions form the starting point for meaningful learning.

Learning is situated in real-life contexts.

Learning is a social enterprise.

In-depth understanding of a few topics is more important than superficial knowledge of a wide range of topics.

Every chapter in the book starts with a story about the experiences of two children related to that chapter's topic. The intention of this introduction is to place science phenomena in a real-life context and to present a dilemma to the children that involves them in the interpretation of such phenomena. For example, in the chapter about color and light, the introductory story is about a girl and a boy who go to a shop to buy the boy a sweater. The girl takes a red sweater outside to inspect the color in daylight and is, as a result, nearly taken into custody as a shoplifter. However, after her explanation, the shopkeeper understands the reason why she took the sweater outside. Her boyfriend, though, thinks that the girl is very stupid because, according to him, red is red, whether you see it inside or outside.

The suggestion in the teacher's guide is to discuss this issue with the class. After this story, the textbook continues with cartoons of children expressing their conceptions of the

FIGURE 5.2 *Ellen's conception*
Ellen says that if you shine a blue light on a red sweater it becomes light red.

relationship between color and light. Two of these cartoons are pictured in Figures 5.2 and 5.3. The teacher's guide suggests discussing these conceptions with the children.

CLASSROOM REALITY OF *BIRD'S-EYE VIEW*

In the framework of the MUST project, a lesson series on the topic color and light was video-recorded in the upper elementary grades of a multiethnic elementary school. The ability levels within the class varied widely.

The teacher started the lesson with the introduction story. A student was asked to read the first part of the story aloud. Another child was then asked to continue. After the reading was finished, a whole classroom discussion started about the issue in the story: whether or not Ellen was right to take the sweater outside to examine its color in daylight.

FIGURE 5.3   *Randy's conception*
Randy says that if you put a light on a red sweater in a dark room, the sweater
starts glittering.

After this discussion, the teacher read the conceptions of the cartoon children in the
textbook, and again a classroom discussion took place, in which the students expressed reasoning on why they did or did not agree with one of the children in the book. On the videotape, the lessons look like an ordinary reading lesson. Moreover, it was rather boring to
view.

DISCUSSION IN THE MUST TEAM

The main issue of the discussion in the MUST team was whether the edited videotape represented innovative practices in elementary science in a real classroom context. The videotape

caused a rather furious debate between José and Martin, another MUST team member. Martin, a former elementary teacher, has a master's degree in educational technology and has experience in professional curriculum development in elementary science. He is a strong advocate of a hands-on science approach.

Martin could hardly wait until the video ended and nearly shouted, "This is a reading lesson and has absolutely nothing to do with elementary science. It is a shame to devote precious science time for reading!"

Joop replied, "Well, I don't like the way our book is portrayed in the video; it's boring to look at. But the meaning of all this is to open students' science concepts."

José added, "We think it's better that the children do the reading in small groups and discuss the different conceptions."

But Martin was still upset and responded, "Well to me, it is, it looks like lessons I saw fifteen years ago, reading, answering teacher questions."

Now José lost her calm and said, "Come on, there have been a lot of changes in the ideas of elementary science since. Addressing students' concepts is rooted in constructivism. You know what that means, don't you?"

However, after this discussion, all team members admitted that the videotape represented teacher behavior that is quite common in the Netherlands. When the textbook presents a story, most teachers will handle it much in the same way as Bill, the teacher in the videotape. And after all, Bill did address students' conceptions about the relationship between color and light, and that is far away from a traditional "teaching is telling" approach.

FOR REFLECTION AND DISCUSSION

1. Do you think it is a good idea to open a science lesson with a story in which the topic of the lesson is placed in a real-life context and a dilemma about the topic is woven into the story? Why or why not?

2. What do you think of including cartoon children expressing their conceptions into a textbook?

3. Consider the following statements and formulate your own opinion:
   - It is OK that the teacher in the video started with whole class reading and discussion. In his opinion, small group activities are not an option, because the students' ability levels vary too widely in his class. As a consequence, some groups would finish the reading and discussion much faster than other groups.
   - Constructivism is a beautiful theory, but for an elementary teacher with no special background in science, it is too difficult to guide students' preconceptions and misconceptions to understandings accepted by the scientific community.
   - Substantial learning in science will not take place unless we take students' conceptions seriously.

4. If you were a member of the MUST team, what would be your contribution to the discussion that took place after viewing a science lesson on video that (according to some) looks more like a reading lesson?

5. Should we draw a line between reading and science instruction? If so, how should we do this?

■ **COMMENTARY**

Constructing Constructivism and Checking Reality Checks

Wolff-Michael Roth

"Constructivism: Time for a Reality Check?" is full of interesting issues. I agree with the contention that constructivism and constructivist reform are caught up in problems, but I see these differently than Ellen van den Berg. Pertaining to her case, constructivist reform is associated with at least four problematic issues. First, constructivism does not provide for a specific model for the relationship between a material activity and the associated theoretical discourse; constructivism cannot automatically mean hands-on (as Martin appears to suggest). Second, constructivism focuses science educators' attention too much on the individual and his or her deficits and not sufficiently on the social and material world into which each individual human being is always and already thrown from the beginning. Third, many "constructivist" science educators seem to take a behaviorist approach in designing curricula that make (force?) students to abandon their commonsense discourse (alternative conceptions) about the world in favor of the scientific discourse (conceptions). Finally, reformers and technocrats have imposed constructivism on teachers in ways that do not seem to be compatible with such constructivist ideas about learning as autopoiesis. In checking the reality check, I lump these four points into two issues with which I have wrestled over the past decade, both as a practicing classroom teacher and as a co-teaching researcher. My first point pertains to learning and its relationship to learning theories such as constructivism. My second point deals with the nature of change in teaching and the locus of control for bringing about change in teaching practices.

CONSTRUCTIVISM, LEARNING, AND ACTIVITY

Constructivism is a theory of learning. At its core is the assumption that learning is an autopoietic process in which organisms—in our situation, students and teachers—change the contents of their minds to be better adapted to their circumstances. Constructivism cannot suggest that one teaching method is better than another. Students adapt even to the most boring lecture situation and do well on exams; that is, they successfully adapt to their environment, which is a sign of construction and learning. The conflation of constructivism with hands-on activities is therefore unfounded. There are at present no concrete constructivist models that show how the manipulation of objects allows students to subsequently talk theoretically about them. Why, for example, should illuminating a sweater with light help students master the discourse of light, interference, refraction, and reflection?

Perhaps science educators and teachers should think differently about learning science in at least two respects. First, an individual has learned when his or her relationship to and participation in the social and material world (which is not neatly separated into science, reading, etc.) has changed. Participating in conversations about light and, in the process, changing what one has to say is certainly learning. Changing what one has to say about light is likely to be associated with many other aspects of students' lives. Dogmatically separating "talking science" from "talking poetry," "talking love," "talking soccer," or talking whatever else one talks in a reading lesson does not help us in changing teaching or learning. Second, the most fundamental human characteristic is the power to act. This means that we are not simply determined by internal psychological or external (sociological) factors. That is, human beings do not just construct knowledge but also construct and change the contexts of their activities and thereby become successfully adapted. Students and teachers ought to be able to shape their worlds by participating in decision making about their learning rather than being treated as behavioral dopes subject to the environments someone else sets up to determine and change their behavior.

ENACTING VERSUS IMPOSING CHANGE IN TEACHING SCIENCE

As in earlier reforms, those vested with institutional powers imposed constructivism on teachers. Constructivist reform has often been undemocratic, imposing on teachers ways of understanding the world and acting in it without consideration of their current understandings. Constructivist reformers construct not only children in a deficit mode (misconceptions, naive conceptions), but also teachers (misconceptions; lack of content knowledge, pedagogical skills, and confidence). From the perspective of teachers, however, ivory-tower-based armchair philosophers and governmental technocrats conceptualize and mandate change without consideration of the contexts that mediate teachers' everyday work in the classroom and transformation potential. To put it bluntly, constructivism turned out to be mere rhetoric, and reformers often disregarded the nature of teachers as learners in their own right. Reformers talked the talk rather than walking the walk. Learning as changing participation in the social and material world, in the way I outlined above, suggests that teachers too will not switch from enacting a set of practices one day to enacting a very different set of practices another day. Practices are very stable, being produced by dispositions that are the residue of the individual teacher's lived experience (something that is really real to all of us). Change therefore does not come easily even if a teacher is totally committed to this change.

When I began classroom research as a science teacher and used videotaped lessons to analyze aspects of my own teaching, there were things that I wanted to change. In particular, I noticed that I could do better by listening to students before jumping to conclusions about what they knew or what they wanted to say. I decided to change my practices of interacting with students, particularly the way I enacted conversations. Change did not come easily, and it took me a long time, despite daily reflection, analysis, and writing about this issue—that is, despite this best-case scenario in which a teacher was committed to change. How much more difficult will it be to change teaching practices when these are mandated from the outside as technocratic solutions to problems that the individual teacher might not even construct as such? Like many participants in the Scandinavian labor movement, I believe that imposing rather than co-participating in change is fundamentally undemocratic. Are there any alternatives? My colleague Ken Tobin and I have practiced such an alternative for some time now (Roth & Tobin, in press). Co-teaching/co-generative dialoguing is a way of participating in teaching and learning to teach in a fundamentally democratic context.

Co-teaching/co-generative dialoguing practice is based on two fundamental principles: (1) Praxis can be understood only from the inside, by being part of it, and (2) changes in praxis have to be rooted in, and come out of, that very praxis. As a consequence, university professors (researchers, supervisors, methods teachers), regular teachers, teachers in training, and other school personnel participate equally in planning, enacting, and evaluating teaching with a particular focus on student learning. We do not allow "observers," who tend to judge teaching from an outside perspective. We do not critique another co-teacher (as observers) for not having acted when we have failed to act in the particular situation. After lessons, we co-teachers meet, also inviting student representatives, to make sense of and theorize our experience. We strive to derive practically viable actions to change what we have done and test these new actions in subsequent lessons. Change is therefore not something that is possible only in theory; change is part and parcel of everyday practice. We do not mandate new practices but participate with teachers to enact teaching that better addresses student learning.

Over the years, I have personally taught in such a way with several elementary teachers who thought that they were not well prepared to teach science. However, my research shows that co-teaching/co-generative dialoguing is a rich context in which all teachers involved learn and change irrespective of their experience, which ranged from beginning teacher to thirty-five-year veteran. It is typical for my teachers to say things like "I just improved so much. I don't think three university courses could have given me what [co-teaching] gave me in these two months." In our case, the MUST team members would not be allowed in the classroom unless they were participating in teaching and contributing to bringing about change. They would have to be there in the classroom and, with the teacher, enhance students' learning. In this process, their own participation in the social and material worlds of the classroom changes; they learn and engage in a continuous trajectory of becoming in the classroom. Martin and Joop would have had to participate with the teacher, not replacing Bill, but doing a less-boring lesson with him and thereby allowing him to become a different (better?) teacher. As "organic intellectuals," they would have participated in "re/constructing elementary science" (e.g., Roth, Tobin, & Ritchie, in press) rather than talking change removed from the classroom.

References

Aikenhead, G. S. (1998). Bordercrossing: Culture, school science, and assimilation of students. In D. A. Roberts & L. Ostman (Eds.), *Problems of meaning in science curriculum* (pp. 86–100). New York: Teachers College Press.

Duran, B. J., & Dugan, T. (1997). Increasing teacher effectiveness with language minority students. *High School Journal, 80,* 238–246.

Helms, J. V. (1998). Science and/in the community: Context and goals in practical work. *International Journal of Science Education, 20*(6), 43–53.

Meir, T., & Nelson-Barber, S. (Spring, 1990). *Multicultural context a key factor in teaching.* New York: Academic Connections, Office of Academic Affairs, The College Board.

Menken, K., & Look, K. (2000). Making chances for linguistically and culturally diverse students. *The Education Digest, 65*(8), 14–19.

Moll, L. C. (1992). Bilingual classroom studies and community analysis: Some recent trends. *Educational Researcher, 21*(2), 20–24.

Pallas, A. M., Natriello, G., & McDill, E. L. (1995). Changing students/changing needs. In E. Flaxman & H. Passow (Eds.), *Changing populations, changing schools: Ninety-fourth yearbook of the National Society for the Study of Education* (pp. 30–58). Chicago: University of Chicago Press.

Roth, W.-M., & Tobin, K. (in press). *At the elbows of another: Learning to teach by coteaching.* New York: Peter Lang.

Roth, W.-M., Tobin, K. G., & Ritchie, S. M. (in press). *Re/constructing elementary science.* New York: Peter Lang.

Style, E. (1988). *"Curriculum as window and mirror": Listening for all voices.* Summit, NJ: Oak Knoll School Conference Booklet.

U.S. Bureau of the Census. (1993). *Foreign-born population in the United States.* Washington, DC: U.S. Government Printing Office.

*Resources to Consider*_____

Barba, R. H. (1998). *Science in the multicultural classroom: A guide to teaching and learning.* Boston: Allyn & Bacon.

This book is a comprehensive guide to teaching practices designed to meet the learning needs of diverse student populations. Chapters focus on topics such as "Motivation in the Multicultural Science Classroom," "Ways of Knowing Science," "Instructional Strategies for Culturally Diverse Learners," "Constructing a Knowledge of Science and Language," and "Math/Science Integration in the Multicultural Classroom."

Eisenhower National Clearinghouse. *Equity.* [http://www.enc.org/topics/equity]

This site is a resource for teachers interested in promoting equitable science learning opportunities for all students. Links at this site provide access to on-line materials and information, essays, and checklist and rubrics for assessing equitable science classroom conditions.

Heil, D., Amorose, G., Gurnee, A., & Harrison, A. (1999). (Eds.). *Family science.* Portland, OR: Portland State University.

Ideas for organizing family science community events and strategies for promoting the doing of science in the community are described in this book.

Rollnick, M. (1998). The influence of language on the second language teaching and learning of science. In W. W. Cobern (Ed.), *Socio-cultural perspectives on science education* (pp. 121–137). Dordrecht, The Netherlands: Kluwer Academic Press.

Rollnick discusses issues for second language science learners with particular emphasis on cultural factors that are intertwined with language. She describes different strategies that can be used to assist second-language learners.

Singelis, T. M. (1998). (Ed.). *Teaching about culture, ethnicity and diversity: Exercises and planned activities.* Thousand Oaks, CA: Sage Publications.

This book is a rich resource of exercises and activities for teachers concerned about issues involving culture, ethnicity, and diversity. Each chapter includes a literature-based essay, followed by exercises for exploring relevant concepts.

Winebrenner, S. (1996). *Teaching kids with learning difficulties in the regular classroom: Strategies and techniques every teacher can use to challenge and motivate struggling students.* Minneapolis, MN: Free Spirit Publishing.

The learning needs of diverse students are considered in the variety of activities and strategies that are illustrated in this book.

6

Elementary Science Teaching for Understanding

To learn science means something very different today than it did just a few years ago. In the past, students were considered empty vessels to be filled with ideas, and science concepts learned by students were envisioned as duplicates of reality presented by the teacher or textbook. Student learning based on this transmission model too often consisted of knowing scientific facts and information that had little value beyond the walls of the classroom. Today, this transmission model of learning has given way to other ways of thinking about learning. One epistemology that is currently favored by many educators as a referent for teaching and learning stresses the active construction of science understandings. An assumption that is central to this constructivist epistemology is that students construct their own meanings of science concepts and phenomena through engaging in a variety of learning experiences in diverse learning contexts. This epistemology of learning also recognizes that learning involves social interaction and is greatly influence by what the learner already knows. The outcomes associated with learning based on constructivism are science understandings that highlight how science concepts are related to each other and to the discipline and develop from the use of scientific reasoning and critical thinking (Bybee, 1997).

Consistent with this constructivist epistemology of learning is the realization that students come to science class with personal mental models of the world and how it works that more often than not arise from their experiences outside of school. For students to construct science understandings, teachers need to make use of instructional strategies that challenge students' personal ideas and also socialize them into a community of science knowledge (Driver, Asoko, Leach, Mortimer, & Scott, 1994). Creating a science learning environment that incorporates both these individual and social processes can be very challenging for teachers. Children's mental models are often rooted in the concrete and observable experiences of their daily lives and are not easily changed by the abstract representations often associated with science instruction. When science lessons are not linked to students' life experiences and engage them in discourse that focuses on conflicts between common sense and scientific views, learning tends not be meaningful, motivational, and developmentally appropriate. Teachers must additionally consider that changing students' mental models will take time and may involve trading one mental model for another and later still another.

A constructivist epistemology may also serve as a referent for teacher learning. Not unlike the children they teach, elementary teachers may hold mental models about science and science teaching methods that reflect different stages in their pathways of understanding. This is to be expected because of the demands placed on elementary teachers to be well versed in so many curricular areas. Teachers who wish to develop science understandings and improve their science teaching practices need to seek learning opportunities that incorporate personal and social processes and reflect on the nature of the science learning environment they construct for students.

The four cases in the chapter address several issues associated with science teaching for understanding. Tenets of constructivism central to dilemmas highlighted in these cases include the following: Individuals construct their own meaning, what is already in the learner's mind matters, the construction of meaning is a continuous and active process, errors are critical to learning, and learners have the final responsibility for their learning (Driver & Bell, 1986). In the first case, "Seasons Change and Conceptions Shift—But Not Always as Expected," John Settlage describes his experiences in helping third graders develop a scientific explanation for the seasons and his feelings of frustration when his lessons failed to produce the expected results. In the second case, "What Is the Shape of a Star?," Molly Weinburgh explains what can happen when a student teacher's desire to use a popular children's book is coupled with her naive understandings about stars. In "No Bones about It!," Stacey Neuharth-Pritchett and Jennifer Bellnap recount the unrealized expectations of a prekindergarten teacher as she attempts to integrate science activities into a theme-based instructional unit. The dilemma raised in this case centers on Julie's ineffective attempt to put into practice the teaching strategies presented in a workshop and how the staff development coordinator can help Julie do so successfully. In the final case, "And God Made the Little Birdies, Too," Andrew Paolucci tells about the test question he wishes he had never asked. The case focuses on the issues that a teacher must face when students' religious beliefs affect their construction of science understandings.

■ **C A S E 6 . 1** ■

Seasons Change and Conceptions Shift—But Not Always as Expected

John Settlage

■ *John, a university professor, regularly volunteers to coteach science with Deanne Urry, a veteran third grade teacher in Cleveland, Ohio. In this open case, John tells about his own experiences in helping Deanne's students develop a scientifically accurate explanation for the seasons. His knowledge of learning theory and use of a computer simulation and hands-on materials in his lessons would seemingly guarantee student conceptual change in the desired direction. However, despite John's best efforts, assessment results reveal that most of the students hold firmly to the belief that the seasons are caused by changes in the distance between the earth and the sun. In fact, some students, who had initially explained the seasons in terms of the tilt of the earth on its axis, describe the seasons in the same way as most of their classmates. The experience leaves both John and Deanne questioning their own teaching practices and trying to figure out why the lessons failed to produce the expected learning outcomes. The case is based on actual events and is followed by commentary from science teacher educators Tom Koballa and Leslie Upson.*

I was very fortunate five years ago when Deanne Urry agreed to let me team-teach science in her classroom. Since the beginning, our working relationship has been a comfortable partnership because we are in the room to support each other's science teaching. Also, when we wonder about the success of a particular lesson, we have the luxury of being able to rely on each other's help to make sense of every event.

We had decided that I would begin my time as lead teacher with the class this year by doing a brief unit on seasonal change. Deanne and I chose to center our unit on the the the *Seasons* program from Tom Snyder Production's *Science Court* materials (Snyder & Dockterman, 1998), even though it is intended for use with fourth grade students and older. We thought that it was an appropriate learning resource for our students and would extend and enhance previous textbook readings about the seasons. Before my first lesson, I asked students to show me what they already knew about the seasons by completing a preassessment instrument. By asking the students to draw and write, I hoped to discover what they knew about the seasons.

On the same day that the preassessment was administered, Deanne and I looked them over while the students were at P.E. I was struck by the wide variety of responses. About one-third of the children drew pictures, as Joyce did, of activities they enjoy doing during the summer and winter (see Figure 6.1). To explain why we have seasons, one child wrote, "The first people who walked the earth named the seasons and we still call them that." Although this would explain why we have the names that we do for seasons, it really doesn't explain much about the cause for seasons.

The remainder of the class drew pictures showing the sun and the earth. Of these, I was surprised that almost half had divided their pictures into quadrants, labeling each corner with

What Causes Seasons?   name

Everybody knows it is hot in the summer. Winter is when it is cold outside.
We also know the sun makes us warm. But why do we have different seasons?

Draw a picture that shows why we have seasons. Use words to label your
picture.

Write a sentence that explains why we have seasons.

Why we have seasons is that sometimes when
it's winter it will go around an till it comes back
to winter because some times we will need
these season because when it's winter we want the other seasons.

FIGURE 6.1

the name of a season and including the earth in each section. Deanne said that she believed that her students were most likely trying to replicate a textbook diagram they had studied during a recent reading lesson.

I was glad we had asked the students to write about the seasons in addition to drawing pictures. The children's written statements served as a second window into their thinking. Of the fourteen papers showing a relationship between the earth and the sun, five children depicted the tilt of the earth and used the idea of the tilt to explain the cause for summer and winter. The results of the preassessment suggested to Deanne and me that about 20 percent of the class understood the seasons in terms of the tilt of the earth on its axis.

As I began my first lesson, I was fairly confident in my ability to help all the children in the class develop sound scientific explanations for the seasons. After all, as revealed by the preassessment, one student in five was already there. I was fully aware that *Benchmarks for Science Literacy* (American Association for the Advancement of Science, 1994) reserves the learning of this concept until middle school, but I couldn't forget my initial reaction to the videotape *A Private Universe* (Harvard-Smithsonian Center for Astrophysics, 1987), which showed Harvard graduates unable to articulate why it is hot in summer and cold in winter. I wanted to make sure that all our third graders understood seasonal change, and I thought that there were several factors that would help my lessons succeed.

First, I had the benefit of having Deanne in the room while I was teaching. Because she was a veteran teacher, I knew that I could depend on her to restate any explanations or directions that might be unclear to the students. Second, I already had evidence that even with traditional, textbook-based instruction, some of the children in this class could draw and compose sound written explanations for the seasons. This was evidence to me that the concept was within their grasp and that competent teaching should be able to guide even more students to the desired learning outcome. Finally, I had many pedagogical, intellectual, and technological tools at my disposal. The activities I had chosen to use were highly experiential, grounded in conceptual change pedagogy, and would include cooperative learning, demonstrations, and class discussion. I even had the lure of using the animated computer program (with stereo sound, no less) that is the core of the *Science Court* materials. Surely, if a textbook lesson resulted in five students learning about the seasons, all the resources that I was pouring into my lessons would be at least as fruitful.

The *Science Court* materials start with a challenge or mystery that has a comical twist. The *Seasons* episode begins with a character's vacation to Australia in June. The temperature there is much cooler than she had expected, and the locals explain that winter is coming. She also learns that the earth is moving farther from the sun. The cooler temperatures not only spoiled her vacation, but, on her return to North America, prompt her to file a lawsuit against the person from whom she was to have taken swimming lessons while in Australia. In essence, *Science Court* becomes the stage on which the dilemma faced by the character is debated.

In the courtroom scene, the prosecuting attorney supports the idea that the distance that the earth is from the sun is responsible for the seasonal changes and their effect on daily temperature. The defense attorney represents the swimming instructor, who is alleged to be collecting money for lessons he knows will not be taught, since it would not be summer. With a female astronomer on the stand, the prosecution shows that because of the elliptical orbit of the earth, June is when the distance between earth and the sun is greatest. However, the astronomer explains that the distance, while seemingly large, is equivalent to adding three city blocks to a five-mile bike ride. This testimony is intended to show that the distance explanation is inadequate for explaining the warming that we experience in the summer.

The program contains built-in pauses at various points, and I used these pauses to organize the students into groups of four and focus their attention on six questions raised by the main character's dilemma. Within a group, each child had a different paper identified by a letter of the alphabet. Even though the questions on their handouts were identical, the papers had different bits of information appearing as quotes from the characters featured in the program. The students shared the quotes by reading them to each other. For example, Question 1 asked, "What is the earth's curved path around the sun called?," and the answer appeared in the quote on paper B. The students were obliged to help each other to answer all six questions.

When all groups had finished, I used the computer to randomly select a child to answer the question. The computer program would first choose a group number and then a letter. The designated child would answer the question, and I would then show the correct answer on the computer. I was astonished by the children's enthusiasm for this activity. After Sondra offered that the answer to the first question was "orbit" and the computer concurred, the entire class cheered! To preserve our sanity, we directed the class to celebrate less loudly from that point forward.

To supplement and reinforce the ideas presented in the computer program, I relied on some simple demonstrations. I handed a flashlight to Robert and asked him to shine it at the ceiling directly over his head, and we talked about the spot of light. Then I asked him to point the flashlight at a more distant location on the ceiling. I was hoping that the students would notice the difference in the size of the spot when the flashlight was at an angle.

Me: What do you notice about the light spot?

Sharon: It changes.

Patrick: It's an oval.

Me: And what shape was it before?

Class: A circle.

Me: Why do you think it is a different shape?

Dominic: 'Cause Robert tilted the flashlight.

Claire: The light got more spread out.

Building on these ideas, I tried to help students understand that the same amount of light was striking the ceiling tiles, regardless of the light spot's shape. I explained that even though the shapes were different, the amount of light coming from the flashlight was the same. What we could observe was the angled beam creating a large oval in which the light was more dispersed. If we could imagine that this was sunlight, the circle of light would warm a surface more rapidly than the oval would.

At this point, I was worried that I might be reinforcing the idea of a flat earth. Using a borrowed playground ball, I explained the relationship between the angle of the light (either from a flashlight or from the sun) and the warming potential. I asked Mercedes to hold the flashlight while I maneuvered the sphere.

Me: Let's pretend that the ball I am holding is the earth. What do you think Mercedes is?

Class: The sun!

Me: Good. Now, Mercedes, I want you to stand in one place, and I am going to walk around you. Why would I do that?

Michelle: 'Cause the earth goes around the sun.

Me: Yes! And how long would it take, if I was really the earth, to go all the way around Mercedes, the sun?

Brent: A day.

Kevin: A month?

Paula: No, a year!

Me: Yes, it takes a whole year to go around the sun. Who can tell me why I am holding the ball crooked like this?

Wayne: The earth is tilted.

Me: Great! Now Mercedes, I want you to shine the flashlight on the top half of the ball, the part I am tilting toward you.

Even though it was difficult for everyone to see, I tried to help them understand that when Mercedes was shining the flashlight at the top half of the ball as it was tilted toward her, the spot of light was more concentrated. When she directed the light at the lower half of the ball, the spot was oval, and the light was more diffuse: This represents winter in Australia.

To work our way through the entire *Science Court* program required almost three entire class sessions. Not rushing through the materials was important if the students were to have a chance to learn the concept meaningfully. From my observations, it seemed as if the majority of the class had grasped the major idea. They were inquisitive, they appeared to be genuinely interested in the computer program, and they acted as if they were sincerely trying to sort through the competing ideas (i.e., distance as opposed to tilt as cause for the seasons). Deanne and I were both pleased by my performance.

The postassessment was designed so that the students did not have to invent explanations for the seasons (See Figure 6.2). I provided them with two competing explanations attributed to two elementary age boys and asked them to choose the one that made the most sense and then to explain their choice. The first explanation, given by Terry, was that it becomes warmer in summer because the earth and the sun are closer together, while Billy, using the scientifically acceptable explanation, claimed that the tilt of the earth causes changes in seasonal temperatures. Wanting to avoid the possibility that one explanation would be chosen over the other because it was worded more simply, I wrote them so that they were approximately the same length and were similar in tone. I read both explanations aloud to the entire class, and they were given about ten minutes to write their responses.

Painful as it is for me, I must report that on the postassessment, eight students selected the correct explanation of the cause for the seasons, and thirteen chose the explanation that the distance the earth is from the sun causes the seasons. Recall that five children seemed to understand the concept before my lessons began. One of the five did not complete the postassessment, two remained committed to the tilt factor, but two others moved to a "distance from the sun" explanation. Here is what they wrote on their two assessment sheets.

FIGURE 6.2

Seasons Post-Assessment   **Name** _____

Two children were asked to explain why we have seasons. Here is what they said. Read the ideas of Terry and Billy. Think about which idea makes more sense.

Terry knows why we have seasons. When the Sun is closer, it makes the Earth warmer. This is when we have summer. July is a hot month because the Earth is near the Sun. When the Earth moves away from the Sun, then the Earth gets colder. In February it is cold because the Sun and Earth are further apart. Winter is cold because the Earth is far from the Sun. If the Earth and the Sun were the same distance apart all year, then we would not have different seasons. Terry says, "Earth gets more heat when it is close to the Sun. That is why summer is warm and winter is cold." Terry thinks the distance is the reason for the seasons.

Billy knows why we have seasons. The tilt of the Earth makes it warmer or colder. When it is summer in Ohio, the top part of the Earth is tilting toward the Sun. This happens in July. The light from the Sun makes in warmer when we are tilted toward the Sun. Winter is cold in Ohio because we are tilted away from the Sun. In February the light from the Sun does not make it as warm in Ohio. But in Australia, February is a summer month. Billy says, "The tilt of the Earth causes the seasons. When your part of the Earth is tilted toward the Sun, then you are having summer. That is why Australia and Ohio have opposite seasons." Billy thinks the Earth's tilt is the reason for the seasons.

I think the one who makes more sense is Terry or Billy (circle one). Explain your choice.

_____

_____

_____

_____

_____

_____

_____

_____

_____

_____

_____

_____

_____

_____

Latoya

Preassessment.   It is hot in the summer because the earth is tilted towards the sun. It is cold in the winter because we are away from the sun.

Postassessment.   I think Terry's story about seasons is right because it does not cause seasons because of the tilt. The reasons we have seasons is because the earth moves away from the sun.

Rolanda

Preassessment.   It is warmer in the summer because the earth is tilted close to the sun. It is cooler in the winter because the earth is tilted away from the sun.

Postassessment.   I think Terry makes more sense. Because in class we read a book about seasons, and it said that when the earth is far from the sun it's winter and when it's close it's summer.

There were six other children who endorsed the tilting earth explanation even though they had not used the idea of the tilt of the earth in their preassessment explanation for the seasons. But even some of these explanations seemed to reveal some confusion: "Billy is right because the tilt is what causes seasons because the earth faces the sun on each side. And every time Ohio faces the sun we get summer." "I think Billy is right. Because when the sun tilts toward the earth it gets hot. When the sun tilts away from the earth it gets cold." Although some children understood the idea of tilt, it was applied to the sun and not the earth.

Several other interesting explanations appeared on the postassessment. Damon wrote, "I think it is Terry because he is giving more than Billy," and Jerome wrote, "I think that Terry's right because once the earth gets closer to the sun it makes the earth hotter and I learned that from my teacher in school. In science today." This last comment indicates that, not only are students' ideas often resistant to change, but students are also capable of reinterpreting information given by the teacher such that it is consistent with their preexisting notions. This experience leaves me uncertain about attempting to teach this concept to next year's third graders.

FOR REFLECTION AND DISCUSSION

1. Is the idea that the earth's tilt is the cause for the seasons a concept that is unreasonable to expect third graders to understand?

2. How can the apparent backsliding of Latoya and Rolanda be explained? What happened that caused them to apparently unlearn the scientifically acceptable explanation?

3. Were the differences in the preassessment and postassessment results related to the nature of the assessment tasks (i.e., draw and describe versus select and defend)? Should identical instruments have been used for the preassessment and the postassessment? Is that a reasonable practice for teachers?

4. Is it any coincidence that the two students who backed away from the tilting earth explanation were girls? Is this evidence of the debated notion that girls are less able to think spatially? Or was there something in how the lessons were taught that made the concept easier for the boys to learn?

■ **C O M M E N T A R Y**

A Letter to John

Thomas Koballa, Jr., and Leslie Upson

Dear John,
There is no doubt in our minds that you are an exceptional teacher. Your thoughts focus on your students and their learning. You carefully consider what you wish to accomplish in your lessons and prepare accordingly. We admire you as a science teacher educator. Through your work with Deanne, you have established the type of school–university partnership that reform leaders agree is necessary to bring about meaningful change in science education. This partnership enables you to keep in close contact with science learning in schools and model the classroom practices that you advocate in your science methods classes. We believe that you represent the very best of the science education community and that both the city of Cleveland and Cleveland State University are very fortunate to have you working with their students.

Your dilemma of not achieving the success in your lessons that you had hoped for highlights for us the reality of science teaching. In preparing and teaching the lessons that you describe in the case, you no doubt made hundreds, if not thousands, of decisions. Your decisions centered on your students' dispositions and motives, what they know about seasons, and how best to help them construct more scientifically accurate understandings about the causes of seasonal change. We find no fault in your decisions. Put in your position, we can only hope that we would have made decisions as professionally sound as the ones that you made. However, given the luxury of being able to act as Monday-morning quarterbacks with time to reflect on and second-guess your decisions, we would like to offer some ideas for your consideration. Our ideas might help you to decide whether and how to teach third graders about what causes the seasons next year.

First, we applaud you for gathering information from the third graders about their understanding of seasonal change. The preassessment results revealed that a number of students seem to recognize that interactions between the earth and sun are in some way responsible for the changing seasons, and some among these even addressed tilt in either their drawings or explanations. Given these results alone, we too would have chosen instructional interventions that present "distance between the earth and the sun" and "tilt of the earth in its axis" as competing propositions, as is done in the *Science Court* episode. However, the preassessment responses of other students that focused on seasonal activities and not the causes of seasonal change suggested less sophisticated understandings. It is very possible that these students were not ready to consider the competing propositions that were the focus of your lessons. Research by Baxter (1995, p. 163) indicates that young children use their observations of near and familiar to explain the seasons. Deeper probing of selected students from among those whose preassessment results focused on seasonal activities might have led you to focus your lessons to address other naive understandings of seasonal change. If probing via individual or group interviews is not possible, then you might wish to consider developing a preassessment instrument that enables students to chose among notions for the causes of the seasons elucidated by Baxter (1995, p. 165) based on his own interviews with children:

Notion 1: Cold plants take heat from the sun.

Notion 2: Heavy winter clouds stop heat from the sun.

Notion 3: Sun is farther away from the earth in the winter.

Notion 4: Sun moves to the other side of the earth to give them their summer.

Notion 5: Changes in planets cause the seasons.

Notion 6: Seasons are explained in terms of the earth's axis being set an angle to the sun's axis.

Second, we wish to compliment you on your choice of lessons. We agree that the *Seasons* episode from *Science Court* is a well-designed instructional tool and very motivating for children. Your demonstrations using the flashlight and playground ball are standards that have been used for years to help students develop meaningful understandings about the seasons. Additionally, your instructional style contributed to what we consider to be an excellent classroom climate. On the basis of the dialogue included in your case, we sense that the students felt free to share their ideas and, more important, to change them when they believed they were wrong. Given all that is good about your lessons, we find it hard to find fault. But here are a few things to consider for next year.

An assumption that seems to be inherent in your lessons is that students who participate in class will abandon their own notions about seasonal change in favor of the one that explains seasonal change in terms of the tilt of the earth on its axis. However, your own posttest results suggest that students are not necessarily replacing their existing understandings with this more scientifically acceptable one, but are mixing their ideas with those that are being proffered in your lessons. This is exactly what Gilbert, Osbourne, and Fensham (1982) found in their own work on students' conceptual change. This mixing of ideas is, according to Baxter (1995), associated with illustrative or confirmatory instruction, wherein the teacher presents evidence to show the limitations of commonly held notions about natural events in an effort to bring about conceptual change. Your lessons that focus on dissuading students from explaining seasonal changes in terms of the distance between the earth and the sun seem to be of this type. As an alternative, Baxter (1995) encourages teaching that involves a recursive process of challenging students' personal notions about the seasons by providing opportunities for them to test the plausibility of their own assumptions. Using this approach might involve you in developing instructional activities whereby students can individually or in small groups challenge their own ideas about the causes of the seasons. The six notions for the causes of the seasons presented above might serve as a starting point for developing instructional activities. Using instructional activities that roughly correspond with these notions makes the development of a scientifically acceptable understanding of seasonal change a process rather than an event, in which students modify their ideas over time as competing notions are tested and found to be unacceptable.

An important consideration in developing instructional activities to teach this concept is that the activities and their relationship to the concept might not always be well understood by the students who use them. Your concern that you might be reinforcing the idea of a flat earth with the flashlight demonstration is a case in point. Young children might not be able to see beyond the physical objects used in the activities, let alone be able to infer abstract and spatial relationships from their use. Our suspicion is that some of the third graders in the class had difficulty envisioning how the size of the oval created on the ceiling from the flashlight is related to the tilt of the earth on its axis and seasonal change. A related consideration is the need that young children have to manipulate materials as they try to learn science concepts. Next year, we encourage you to allow all students, perhaps working in small groups, to manipulate the playground ball and flashlight. We have found that even among preservice teachers, assuming the perspectives of the earth and sun, rather than observing demonstrations, aids in conceptual change.

Third, we believe that part of the frustration that you are experiencing with the results of your hard work could be due in part to your assessment strategies. The preassessment and postassessment were two different types of activities that measure two different types of knowledge. In the first assessment, students were asked to draw a picture and write one sentence. As was mentioned earlier, many of the students didn't really provide an explanation for seasonal change, but simply drew pictures of what they did during the different seasons. It was difficult to gauge their true level of understanding of seasonal change from this assessment. However, students did use their own experiences as the basis for their answers. In the postassessment, they were asked to listen to you read aloud from the two passages and then analyze which passage was the correct explanation for the cause of the seasons. This assessment was somewhat different from the learning experiences they participated in during the lessons. During the lessons, you used many instructional strategies to try to help students understand the factors that are responsible for seasonal change. Additionally, students worked together during the lessons, making use of a variety of different activities. In contrast, the postassessment asked them to listen, read, and answer. The students were not able to use their own experiences as they had done during the preassessment and classroom activities. This lack of opportunity for the students to use their firsthand knowledge likely contributed to an inaccurate picture of what they learned about seasonal change as a result of your teaching. To gauge student understanding throughout their study of the seasons, you might want to embed assessment tasks within your instructional activities.

In closing, we wish to again compliment you on your efforts to help students develop a deeper understanding of this important concept and thank you for reminding us how complex teaching really is. Although education is once again being elevated to the status of high priority among our nation's citizenry, the model of education embraced by most citizens continues to be an overly simplistic one. The central tenet of the model is that good teaching will assuredly lead to student learning, with good teaching being understood to mean a teacher who is well schooled in the content of the subject making use of appropriate instructional methods. But as your story so well illustrates, this model and the rhetoric associated with it fail to address the complexities of teaching and learning. Thank you for encouraging us to take a more careful and thoughtful look at teaching and learning. We hope our thoughts are helpful to you as you make decisions about teaching seasonal change to students in Deanne's class next year.

Sincerely,
Tom and Leslie

What Is the Shape of a Star?

Molly Weinburgh

■ *In her science methods course, Molly stresses to elementary education majors that young children need to experience and explore phenomena before being engaged in an explanation of the phenomena. She encourages her students to use children's stories as a way of introducing and expanding a science lesson. In this open case, Molly tells about a meeting with Connie, one of her students who used a story by Eric Carle to teach first graders about stars. Connie's description of her lesson reveals her own understandings about stars and presents Molly with a challenge: How can she help Connie to clarify her own understandings about stars and reteach the lesson in order not to leave the students with erroneous information? The case is followed by commentary from Deborah Tippins, a science educator who advocates the use of children's literature to support science instruction.*

Hearing a tentative knock on her office door, Molly looked up to find one of her students waiting expectantly to enter the room and share her news. Connie, a twenty-eight-year old mother of three, had come back to school to get her teaching certificate after her children had entered school. She was excited about becoming a teacher and expressed a deep conviction that she would be a positive influence on her students. She was in her third semester of teacher preparation, attending class at the university two days a week and interning in an elementary school two other days. Throughout the semester, she had expressed her unease with teaching science. She thought that her own science background was poor, and she observed that the cooperating teacher for her two-day internship, Mrs. Smith, did very little science teaching.

Knowing all this, Molly was pleased when Connie volunteered that she had "taught a perfect science lesson" the previous day and had come in early so that she could share her success. Sitting at the small round table in her office, Molly asked Connie to tell her about the lesson. She encouraged Connie to talk freely about her reason for doing the lesson, what she actually did, what the students did, and how she knew that the students had learned the desired content.

Connie began by stating that the lesson was on stars. She explained that her cooperating teacher had given her absolute autonomy in choosing the topic and developing the lesson. However, she was quick to let Molly know that Mrs. Smith had read the lesson plan before Connie taught it and found it to be "very creative, full of fun, and a neat topic for the children." Because Connie was aware that Molly would like to see evidence of what the children had done during the science lesson, she came with a stack of student papers that she believed proved how much the students had learned about stars.

In a voice full of enthusiasm, Connie told Molly about this science lesson. "I knew you would want to know about this lesson. I had the attention of all the children. I stayed late on Tuesday to decorate the classroom so that the students would feel the stars all around them when they came into the room on Wednesday. I hung stars from the ceiling and taped some to the walls. I even put them on the windows, doors, and floor. I began the lesson by reading the story *Draw Me a Star* by Eric Carle."

Molly used a pause in the conversation to ask Connie why she had selected the topic of stars and why she had chosen the book by Eric Carle to begin the lesson.

"Oh, I knew from experience that the children loved books by Eric Carle," Connie replied. She then explained that she had visited the school library and had seen this book on display. It had then become the catalyst for her whole lesson. She was sure that the students would love to know more about stars and that she could use this book to gain their attention. She also explained that stars would be a good topic for first graders because "they had all had real experiences with stars and you have stressed to be sure that young children actually have concrete examples when possible" and that she had a plan that would allow them to continue to experience stars.

The book begins with the main character as a child being asked to draw a star. He draws a five-pointed star, which Carle represents in bright colors in his favorite tissue paper method. Later in the story, the artist shows how to draw a star by showing the steps for doing so and writing "Down, over, left, and right. Draw a star." The illustration again shows a five-pointed star. Connie explained that she gave each of the children in the class a piece of paper on which to draw a star. She read the last pages of the book again slowly so that the students could follow along with the directions. The children "created" a representation of a star, which they then colored. Connie was pleased to report that she did not direct the students about what color to use; giving them choices was very important to her.

After she explained the lesson to Molly, she displayed samples of the students' work. "I have these wonderful examples of what the students learned. Look at these great pictures. And the children had so much fun. They loved this lesson." The pictures revealed that the students had all drawn five-pointed stars and had labeled and colored their drawings. In addition, they had all written a sentence about the shape and color of stars. Connie was pleased with the science that her first grade students had learned. She explained, as she showed their work, "All the students know that stars have points and that they can be any color. My favorite part of the lesson was that I gave the children a real experience with drawing a star so that they now know so much about stars."

Connie's comments took Molly by surprise. The lesson Connie had taught might be fine for art, but it introduced scientifically inaccurate information about stars to the children. Stars are not two-dimensional objects with five points. How can Molly help Connie revisit her lesson without squelching her enthusiasm for teaching science or making Mrs. Smith, Connie's cooperating teacher, appear less than adequate? After all, Mrs. Smith did approve the lesson before Connie taught it. Molly must not only help Connie to understand where this lesson might have fallen short, but also help her to understand more global concepts about teaching science to young children, including the nature of experiential learning and the appropriateness of science topics for young learners. Assuming that Connie understands and develops an instructional alternative, she must then decide, with help from Molly, how to explain to Mrs. Smith why it is desirable for the lesson to be retaught and suggest some ways to help students develop a clearer understanding of the nature and properties of stars.

FOR REFLECTION AND DISCUSSION

1. What should Molly do as a first step in helping Connie to rethink her science lesson?
2. How would you respond to Connie's statement that first graders have had real experiences with stars? How would you respond to her assertion that she created a real experience for students during her lesson?

3. How did Connie's use of the story by Eric Carle contribute to the dilemma that she faces? How might this experience influence Connie's future use of stories to enhance children's science learning?

4. What should Molly suggest that Connie do about her students' understanding of stars following the lesson?

5. How should Connie explain to Mrs. Smith that she needs to reteach the lesson?

6. If you were Connie, what would you say to the first graders in the class when you retaught the lesson?

■ COMMENTARY

Of Stars and Black Holes in the First Grade Classroom

Deborah J. Tippins

There has been an increased emphasis on interdisciplinary teaching and curriculum integration in the past several years. Both the *National Science Education Standards* (National Research Council, 1996) and the *Principles and Standards for School Mathematics* (National Council of Teachers of Mathematics, 2000) stress the importance of helping teachers and students develop science and mathematics understandings through connections to other disciplines. Elementary classrooms, in particular, are learning places where the teaching of science is viewed as an integral context to support reading, writing, and mathematical literacies. Yet for prospective elementary teachers like Connie, the teaching of science appears a daunting task when they are faced with the need to develop in-depth pedagogical and content understandings of multiple subject areas.

Molly, like many science teacher educators who work with prospective elementary teachers, emphasizes the development of science literacy through integration with reading, writing, and mathematics—not as a set of rudimentary skills or isolated knowledge areas, but as literacy in the sense that teachers and students use reading, writing, and mathematics embedded in science inquiry experiences to explore and communicate about their everyday world. As Molly is well aware, childrens' literature can serve as an ideal springboard for building the confidence and skills teachers need to support meaningful science teaching and learning. Thus, Molly was eager to hear how Connie had used Eric Carle's book *Draw Me a Star* as the centerpiece for developing and implementing the "perfect" science lesson. She knew that Eric Carle's books were widely respected by teachers in the local schools as high-quality childrens' literature that was appropriate for use with young learners.

As Connie began to share her "five-point star" story, Molly quickly recognized that the lesson was actually miseducative in nature. Rather than helping students develop a better understanding of the properties of stars, the lesson was a missed opportunity to build on and extend students' prior knowledge of stars. On the one hand, Molly could engage Connie in a discussion of the accuracy of scientific ideas portrayed in childrens' books. Certainly, Connie's story points to the need for science teacher educators to provide opportunities and experiences for prospective teachers that enable them to evaluate the quality of fiction and nonfiction literature as a context for science learning.

On the other hand, this is a story that leads one to question the importance of teaching first-graders about stars. What is the value of science taught in isolation from personal experience or devoid of the passion, feeling, and empathy that are essential aspects of thinking, inquiring, and knowing? There is an inherent danger in reducing the science curriculum of elementary schools to a set of facts that ignores the nature of students' individual experience and their involvement in the world around them. I am constantly reminded of this when I recall Madeline Grumet's (1993) description of a lesson about black holes:

> I have sat in the back of classrooms where students read aloud from science textbooks describing black holes as if they were pot holes. Only someone steeped in the theory of eternal return could pay attention to that text without terror. Neither text nor teacher acknowledged or questioned the horror of the relentless destruction, the area's cavernous suction that the text described. I looked around the classroom. The only terrified person in it was me. The [students], even those taking notes, seemed isolated from the text, from the world and the universe that it described. Black holes were in the assigned chapter with five questions at the end of it to be done for homework. The questions merely mimicked the chapter prose, so they could be answered without even having to even imagine a black hole, let alone worry about one. (p. 18)

Finally, Molly and Connie's story leads me to ponder the nature of the processes that are involved in the transformation of content for pedagogical purposes. What do we have in mind when we encourage teachers to develop "authentic" science experiences for young learners? Would an authentic experience be characterized by tasks embedded in real-world settings or ones that mirror the work of scientists? Alternatively, would an authentic experience reflect the child's ways of thinking, knowing, and understanding stars? Is it possible or even desirable for first grade students to participate in authentic experiences with stars? And what role does children's literature play in formalizing or ritualizing students' personal experiences with phenomena such as stars? These questions, and others like them, highlight the deeper issues of curriculum transformation that are too often missing from traditional elementary science methods courses.

■ **CASE 6.3** ■

No Bones about It!

Stacey Neuharth-Pritchett and Jennifer Bellnap

■ *Julie Marker, a prekindergarten teacher, and her aide Mike Bradley recently attended a district-sponsored workshop on developmentally appropriate practice that highlighted the importance of child-centered teaching. Feeling confident in their ability to put into practice what they had learned, Julie and Mike invite Maggie Allen, the district's staff development coordi-*

nator, to visit their classroom. Julie is particularly interested in having Maggie observe her teaching science to the children. This open case concludes with Maggie observing instruction that is not at all what she expected to see and wondering how she might help Julie and Mike to reflect on their teaching and strive to make their science lessons more appropriate for preschool learners. The characters in the case are composites of people with whom Stacey and Jennifer have worked. The case is followed by a response written by Mark Guy, a science educator with extensive experience teaching science to young children.

"Extra, extra read all about it!" the children exclaimed as they jumped in the air and landed with their arms raised and legs out in the shape of an *X*. Julie Marker's prekindergarten class was two days away from completing an integrated unit on the letter *X* that Julie has recently developed. A teacher for twenty years, Julie was working to change her curriculum to be more appropriate for preschool children. She thought of herself as a rather traditional teacher and was excited by the challenge of teaching in ways consistent with what she had learned in the recent staff development workshop. To Julie, the child-centered teaching strategies that had been presented in the workshop seemed to provide useful suggestions for helping her work more effectively with the sixteen children in her class. With the help of her teacher's aide, Mike Bradley, Julie had revamped her unit on the letter *X* to include more hands-on activities and ones that allowed the children to make choices about their learning.

The interdisciplinary unit included activities for all content areas. One language arts activity involved the children in finding words in magazines that contained the letter *X*, and the children counted the number of different colored macaroni noodles they used to make the letter *X* in a mathematics activity. During outdoor play time, Mike had the children lie head to toe on the grass to make a giant *X*.

On arriving in Julie's classroom, Maggie was immediately struck by the visual transformation. The three large work tables had been pushed near the walls to open the classroom up for activity centers and play space. Julie and Mike had set up several centers to enable the children to engage in explorations related to the letter *X*. Maggie observed children building *X*s using blocks, looking at picture books on the letter *X*, drawing objects whose names contain the letter *X*, and sorting and counting objects that were shaped like the letter *X*. Of particular interest to Maggie was the science area that followed the unit theme by focusing on X-rays. The area was organized like a medical center and contained medical supplies, a heart model, an actual X-ray image posted on the window, and a makeshift examining table.

After scanning the classroom, Maggie turned her attention to Julie and the children. All sixteen of the children were gathered around Julie on the carpet as she began to read the children's book *The Skeleton inside You* by Philip Balestrino. As Julie read, she stopped every so often to question the children about the story. Julie posed her questions quickly, with one student usually having the opportunity to respond before she began reading again. Near the end of the book, the backbone and the flexibility of the body's skeleton were introduced, and Julie and the students stood up and moved their backs to experience the flexibility.

Maggie made a written record of a segment of the question-and-answer exchange she observed:

> **Julie:** What did you say was inside your body? All your bones together are your skeleton. What would your body look like if you had no bones?

Austin: It would be jelly, you couldn't stand up! You'd fall down!

Sarah: Yeah! You'd be a big squishy bag of water!

Julie: Right! Your body holds a lot of water in it. Do you really need a skeleton? So you're not like Play-Doh or clay? You are rigid because your bones are connected to each other. What do we call that?

Walter: Joints.

Julie: Good, Walter, that's right. Joints. We have real bones in us, and so do animals.

Immediately at the end of the story, Julie and Mike talk to the children about different activities in which they could participate for the next several minutes and directed small groups of children to different areas of the classroom. Mike showed one group how to make simulated X-ray images by painting the underside of a child's arm with white paint and then touching it to a black piece of construction paper, while Julie led another small group in building skeleton models using different lengths of white paper sticks cut from the middle of cotton swabs.

"Remember how we are studying the letter *X*, and X-ray begins with the letter *X*," Julie said to focus the children's attention. "We are going to make a model of our skeleton, like what you might see if you looked at an X-ray of the human body. I want you to make a skeleton that looks just like mine. We have more ribs than you see on my model, but we are not going to put them all on because there is not enough room to glue them on the black construction paper."

Julie continues, pointing to the white paper stick on her model that represents the femur, "This bone should be longer than the rest. And, you will need to bend the legs and arms on your model to make it fit on the paper. Start with the collar bones, called clavicles. These are the bones you feel at the top of your chest."

Two of the children selected different lengths of white paper sticks from the pile on the table and begin to glue them to the black construction paper. Others tried to position the sticks on the paper but were clearly unsure of what to do without Julie's step-by-step directions. To help guide the children's work, Julie taped her model skeleton to the classroom wall so that all could see it. Seeing Julie's model and listening to her directions again seemed to be the help needed by all the children, except for Walter. Walter expressed his frustration with the activity by dumping all of his white paper sticks back onto the table.

On observing Walter's behavior, Julie said in a scolding tone, "You aren't suppose to do it like that! You just remove one at a time and then glue."

To which Walter responded, "I don't want to glue."

Maggie watched Julie's lesson with growing disappointment. She was not observing the child-centered, developmentally appropriate learning experiences that she had expected to see. Reading *The Skeleton inside You* to the children was fine, but not allowing them to explore the meaning of the story through extended conversation, drawing, or creative movement limited the activity's effectiveness. Maggie also saw possibilities for learning slip by in Julie's model-building activity. Except for Walter, all the children were building their skeleton models, but the activity did not seem to engage them in thinking about X-ray as a word that starts with the letter *X* or an X-ray image as the product or process useful for gathering information about bones inside the body. She also had concerns about the instructional value of Mike's activity that involved the children in making simulated X-ray images with white paint and black construction paper.

As she prepared to leave the classroom, Maggie thought about the meeting she had scheduled with Julie and Mike after school. She wondered what she would say to the teachers about the relationship between what she observed and what was advocated in the workshop. How would they respond to her critique of their teaching? How might she encourage them to reflect further on their teaching and modify their lessons to make them more appropriate for preschool learners?

FOR REFLECTION AND DISCUSSION

1. Which teaching strategies used by Julie and Mike would you consider appropriate for preschool learners? Which ones would you consider inappropriate? Explain.

2. Do you agree with Julie and Mark's decision to include the human skeleton activities as part of a unit on the letter *X*? Why or why not?

3. How should Maggie initiate a discussion with the teachers about ways in which they might change their science learning activities to make them more appropriate for preschool children?

4. Suppose that it was your intention to have preschool children learn about aspects of the human skeleton. List two learning outcomes related to the human skeleton that you believe are appropriate for preschool children.

■ COMMENTARY

Theme-Based Instruction Does Not Guarantee Science Learning

Mark Guy

The prekindergarten scenario highlights two important aspects of teaching to promote science learning among young children. One has to do with how the planned learning experiences are connected to a theme; and the other has to do with the teacher's instructional role. In this case, how the theme was conceptualized and operationalized in the classroom made it difficult for Julie to create the child-centered, developmentally appropriate learning environment that Maggie expected to observe.

The letter *X* was a topical connection across a variety of activities, including science. Finding *X*s, drawing *X*s, building *X*s, and looking at X-ray images all became a part of exploring the letter through different subjects. In the end, the connections between the letter *X* and science were weak, being created by the teachers rather than by the children. Making a giant human *X* was probably great fun for the children but provided little opportunity for learning. Similarly, having the children assemble the skeleton likely helped them associate the letter *X* with the word X-ray but precluded any investigation of the structure and utility of a skeleton.

In other words, the theme-based instruction limited the benefit of the science activities and served to stifle the children's exploration of underlying concepts.

In the same vein, Julie assumed the role of director and the children acted out her directions. According to Maggie's observations, Julie's level of comfort with this teaching role seems to come from her experiences of being able to engage children in fun science activities while maintaining direct control over all phases of their learning. During the discussion of the book, for example, Julie's questions were narrowly focused to yield predetermined answers. This strategy enabled Julie to move quickly and predictably through the question-and-answer session. In addition, the hands-on activity of making a skeleton focused more on following directions and making a skeleton that looks "just like mine" than on promoting conceptual understandings of bone patterns through the process of building a skeleton. As director, Julie was in total control of the learning environment.

Yet Julie probably felt justified in her actions. The questions she asked while reading the book to the children were intended to solicit what she considered to be important factual knowledge about the skeleton. Her skeleton assembly activity was definitely a hands-on experience for the children. Accuracy of the model was emphasized. To be accurate, the children had to do it the right way, in the right order, and with the right materials. However, simply providing a hands-on lesson to young learners is not sufficient for child-centered, developmentally appropriate teaching, as Maggie clearly recognized. This case presented a teacher who, for the sake of control, seemed to value convention over creativity and imitation over investigation.

Therefore, Maggie's challenge to encourage Julie to teach in ways that are child-centered and developmentally appropriate will likely be no small task. Even if Julie wants to change her style of teaching, the journey can be very unsettling and uncertain. Julie might not feel the need to change her teaching to match Maggie's expectations. After all, Julie has an orderly classroom, relates science to the themes of her units, emphasizes science factual knowledge, and offers hands-on science experiences for her students. For Julie to change, Maggie must, most likely with the assistance of other teachers, help Julie to become dissatisfied with her own teaching. Encouraging Julie to see her actions from the perspective of her students—their need to inquire into something and not just follow directions—may help her to recognize the need for change. Without this perspective and collegial support, Julie will not likely commit to a change process and recognize the need to invite Mike to join her journey, one that will assuredly require great amounts of perseverance and humility.

■   C A S E   6 . 4   ■

And God Made the Little Birdies, Too

Andrew Paolucci

■ *In this open case, Andrew tells about his experiences as a student teacher in a rural community and describes how students' religious beliefs influenced their construction of science understandings. Experiencing no personal conflict between ideas associated with the theory of natural selection and the teachings of the book of Genesis, Andrew assumed that his seventh grade students would also experience none. However, responses to a question asked in class revealed just how wrong he was and the difficulties associated with helping students to develop scientific understandings that conflict with their religious beliefs. The case is followed by commentary from science teacher educator Lawrence Scharmann, who has written extensively about strategies to help students challenge their own thinking on issues related to science and religion.*

I was raised in a suburb of a large American city by Roman Catholic parents. I was taken to church every Sunday. There I learned about God and how he had made Heaven and Earth—and the oceans, and the rivers and lakes, and the forests, and the deserts, and the animals, and even Man—in just seven days.

I was also taken to school every weekday. There, I learned about all kinds of things. My favorite class was science. In science, we studied things like cells and tissues and animals and plants and all sorts of living things. We also learned about a man named Charles Darwin and his theory of natural selection. According to Darwin, every species on the earth had variations among its populations, and the variations that helped those organisms survive to reproduction were passed on to the organisms' offspring. This theory was applicable to all living things, from pond scum right on up to humans.

Never in my young mind was there any conflict while I was learning about natural selection. My father, though a religious man, had no reason to disbelieve these theories that were contradictory to the book of Genesis. To him, there was no reason God could not have been the motivating force behind natural selection. After all, if God is eternal, then what does He care about waiting around a few billion years for Man? I, likewise, had (and still have) no internal conflict regarding evolution.

My conflict, as it would turn out, was external.

Last winter, I was assigned to be a student teacher in a seventh grade class in a rural town I will call Yardley. This town has several thousand people, a few hundred cows, a thousand hound dogs, a gazillion pickup trucks, and a Wal-Mart. Although there are people who live there that commute to the city to work, the majority of the citizens are farmers, local business owners, and the like. Yardley definitely has a small town feel, and everyone is devoutly Christian.

My cooperating teacher at the school taught life science. On my first day there, she was wrapping up her unit on the dreaded "E" word. She handed me a letter. It read as follows:

Dear Mrs. _____,

   I do not want my daughter subjected to the teaching of evolution in your class. She was born and raised in a good Christian family. The theory of evolution goes against her beliefs. Please do not fail my daughter if she refuses to participate. She is an "A" student and will gladly do any alternative work you give her. Your cooperation would be greatly appreciated.

   Sincerely,

   _____

"I get at least one letter like this every year," the teacher told me. "I never even teach the chapter on human evolution anyway. We cover Darwin and natural selection, and then we go through the animals all the way up to mammals, but I never connect it to humans. Besides, you won't have any problems. We already did that. You'll be going over viruses, monerans, protists, invertebrates, and some vertebrates. You'll be leaving right about the time we get to amphibians."

For the most part, she was right. I didn't have any religious conflicts until the last week. I was teaching the chapter on amphibians. On the day before the test, I was reviewing the chapter with the class when I noticed that I had made a big error. On the test (of which I had already made many many copies), there would be a question involving the migration of amphibians onto land. Because the question was kind of tricky, I read it straight from the text: "When the first amphibians moved onto land, what dangers did they face?"

This was the last class of the day, and the students were always restless and exuberant. I got a barrage of answers shouted in my direction:

"Breathing air!"

"Getting food!"

"Drying up!"

"Being eaten by predators!"

This last response, as I was about to discover, was booby-trapped.

I have this annoying preoccupation with what I believe to be true. If someone asks me a question, I will answer it thoroughly and to the best of my abilities. I cannot lie, nor can I withhold information. In this case, I thought the "being eaten" response was wrong, and I had to tell the class why it was wrong: There were no land-dwelling predators to eat the first amphibians because no animals had evolved onto land yet. However, to say this directly would be an invitation to disaster. I tried to approach the issue subtly: "You guys have studied natural selection, right?"

"Yes. . . ."

"Okay. Think about this question from that point of view. What kinds of predators would be on land when the first amphibians left the water?" I thought this would make them see my point. It didn't.

"Birds!"

"Lizards!"

"Other amphibians!"

"Dinosaurs!"

I knew I would have to try another approach. "Okay," I said. "What are the five types of vertebrates?"

"Fish!"

"Amphibians!"

"Mammals!"

"Birds!"

"Reptiles!"

"Good!" I said. I wrote them on the board. "Now, which of these are the least complex organisms?"

"Fish?" said one girl.

"Right! And which ones are the most complex?"

"Mammals," said a boy in the back.

"Exactly!" Oooh, I was on a roll. I was running for the goal line. Nothing could stop me now. "So, how would you order these from least complex to most complex?"

"Fishes, amphibians, reptiles, birds, and mammals," said someone up front.

"And which ones were the first animals to move onto land?" I asked the class.

"The amphibians?"

"Yes! The amphibians!" I was amazed at how well they were doing. We were first-and-goal on the one-yard line. All we had to do was run the ball into the end zone. "Now, with all this in mind, what types of predators were living on land when the first amphibians left the water?"

"Reptiles!"

"Birds!"

"Snakes!"

"Saber-toothed tigers!"

Fumble!

"No!" I said, barely able to contain my frustration. "You just agreed with me that amphibians were the first animals to leave the water . . . !"

"Right. So . . . ?"

"So if the amphibians leave the water before any other animals, how could there be birds and snakes and saber-toothed tigers already on land waiting to eat them?!?!!"

"God put them there," said a girl.

God put them there. It was not the response I wanted to hear. Nowhere in Darwin's theory of natural selection does he say, "and God puts these animals here." I knew I had to drop the subject. I wasn't going to cross that line. I had to forfeit the ball game to God.

My talents lie elsewhere. They have to. They certainly don't lie here. If anyone knows how to make students confront their "alternative conceptions" where God is concerned—without getting struck down by a bolt of lightning—please let me know.

FOR REFLECTION AND DISCUSSION

1. What are some common science misconceptions or "alternative" conceptions? Are there any misconceptions you have previously held? Explain.

2. What teaching methods can be used to help students confront and overcome their alternative conceptions?

3. Would you confront the students' alternative conceptions in the case described above? If so, how?

■ COMMENTARY

Enhancing Instructional Success in Teaching Evolution

Lawrence C. Scharmann

Frameworks that seek to understand how knowledge restructuring occurs and how to build a learning environment that facilitates this restructuring raise important philosophical, psychological, and pedagogical questions . . . about how conceptual change occurs. . . . Implicit in emphasizing the **how** is a shift in . . . perspective from one that embraces "scientists' ways of knowing" as the dominant objective towards one that favors "positioning the learner for the next step." This change in perspective and approach represents a radical and complex departure from common practice. (Duschl & Gitomer, 1991, p. 839)

The opening quote represents a partial description of what is known as the conceptual change instructional model (Posner et al., 1982). In interpreting the implications of this model, Duschl and Gitomer suggest that for conceptual change to take place, four conditions must be met:

- Existing ideas must be found to be unsatisfactory.
- The new idea must be intelligible, coherent, and internally consistent.
- The new idea must be plausible.
- The new idea must be preferable to the old viewpoint on the grounds of perceived elegance, parsimony, and/or usefulness.

In analyzing the case entitled "And God Made the Little Birdies, Too" against these four conditions, it is clear to me that the students did not find their existing ideas to be unsatisfactory. Hence, because the first condition was not met, the remaining three become all but impossible to achieve. Where did this student teacher go wrong? Perhaps it was in trying to get students to adopt "scientists' ways of knowing" rather than in "positioning the learner for the next step." In other words, instructional decisions were not made to permit students to experience ideas that were in conflict with their existing notions; hence, conceptual change was not initiated. Attributes that enhance the potential for conceptual change include, but are not limited to the following:

- Providing opportunities for students to express their initial thoughts on an issue/topic (engagement → exploration)
- Encouraging peer interaction in which alternative conceptions arise (exploration → small group discussion)
- Facilitating student-to-teacher interactions in which alternative conceptions are recognized, discussed, and compared to views held by the scientific community (explanation/ debrief of small group discussion)
- Providing opportunities for students to express themselves in a reflective manner and/or make applied use of key concepts (explanation → elaboration). (BSCS, 1992; Lawson, Abraham, & Renner, 1989)

In relation to the final statement of the case, "If anyone knows how to make students confront their 'alternative conceptions' where God is concerned . . . please let me know," how might these attributes be translated into instructional practice? A successful strategy I have employed in introducing evolution is the use of a small group, peer discussion. Foreshadowing current reform efforts, as exemplified in the "Teaching Standards" section of the *National Science Education Standards* (National Research Council, 1996), Schwab (1962) cited three reasons for the effectiveness of small group discussions:

- Students are most active and individually engaged in learning when working in small groups.

- Discussions evoke, as reinforcers of learning, a host of more desirable affective outcomes (e.g., working, belonging, and identifying with a peer group).
- Teachers can establish greater instances of interpersonal relations (both student–student and student–teacher) during a given instructional period compared with most other teaching methods.

I urge teachers to consider the use of a peer discussion, with respect to evolution, as soon as students exhibit expressions of anxiety, confusion, anger, withdrawal, or other nonverbal indicators because it

> enhances participation in the learning process and provides potential resolution and reinforcement for previously misunderstood value positions. These value positions were previously based on a student's perceived need to make a dichotomous choice between scientific versus religious viewpoints. In fact . . . direct student involvement is critical to the success of the resolution of this issue [evolution] in particular and an understanding of the nature of scientific theories in general. (Scharmann, 1990, p. 99)

The following lesson provides a synthesis of the use of cooperative learning, an application of the learning cycle to teaching biology (BSCS, 1992), and a goal of enhancing conceptual change.

ENGAGEMENT

Ask students to respond in writing to the following (individually):

1. Consider what you have read or been taught and summarize your understanding of evolution.
2. Summarize your understanding of creation origins.
3. Do you perceive there to be a conflict in your responses to questions 1 and 2? Why or why not?

Note: The engagement can be used as either an in-class or out-of-class activity.

EXPLORATION

Assign students to small discussion groups of three to five individuals. Have them share with classmates their responses to the engagement activity. Once it is completed, have groups consider two additional questions:

1. What reasons support the teaching (in science classes) of:
   - Only evolution?
   - Only creation origins?
   - Both evolution and creation origins?
   - Neither evolution nor creation origins?

2. Examine the merits (i.e., the strengths and weaknesses) of each set of reasons in question 1. Is one set of reasons more compelling (or stronger) than the others? If so, which one? Why?

The teacher's role during discussion is to monitor group progress. It is neither to lead groups nor to provide limitations on the direction of discussion; instead, it is to maintain on-task behavior and mutual respect. In monitoring groups, teachers should note obvious instances of misinformation and sources of student disagreements. The only exception, regarding direct teacher intervention is to remind students that the intent of discussion is to listen to and respect the opinions of other group members. Ultimately, discussions, unlike debates, do not require winners and losers; a well-constructed discussion produces nothing but winners.

EXPLANATION/ELABORATION

Each group should select a spokesperson to share the group's consensus (from question 1 in the exploration task). On completion of reports and any final intergroup clarification, teachers should bring the class together to conduct an interactive, large group discussion. The teacher should plan to address any misinformation, especially related to competing knowledge claims resulting from different ways of knowing (e.g., religion versus science); in other words, it is very important for teachers and students to distinguish between when they are using science and when they are using religion as explanatory tools. The compatibility of these ways of knowing is left strictly as an individual choice. It is at this point, nonetheless, that I share with students some products of evolutionary thinking (Scharmann, 1994): (1) antibiotics and why we are instructed to take them over seven to ten days even when we begin feeling better after only two to three days (i.e., application of natural selection); (2) more efficient identification of "new" diseases by the Centers for Disease Control and Prevention by noting potential precursors or common ancestry with other diseases (i.e., application of modification with descent); or (3) herbicide/pesticide rotations used in agriculture to prevent resistance to any single chemical (i.e, application of natural selection). Thus, even if students don't wish to "believe" in evolutionary origins, they might begin to more readily recognize that we all accept products of the use of this powerful theory to solve problems. Finally, students should be given time to reflect (i.e., by writing a journal entry) on what they individually gained as a result of participation in the small group discussion.

In the end, teachers cannot *make* students confront their conceptions. Students can only be *invited* to consider alternatives to their conceptions. Ultimately, students must confront and recognize alternative conceptions themselves. Peer discussion represents an excellent teaching method to initiate such an invitation because it demands more direct participation by students than most other instructional choices. I have found that a peer discussion model also increases students' desires for more information associated with evolutionary theory than does the use of more traditional teacher-centered instructional approaches (Scharmann, 1990). Finally, I have repeatedly noted that peer discussion enhances opportunities for students to introspect, reflect on, and reconstruct personal knowledge and attitudes concerning evolution in a direction that possesses greater scientific integrity.

References

American Association for the Advancement of Science. (1994). *Benchmarks for science literacy.* Oxford, UK: Oxford University Press.

Baxter, J. (1995). Children's understanding of astronomy and the earth science. In S. M. Glynn & R. Duit (Eds.), *Learning science in the schools: Research reforming practice* (pp. 155–177). Mahwah, NJ: Lawrence Erlbaum.

BSCS. (1992). *Biological science: An ecological approach* (7th ed.). Dubuque, IA: Kendall/Hunt.

Bybee, R. W. (1997). *Achieving scientific literacy: From purpose to practice.* Portsmouth, NH: Heinemann.

Driver, R., Asoko, H., Leach, J., Mortimer, E., & Scott, P. (1994). Constructing scientific knowledge in the classroom. *Educational Researcher, 23*(7), 5–12.

Driver, R., & Bell, B. (1986). Students' thinking and the learning of science: A constructivist view. *School Science Review, 62*(240), 443–456.

Duschl, R. A., & Gitomer, D. H. (1991). Epistemological perspectives on conceptual change: Implications for educational practice. *Journal of Research in Science Teaching, 28*(9), 839–858.

Gilbert, J. K., Osbourne, J., & Fensham, P. (1982). Children's science and its consquences for teaching. *Science Education, 66,* 623–633.

Grumet, M. (1993). The curriculum: What are the basics and are we teaching them? In J. L. Kincheloe & S. R. Steinberg (Eds.), *Thirteen questions: Reframing education's conversations.* New York: Peter Lang Publishing.

Harvard-Smithsonian Center for Astrophysics. (1987). *A private universe.* Washington, DC: Annenberg/CPB.

Lawson, A. E., Abraham, M. R., & Renner, J. W. (1989). *A theory of instruction: Using the learning cycle to teach science concepts and thinking skills* (Monograph No. 1). Columbus, OH: National Association for Research in Science Teaching.

National Council of Teachers of Mathematics. (2000). *Principles and standards for school mathematics.*

National Research Council. (1996). *National science education standards.* Washington, DC: National Academy Press.

Posner, G. J., Strike, K. A., Hewson, P. W., & Gertzog, W. A. (1982). Accommodation of a scientific conception: Toward a theory of conceptual change. *Science Education, 66*(2), 211–227.

Scharmann, L. C. (1990). Enhancing an understanding of the premises of evolutionary theory: The influence of a diversified instructional strategy. *School Science and Mathematics, 90*(2), 91–100.

Scharmann, L. C. (1994). Teaching evolution: Past and present. In J. S. Simmons (Ed.), *Censorship: A threat to reading, learning, thinking* (pp. 148–165). Newark, DE: International Reading Association.

Schwab, J. J. (1962). The teaching of science as enquiry. In *The teaching of science* (pp. 1–103). Cambridge, MA: Harvard University Press.

Snyder, T., & Dockterman, D. (1998). *Seasons.* Watertown, MA: Tom Snyder Productions.

Resources to Consider

Duit, R., & Treagust, D. (1995). Students' conceptions and constructivist teaching. In B. J. Fraser & H. J. Walberg (Eds.), *Improving science education* (pp. 46–69). Chicago, IL: National Society for the Study of Education.

Duit and Treagust discuss the nature of students' science conception in relation to constructivist views of teaching and learning. They conclude with a list of recommendations for improving science education.

Gallas, K. (1995). *Talking their way into science: Hearing children's questions and theories, responding with curricula.* New York: Teachers College Press.

This book examines how children think and construct knowledge about their world. The role of language and thinking are discussed as critical dimensions of engaging young children in scientific thought.

Lowe, T. L., & Matthew, K. I. (2000). Using puppets and children's literature in the science classroom. *Science and Children, 37*(8), 41–45.

These educators provide a rationale for using children's literature to teach science at the early childhood level. Their article also stresses guidelines for selecting appropriate fiction and nonfiction books with selected examples.

National Science Teachers Association. [On-line] *Outstanding science tradebooks for children.* Available at: http://www.nsta.org/pubs/sc/ostblist.asp
This site presents lists of science trade books that have been identified as outstanding by a review panel appointed by the National Science Teachers Association in cooperation with the Children's Book Council. Titles are organized by topic (biography, life science, earth and space science, technology and engineering, etc.), and each is accompanied by a brief description.

Shapiro, B. (1994). *What children bring to light: A constructivist perspective on children's learning in science.* New York: Teachers College Press.
Shapiro explores how young children make sense of concepts associated with light energy. This book is an in-depth look at the sense-making process of elementary school students.

Smith, D. C., & Wesley, A. (2000). Teaching for understanding: Bridging the gap between student understanding and state and national tests and standards. *Science & Children,* 38(1), 36–41.
This article describes how a fifth grade teacher and an elementary science educator collaborated to explore tensions between teaching for understanding and teaching to the test. Also discussed is the student-centered approach they used to negotiate these tensions.

7

Assessing Student Learning in Science

How do you determine whether or what children have learned in your science classroom? Assessment practices, those information-gathering and decision-making processes in which teachers engage, especially as implemented in science classrooms, are undergoing real and meaningful changes. Changes are evident in both why and how assessment is done. The forces that have brought about these changes stem primarily from efforts toward educational reform. This rethinking in science education was epitomized by publication of the *National Science Education Standards* (National Research Council, 1996). Influenced by the culture of reform, teachers in increasing numbers are no longer asking students to memorize isolated science facts and formulas; instead, students are being asked to construct new and meaningful science understandings for themselves. In many of today's elementary classrooms, teachers take on new roles as facilitators of student knowledge construction rather than givers of information; they encourage the development of communities of learners, multiple perspectives, critical thinking, and diverse approaches to solving real problems. To match the sophistication of the science learning expected of students, significant changes are occurring with regard to assessment practices.

Over the last decade, we have seen movement toward a somewhat nontraditional philosophy about educational assessment. Traditional paper-and-pencil tests, quizzes, and end-of-chapter questions provide only a portion of the data needed to indicate student progress in science. Traditional tests do not adequately measure students' abilities and skills as they engage in processes that lead to final products as a part of a complete learning experience. Various techniques of assessment must be used to determine how students work, what students are learning, and what students can produce as a result of learning. According to the *National Science Education Standards* (National Research Council, 1996), assessment tasks must make use of a broad array of data collection methods that provide in-depth information about what students are learning. They must be free of bias, have clear purposes, and serve to blur the distinction between instruction and assessment. Assessment in science must also provide students with opportunities to practice problem-solving skills and refine their science understandings in authentic contexts. In addition, the authors of the standards assert the idea that teachers, students, educational administrators, parents, the public, policymakers, institutions of higher education, business and industry, and government are all consumers of information about student performance in the science classroom (1996, p. 76). Although the basic elements of authentic assessment are not new, they are being organized in new ways that should provide stronger links between teaching, learning, and assessment. The closer the assessment approximates the teaching–learning situation, the better will be the validity of the assessment (Payne, 1997). A variety of systems of assessment has evolved, is still evolving, and will likely continue to evolve throughout your professional career in teaching.

The three cases in this chapter represent just a sample of the many dilemmas that elementary science teachers wrestle with when attempting to use alternatives to traditional assessment. In the first case, "Talking Together about the Moon" by Emily van Zee, a first grade teacher questions how she should respond to a child's answer that differs from all others. The case focuses on the child's ongoing conversations about the moon and the class's shared observations, experiences, ideas, and questions. In the second case, "Daring to Be Different," Nancy Davis and Rose Pringle recount how an elementary student teacher, with the support of her science methods course professor, wrestles with the skepticism of the supervising teacher and student opposition when she proposes peer assessment for a science project. An important dilemma in this case is associated with teacher and students sharing authority to evaluate student work. The final case, "The Light at the End of the Hands-on Tunnel" by Virginia Wilcox and Michael Kamen, raises assessment concerns and frustrations of the fourth grade teachers in an elementary school that has eliminated science textbooks and adopted modular science kits. The teachers question whether they are really assessing the students' understanding of concepts or simply their ability to perform a certain task.

■ **C A S E   7 . 1** ■

Talking Together about the Moon

Emily H. van Zee

■ *Akiko Kurose, a first grade teacher in an urban public school, graciously welcomed me to her classroom to observe the many ways that she used science as a focus for learning. We had met in physics programs for teachers in which she had participated in trial-testing some of Lillian McDermott's* Physics by Inquiry *(1996) materials. She received the Presidential Award for Excellence in Teaching of Science and Mathematics in 1990. Aki and her family had been forced to live in a Japanese internment camp during World War II. These experiences underlay her commitment to fostering global understanding and peace. One way in which she encouraged global perspectives was to invite her students to watch the moon. During their ongoing conversations about the moon, the children shared observations, experiences, ideas, and questions. Such conversations often require skillful navigation. What should a teacher do, for example, if one child's response differs from the others? This case is dedicated to Aki in loving memory of the joyful ways in which she nurtured her students' thinking. It is followed by commentaries from Emily van Zee and Lynn Bryan, a science teacher educator who regularly engages her classes of prospective elementary teachers in investigations of the moon.*

Aki Kurose's first grade students began each day by singing "good morning" to each other in several different languages. They could choose to sit down anywhere in the world when they gathered around Aki to plan the day's activities. An artist had made about a third of the floor area in Aki's classroom into a colorful map with continents big enough to sit on. A large green banner proclaimed PEACE. This was a classroom in which the students learned to think with a global perspective.

Aki wrote (in press) that "observing the moon is a way to give children experience in making discoveries in a cooperative and sharing way which allows them to discover that everybody on the planet Earth is sharing the same phenomena." Her students knew that children everywhere can look up in the sky and see the moon because Aki read her students moon legends from many cultures. A favorite was "The Truth about the Moon" by Clayton Bess (1983), in which an African child hears many stories about the moon as he seeks answers to his questions.

The students in Aki's class frequently made up their own legends about the moon. One day, for example, I observed a child dictating a long story about a fox named Maii who encountered a bee in his search for a way to climb to the moon. This student watched carefully as Aki wrote the words, asked for corrections when Aki omitted a question mark or slipped into cursive ("I don't read cursive"), and instructed Aki to write in special ways, such as making very small letters for what the bee said to the fox.

When the moon was visible during the day, Aki often would take her students outside to make observations. They drew not only the moon, but also where it was with respect to the houses and trees on their horizon. As they became more experienced observers, they began to take care in recording its shape accurately and its position in the sky with respect to the sun.

Aki provided paper strips of seven circles that the students could use to record the shape of the moon each week even if they happened to see the moon outside of school hours. Some of the parents became so intrigued with this moon watching that they came in to talk with Aki to clarify their own understandings of what they were seeing in the sky. In this way, Aki created a sense of community in which students, parents, and teacher were observing, thinking, and learning together.

The children began watching the moon, sun, and stars early in the school year and talked together about what they had seen several times a week. These conversations often began with the children drawing on the board the shape of the moon that they had seen during the preceding twenty-four hours. Then Aki would ask questions such as "What did you see?," "When did you see this?," and "Where did you see the moon?" Such questions provided incentives for these first graders to orient themselves in time and space. They wanted to learn how to read clocks so that they could report to the class what time it was when they had seen the moon.

One day, I was watching the students drawing crescent moons on the board. The evening before, a waxing crescent moon had been visible in the western sky. Most of the students drew crescent moons lit on the right that looked like backward C's. One student, however, drew a crescent moon lit on the left that looked like a frontward C. This drawing was different from all of the others.

FOR REFLECTION AND DISCUSSION

1. If this happened in your classroom, what would you say and do next? How would you respond if one student seemed to be thinking differently from all the rest? Why would you respond in this way?

2. How would you respond if the student were drawing the moon on paper at his desk rather than publicly on the board? Why would you respond in this way?

◼ COMMENTARY

Reflecting with Teachers about the Student's Response

Emily H. van Zee

During discussion of this dilemma in courses for prospective teachers and in workshops for practicing teachers, a common response has been to assume that the student was wrong. Such responses often focus on ways to protect the student's self-esteem while resolving the issue, for example, "Say it may be tough to remember which side is lit, since it can be seen both ways" or "have the class vote on which side was lit last night." Some suggestions leave the issue open for reexamination: "I would ask this student to copy his/her board drawing onto a piece of paper (if he hasn't drawn his/her observation) and ask him/her to compare it to the crescent he/she observes tonight (or in the next few nights)" or "If we have all the students do this activity, the student may realize that the initial observation was faulty during his/her subsequent observations." This approach involves engaging the student in making and interpreting additional observations in order to figure out for himself what he had done wrong.

However, some responses recognize that the student might be right. Such responses often focus on ways in which this discrepant account might have been generated, for example, "How might the student actually have seen the left-facing moon? Perhaps the student was lying on his back and seeing the moon upside-down. How appropriate is the term upside-down when viewing an orb from another orb?" or "Perhaps the moon was reflected in a window." Some suggestions involve engaging students in thinking about how this might have happened: "Involve the class in discussion of why the moon looks like it does. Can you lie down in one direction and see the moon one way and lie in another direction and see it another way? Why or why not? Does it look different than it would if you were in the Poconos (east coast) or the other side of world?" This approach places responsibility for thinking with the students.

When I transcribed the tape for this conversation about the moon, I was surprised to discover that Aki had prompted the student to draw this different moon. Apparently, the student had told her privately what he had seen, and she had encouraged him to share this different view with his classmates after he volunteered the time of his sighting. [Words in brackets have been added or changed.]

> *Aki:*   [Ken], you want to draw what you saw?
> [Ken] saw something a little different. Let's see what he saw.

Ken drew a crescent shape lit on the left on the board.

> *Aki:*   Do you think it changed?
> In what part of the sky did you see this?
>
> *[Ken]:*   Around [a local park] . . . I saw it in the mirror of my car.
>
> *Aki:*   . . . Isn't that exciting?
> . . . [Ken] saw the moon in his mirror.
> He saw the reflection of the moon . . . in his mirror while [his mother was driving] past the lake and he realized that was the moon.
>
> *[Ken]:*   I thought it was the sun at first and I decided no and then I [leaned] over and told my Mom to stop and she said, "Oh, that's the moon! "

This conversation illustrates the importance of listening carefully to what students are saying. What appears to be wrong may in fact make good sense if one can elicit the details of a child's experiences and interpretations. By creating a classroom climate that welcomed student thinking, Aki was able to hear about this student's experiences privately and then to choose to engage all of the children in thinking about something intriguing together. What she might have perceived as a wrong answer she instead recognized as a special circumstance that merited not only discussion but also celebration.

Another example of the complexity of these students' thinking occurred when one of Aki's students went to visit Australia. This student continued observing the moon there while her classmates observed the moon at school and at home. When she returned and they compared their drawings, they discovered that what we see depends on where we are. While people in the United States were seeing a waxing crescent moon appear to grow bigger on the right, people in Australia were seeing a waxing crescent moon appear to grow bigger on the left. This led one of the children to ask, "How does the moon look if you're on the equator?" Such abstract questions emerged from the deep knowledge these children had acquired during their ongoing inquiries. As Aki wrote (in press) in reflecting on this conversation, "Several children were also curious about how the earth appears from the moon. These experiences engender thoughts about the moon from different places, granting the students the gift of a global perspective."

From Reflections of the Moon to Reflections on Science Teaching

Lynn Bryan

I wonder what was going through Ken's mind when he was drawing his picture on the board. Was he excited that his picture was different from the others, because he knew that he saw the moon in a different way (in the mirror)? Or was he wondering whether he was wrong because his picture was in the opposite direction from the others? As I think back to years ago when I was Ken's age, I would probably have felt timid about sharing my picture of the moon knowing that it was different from my peers' pictures and they would have thought I was wrong.

In contrast to my own science experiences, I imagine that Ken and the other children in Aki's classroom are in the "comfortable neighborhood of science" (Roth, 1991): They feel free to express their thoughts, share their ideas, ask questions, and enjoy learning. I imagine that daily there is an eager buzz in the classroom as children excitedly yet carefully draw the moon that they saw the night before. I imagine that the children are not focused on the "right answer," but rather are enthused about figuring out and making sense of new phenomena in the world that surrounds them. Finally, I imagine that Aki's students unabashedly explore their hunches, explain their theories, and accept alternative solutions. Does this describe your science classroom?

One important aspect of Aki's classroom is that by orienting her science around a global perspective, she is helping students to develop an accurate conception of the nature and processes of science. The message that children most likely take away from her lessons is that science is more than just a collection of facts. Science involves perspective and multiple ways of knowing. Science involves skills that are essential to the processes of and thinking about science. Specifically, Aki's case illustrates the importance of reasoning and communication in science as she helps her students become aware of their environment and its connections to science. Because Ken is allowed to share and explain his observation of the "backward moon," the class learns about carefully considering data and drawing conclusions based on observations. They learn how to analyze and evaluate the merits of an explanation on the basis of information provided, checking each others' assertions against accepted scientific knowledge. Finally, the inquiry orientation of this lesson also fosters question posing. Students were inquisitive and curious. Undoubtedly, the short classroom conversation that we read in the case continued with children wondering about questions such as "Why does the moon look backward in a mirror?," "How do mirrors work?," and "How can you tell if the moon is backward if it is full?" An attitude of curiosity and inquiry is fundamental to science, and Aki seems to nurture this disposition in her students.

The circumstances that are described in this case are often uncomfortable for even the most veteran teacher. How would you handle a response like Ken's—a response that is unexpected or appears to be incorrect? What would have been your reaction? Aki's case strongly suggests that as teachers, we need to develop and nurture our skills not only in hearing children, but also in listening to children's ideas and explanations. Furthermore, we need to provide multiple opportunities for children to demonstrate what they know and how they know. Discerning what a child knows and how he or she reasons is not possible without appropriate means of communication. We need to allow children to explain orally, in writing, by demonstrating, and through drawing. Allowing Ken to draw a picture and explain his observations in his own story not only enabled Aki to listen and understand his perspective, but also communicated to all the students in class that day that their experiences and ideas are valuable. Rather than judging or discounting their observation, Aki treated her students as serious learners, enabling them to come to understand and apply the processes and practices of science.

As you reflect on this case, think about the learning environment that Aki created in her classroom and think about your own science classroom. In particular, consider the following questions:

- Aki purposely chose to teach science from an orientation that fostered peace and a global understanding. What perspectives guide your science teaching?
- What goals do you have for your students in science classrooms? What attitudes, skills, and understandings do you want them to develop?
- What do you do in your own classroom to foster a disposition of curiosity and inquiry in your students?
- How do you model the attitudes and standards of scientific practice for your students?
- What are ways in which your students communicate their explanations and understandings to you?
- What are ways in which you can listen more carefully?

■ CASE 7.2 ■

Daring to Be Different in Assessment

Nancy T. Davis and Rose M. Pringle

■ *This case describes an attempt by June Wilson, an elementary intern, to introduce peer assessment in her science class. Recent discussion about the influence of standardized testing has caused June to think about alternative ways to conceptualize assessment within her class.*

Keeping the goal of creating learning communities in mind, she attempts to align her assessment practices with her goals. On the advice of her university supervising teacher and in subsequent discussions with the classroom cooperating teacher, June decides to work with the students in developing criteria for assessing their science projects. This idea of peer assessment is met with some skepticism from the cooperating teacher and opposition from the students. June is a composite of teachers with whom Nancy and Rose have worked. The case is followed by a response written by science teacher educator Gilbert Naizer.

"What grade did you get on your science report? I got an A," Brad boasted loudly as June Wilson passed out papers to her sixth grade class. She saw Sara fold her paper and withdraw from the group as she hid her paper in shame. This incident bothered June, but she didn't have time to deal with it in the fast pace of teaching class. Switching gears, June began to introduce the individual science research projects the students were going to be involved in for the next six weeks. She planned for students to investigate machines found in and around the home and to design a model of a simple machine that would be useful in the kitchen. Students' individual projects would form the basis for teaching the unit on simple machines in the coming weeks.

"Are we getting graded on this?" June's students inquired as she tried to infuse enthusiasm for the projects. Again this issue of assessment was raised in June's mind. But again she could not deal with it right then; this was something to talk over with her supervising teacher.

June is an intern whose supervising teacher encourages her to think about the classroom she wants to create. In recent conversations, they had established that they wanted to create communities of science learners in the classroom. This was consistent with June's experiences in her university science methods courses and current beliefs about teaching and learning science. "What do I need to do to help create the classroom I want—a community of learners?" was the question June was using as a referent for her teaching. Images of Sara's reaction as she looked at her grade came quickly into her thoughts. As she reflected on the dilemmas of getting students to really learn together and develop into a community of science learners, she identified assessment practices as one of the most problematic.

Because June wanted her class to be a place where all individuals come to learn, she was concerned about the role that assessment played in setting teachers up as experts and students as novices. She realized that with many topics in science, she would be learning along with the students. How could she create assessment practices that reinforced the notion of all members of the class being learners? As she thought more about how assessment is traditionally interpreted, she realized that most students tended to look at grades as a reflection of their personal value. Students thought of themselves as "A students" or "B students" and sometimes even "D or F students." Students performed for the grades rather than for learning. She realized that many students valued their assignments only for the grade they would receive, not for the learning opportunity provided.

"How can I make assessment in science be about helping each person to improve rather than a value judgment?" was a question June brought to her supervising teacher during their weekly practicum session at the university. In conversation, they explored options and anticipated student responses to the proposed change. June decided to make some changes in the class assessment practices and to explore how these changes affected the learning environment. At first, June shared the ideas with her cooperating teacher.

"Well, I am not sure how this will work at this school," said Ann, her cooperating teacher. "We have tried so many new things here: portfolio, journals, you name it. But we have to go right back to the test and the grades that the parents want. The parents have a strong influence here, and they want the students to do well on the standardized tests. With any new development, the first thing they ask is 'How will this help the students on the state tests?' "

However, Ann gave June the go-ahead to try the peer assessment. June decided to implement these changes as students conducted individual science research experiments. She selected this unit in part because of observations she had made of the competitiveness that was often established when students were doing science fair projects. Assisting each other to improve would be a good metaphor for how she wanted her students to think about learning with each other. Students were familiar with science fair projects from competitions in previous years. June was determined to make it a better learning experience for students. She decided to introduce peer assessment as part of the practices for this unit. In doing so, she knew that the students would have to be part of the negotiation process.

The next day, when the students were working on their projects, June told them to choose a partner. She instructed them to make a list of pointers that could be used to identify a superb science project. To get them started, she asked, "What are some features that a project should have for it to be rated highly?"

"I know," Mark shouted out immediately.

"No, Mark, I want you to talk with James. Isn't he your partner? Write down the decisions you make."

"Okay, we will," Mark replied.

As June walked around the room, she was pleased with the conversations she heard taking place among the student pairs. Not only were they talking to each other, they also had fairly long lists.

As she approached Brad's desk, he asked, "Ms. Wilson, what are you going to do with our list?"

"In a minute, we will be putting all of our lists together," she replied.

During the whole group discussion to elicit the students' responses, June compiled a list on the display board. In the first round, each group was asked to share one point. This continued until the students had exhausted their suggestions.

"Wow," June said looking at the list. "You all did well. What about using this list that you have made to assess each other's science research projects?" she asked, as she pointed to the list of criteria including objectives, clear introduction, good description of the machines, at least eight examples, labeled drawing, and good organization.

"What?" Brad said, almost instantaneously. "Do you mean us assessing our projects?"

"Yes," responded June. "We could use these criteria to assess the research projects of our peers," she continued as she wrote the words Peer Assessment on the display board.

"Peer assessment?" a number of students questioned as they read the words aloud.

"Do you mean that we give each other a grade on the project?" Julie inquired.

"Oh, no," chirped Mary. "My mother won't like that."

"Why not?" June asked.

"Teachers are the ones who mark our work and give us grades," said James. "Isn't that what they are paid for?" he continued under his breath.

"If our peers give us grades, how will you know who will be promoted next year?" Mary said as she got out of her chair to talk to Brad. All eyes turned to them as she whispered in Brad's ear.

"What's with you and Brad?" June asked Mary.

Just then Brad turned and said, "How can our peers decide what you want? You gave us the assignment in the first place."

Pointing to the display board, June said, "How about using these criteria as a guide to provide comments to our peers to help them to improve?"

There was a pause in the class as if the students were repeating what they had just heard. Then a chair screeched as Sara rose to the floor. "Ms. Wilson," she said, "I know just as much as my peers, so how can I assess their work? How can they assess mine?" She then turned and looked in the direction of Brad and James and continued, "I am prepared to take corrections from my teacher who knows more than I do. In fact, she is the person I should be learning from."

FOR REFLECTION AND DISCUSSION

1. What is the role of assessment in science learning?
2. How does assessment detract from creating communities of learners?
3. How might assessment serve to foster the development of learning communities?
4. How would you respond to Sara's comments about teachers knowing more than the students?
5. How would you respond to James's comments about assessment being what teachers get paid to do?
6. How would you deal with questions from parents about peer assessment?

■ C O M M E N T A R Y

Creating Community in the Elementary Classroom: A Question of Peer Assessment in Science

Gilbert Naizer

The major concern of the teacher intern in this case is the desire to move the class toward becoming a community of learners with a focus on learning instead of getting a grade. Additional problems surface as the students object to the use of peer assessment. Establishing an environment of collaboration, shared authority, and positive interactions is not an easy process. June's desire to align practices with reform movements such as that advocated in the *National Science Education Standards* is an admirable goal for a teacher intern. The standards advocate establishing a community of learners and encourage situations in which students are engaged in ongoing assessment of their work and the work of others.

In a classroom with the competitive nature described in this case, it will take concerted effort to establish the desired learning community. It is not evident from the case whether opportunities for working with peers have been used as instructional processes in the past. The description of Mark shouting out an answer when the children had been asked to work with a partner indicates that this may be a rare occurrence for this classroom. If most activities have been performed individually, students would naturally focus on competition rather than collaboration. Using cooperative group projects would aid in the establishment of the class as a community. However, simply putting students into groups does not guarantee that there will be cooperation and collaboration. Specific measures can be taken to ensure that groups are actually working together rather than merely sitting together while working (for examples, see Baloche, 1998; Johnson & Johnson, 1994; Slavin, 1995). If a collaborative atmosphere is the norm for the classroom, accepting feedback from peers would not be an intolerable circumstance.

Perhaps the biggest challenge in moving toward the community environment is the class's view of the teacher as the expert and the students' role as the ones searching for the answer that the teacher wants. Changing the focus to "meeting the established criteria" as opposed to doing "what the teacher wants" is a significant hurdle. Altering this perception is vital in establishing the desired learning community. Efforts by the teacher to stress the value of thinking and the process of problem solving rather than the right answer would assist in establishing the value of learning. Providing opportunities for students to expand on, support, or contradict each other's answers to questions in class rather than the common practice of the teacher accepting or rejecting answers is a possible step toward this goal. Clearly, the students in this class were focused on grades, not on learning. Student involvement in establishing the project criteria as described is a necessary step toward establishing the shared authority and the desired focus on learning. However, the teacher immediately judging the criteria and suggesting the use of the list supported the "teacher as expert" notion. Giving the class the opportunity to discuss and comment on the list and provide suggestions for its use might aid in the move toward valuing their knowledge as well as that of the teachers.

Self-assessment is one step that leads students to taking responsibility for learning. Providing opportunities for self-assessment before moving into peer assessment might make the transition easier. If students began to see that they can effectively assess their own work, they may be more willing to accept feedback from peers. Additionally, using established criteria to assess another's work increases familiarity with the criteria and will be helpful as students revise their own work. Discussing the value of pointing out strong and weak points, suggestions for improvement, and ideas for clarification instead of giving a grade could help the class understand the desired purpose of peer assessment.

Students are naturally resistant to changes in classroom practices. June should not be discouraged by such resistance and should strive to stay committed to matching her practices with her beliefs. Easing into changes and thinking through possible areas of resistance in advance will be helpful in making significant changes.

■ C A S E 7 . 3 ■

The Light at the End of the Hands-On Tunnel

Virginia Wilcox and Michael Kamen

■ *The adoption of modular science kits raises concerns about assessing students' science learning for Virginia and her grade-level colleagues. The teachers consider the background information and assessment suggestions provided with the kits woefully inadequate. Their lunchtime discussion highlights several assessment-related issues with which the teachers are grappling as they use the kits for the first time but provides no quick and easy solutions to their assessment dilemma. Virginia and Michael's long-term investigation of Virginia's authentic assessment practices helps Virginia and her colleagues to focus their concerns about assessing student learning. This open case is followed by commentary from Barbara Spector, a science teacher educator with vast experience in issues of science assessment.*

Last year, Grungewood Elementary School, a rural elementary school of about 500 students located in the Southeast area of Portland, Oregon, eliminated science textbooks and adopted module kits for all science classes. The kits were purchased from several vendors and were selected primarily for the quality of their hands-on science experiences. At the beginning of the year, we were eager to use the new kit-based curriculum materials. However, after several months of use, we are having some doubts as we struggle with several problems that have emerged relating to assessment.

A recent fourth grade team meeting was dedicated to an informal discussion of these assessment issues. As we began to share some of our frustrations related to assessment, Pam brought up a concern about the performance assessment task included in a module on electricity. The conversation that took place follows:

Pam: I was using the skills checklist that came with the kit. It includes the item "successfully lights a bulb with one wire and a battery." I circulated around my classroom and checked off the names of students who were able to light the bulb. I was not surprised when Joe was one of the first students to accomplish the task. I checked his name and then noticed that Adam, sitting across the table from Joe, was copying Joe's model and was then also able to make the bulb light. I checked Adam's name off as well but was left with a feeling that I wasn't being fair. I wondered whether Adam had a true understanding of a closed circuit. Should Adam receive the same evaluation as Joe when Joe was able to complete the task on his own and Adam simply copied Joe?

Jan: As I see it, each child needs to progress through his or her own levels of wrongness, and it really doesn't matter whether Adam copied. I actually think that we should encourage children to learn from each other. The point is not *how* he learned to make the bulb light, but that he did make it light.

Bill: Is that really the point? Do we want to create students who just blindly perform tasks without the proper understanding of the concepts that are taking place within that task? I'm not sure Adam understands as much as Joe about simple circuits. Just because he copied the circuit does not mean he knows how to make the bulb light on his own or even understands much about circuits or electricity at all.

Jan: I agree, but can we automatically assume that Joe understands more just because he did it first? He may have stumbled onto a way to light the bulb without really understanding much about what he was doing. It is even possible that Adam understands more than Joe after applying what he saw to solve his own problem.

Virginia: It seems to me that there is some confusion about what we are trying to assess. The kits do not really provide sufficient teacher background information about the concepts being studied, and I am left wondering whether we are talking about assessing students' understandings of the concepts, their ability to make circuits, or both. Ultimately, don't we want students who are not just mindlessly performing tasks but are able to discuss or explain the task intelligently?

Pam: It seems that we want to assess what children can do *and* what they know. I am frustrated because I don't feel like I am getting at what students have actually learned. The skills checklist that came with the kit is the simplest assessment tool to use. All I have to do is make a copy for each child and check off the skills as I observe them completing them. There are other assessment suggestions in the teacher's guide, such as concept webbing and student-generated questions and answers, but they come with little guidance about what to look for or how to score and evaluate them. I don't know whether the checklist alone is enough to really get a true picture of what the student knows.

Bill: Yeah, I know what you mean. I also had some difficulty in knowing how to follow up with some of the students' work. As recommended in the teacher's guide, I recently encouraged children to create their own theories about what they discovered about conductivity though liquid solutions. One group came to the conclusion that electricity did not travel through a saltwater solution. I think it was because they didn't leave it in long enough or maybe didn't have enough salt in their solution. Whatever the case, the rest of the class either agreed with the statement or hadn't gotten that far yet. When no other group protested, it was added to our "what we learned" sheet. I then checked off the goal for that lesson, "understands the principle of electricity traveling through various liquid solutions," on my checklist. The next day I received a note from a parent with a physics degree expressing concern about allowing students in my class to learn misconceptions. Now I'm not sure when to correct students and when to allow their own personal theories to be documented and shared with the class. I wish the kits provided us with more guidance as to what concepts fourth grade students should be able to understand.

Virginia: I see your point, Bill. You thought you knew why they came up with that theory but didn't see it as necessary to point out the misconception. What worries me are the teachers who would not see a problem with that at all. There are teachers who wouldn't have even known that was an incorrect theory until that parent's note pointed it out to them. Is the process students go through to discover something ultimately more important than the actual information being obtained? Once again this boils down to: Are we assessing their understanding of a concept or their ability to perform a certain task?

The discussion continued even as the bell rang, bringing the lunchtime grade-level meeting to a close. Pam summed up the group's concerns related to assessment and evaluation of the kits in comparison to materials used in the past:

The consensus seems to be that we need more information. The checklist provides an easy way to score each child but leaves too many unanswered questions. As a grade-level team, we all seem to be struggling with several issues. Although we don't want assessment to stand in the way of a student's inquiry, we need to find a way to get beyond what children do and gain insight into what they understand. Furthermore, we all share Bill's concerns about knowing when to correct student's alternative conceptions while recognizing that these alternative conceptions are necessary steps in the student's progression toward more sophisticated understandings. We all agree on the need to help parents understand hands-on assessment. So where do we go from here? How do we construct the knowledge needed to develop meaningful science assessments for our students?

FOR REFLECTION AND DISCUSSION

1. When is it appropriate for students to demonstrate what they can do and when is it appropriate for students to demonstrate what they understand?

2. How can teachers help students show what they understand rather than what they can do?

3. Are alternative conceptions a developmental necessity as children progress to more sophisticated understandings? Explain your response.

4. What assumptions about teaching and learning are reflected in the teachers' discussion?

5. Do teachers need to know what children understand?

6. What assumptions about power, stance, and control of learning are implied by the teachers' need to know what children understand or can do?

7. Can a teacher know whether a student has a scientifically accurate understanding of a concept?

■ COMMENTARY

Science Teaching in a Climate of Accountability

Barbara S. Spector

Assessment so often drives instruction in this era of accountability. This case, therefore, can stimulate conversations about a variety of critical aspects of science teaching. Among them are alignment among assessment, learning opportunities, and intended outcomes; assessment embedded in instruction; use of instructional models; the role of alternative conceptions in inquiry learning; the need for multiple assessments; criteria for selection of kits; the need and nature of teacher support for science teaching; differences between hands-on and inquiry activities; and the difference between assessment and evaluation and their uses.

Perhaps the most prominent aspect of this case for me is the issue of alignment. I envision my students in both pre-service and in-service courses engaging in conversations that explicate some of the following ideas when they discuss this case: There is a need to align assessment procedures with learning opportunities and their intended outcomes. The assessment must facilitate learners demonstrating the intended outcome, and the learning experience must provide opportunity for students to reach the intended outcome. When the assessment is embedded in the instruction, as it is in this case, the criticality of the need for clarity about this alignment becomes apparent. These teachers expressed concerns that commonly arise when materials are selected without explicit attention to aligning the three elements. (The teacher's level of understanding of the rationale and intentions of the kit developers and subsequent implementation was the issue that stimulated the question of alignment. It was not whether or not the kit developers built the alignment into their materials.)

The fact that assessment is embedded in instruction allows for authentic opportunities to assess what students are able to do. The case indicates the difference between what students know and what they are able to do. The teachers were astute in questioning whether lighting the bulb—what the student could do—was a result of what a student knew, the nature of that knowledge, mindless mimicry, or happenstance. If the intended outcome was for the children to light the bulb, then the assessment on the checklist was appropriate and provided them that information. If the intended outcome was for the children to understand what a simple circuit is and why it works, the assessment procedure did not align with the intended outcome.

The concerns the teachers expressed point out that authentic assessment can suffer from the same problems that have plagued development of traditional tests. That is, many of the things we value in current science education are often not easy to assess. It is common, therefore, to end up assessing that which is easy to measure and using the assessment as data for evaluation. This can occur even though, as these teachers noted, this evidence may or may not reveal what they want to measure. Thus, one of the key questions in clarifying alignment is "Does the specific performance task measure what we want to measure, or does it measure what is convenient to measure?"

I expect this would segue to discussions about the need for multiple means of authentic assessments and traditional assessments, including the need to engage in dialogue with children, and what each assessment is best able to measure. Pam's comment about the kits not having enough information to enable her to assess concept maps and student-generated questions and answers encourages discussion of ways to generate criteria for using these or other techniques that could be applicable to a variety of topics studied in elementary science.

When assessment is embedded in instruction, the place of a specific activity in an instructional model is likely to influence its intended outcome and, subsequently, the appropriateness of an assessment item. A conversation about the 5E's model (engage, explore, explain, extend, and evaluate) (Bybee et al., 1989) would explore how assessment items would differ for a specific activity depending on where it was placed in the learning cycle.

The question raised about how to handle students' interpretations of data if they are alternative conceptions is addressed when the activity is embedded in a learning cycle. That students' interpretations are tentative is explicit and can be readily understood when students and parents become familiar with the structure of a learning cycle. Bill's comments relating to alternative conceptions reminded me that teachers are often shortchanged educationally in favor of expedience. They are often shown new strategies and techniques without being enabled to understand why those techniques exist. This leaves teachers handicapped in their ability to make productive decisions supporting alignment of intended outcomes and assessment when time runs out or other factors intrude requiring changing instructional plans.

The case begs for answers to the question "What criteria are most useful for teachers to use in determining which kits contain 'high-quality activities'?" Did the teachers use intended outcomes they established for the course of study as criteria to establish whether the kits contained high-quality activities, or were the kits allowed to dictate the curriculum? If they used their own intended outcomes, then these would drive their choice of assessments. Hands-on activities in kits exist on a continuum from closed-ended teacher-controlled "cookbooks" to open-ended student-generated inquiries. Discriminating among activities on such a continuum would be another consideration in selecting a kit. National and state standards would dictate particular preferences.

The teachers voiced explicit need for in-depth understanding of how to adequately explore children's understanding of the topics in the kits. This suggests that an essential criterion for selecting a kit emerging from this case is the availability of ongoing faculty support. This includes human support available on an as-needed basis and the characteristics of material resources provided with a kit.

The need to differentiate between assessment and evaluation and their uses would arise when current and future teachers reflect on that section of the case in which the teachers comment about being "fair." To assess means to measure. This measurement can be used as non-threatening feedback to learners, or a value judgment can be placed on it, in which case it can be used for evaluation and grading. The label "fair" suggests the assessment measure was simultaneously being converted to an evaluation. It seemed to the teacher that it was therefore unfair to say that both the student who mimicked and the student who did the task first should be evaluated (and by extension ultimately graded) equally. The question of how a grade will be used and what it is actually telling the person who will use it is another issue that would reasonably emerge.

This case can be used to emphasize the importance of addressing learning and teaching from a holistic perspective in today's political climate of accountability. Focusing on the centrality of assessment and its inextricable ties to other decisions in the complex phenomenon of student learning is essential for teachers whether they are pre-service or in-service. This case is fertile ground on which to generate many of the necessary conversations.

References

Baloche, L. A. (1998). *The cooperative classroom.* Upper Saddle River, NJ: Prentice Hall.

Bess, C. (1983). *The truth about the moon.* Boston: Houghton Mifflin.

Bybee, R. W., Buchwald, C. E., Crissman, S., Heil, D. R., Kuerbis, P. J., Matsumoto, C., & McInerney, J. D. (1989). *Science and technology education for the elementary years: Frameworks for curriculum and instruction* (pp. 92–93). Andover, MA: National Center for Improving Science Education, the Network Inc.; Colorado Springs, CO: BSCS.

Johnson, D. W., & Johnson, R. T. (1994). *Learning together and alone.* Boston: Allyn & Bacon.

Kurose, A. (in press). Eyes-on science: Asking questions about the moon on the playground, in class, and at home. In J. Minstrell & E. H. van Zee (Eds.), *Inquiring into inquiry learning and teaching in science.* Washington, DC: American Association for the Advancement of Science.

National Research Council. (1996). *National science education standards.* Washington, DC: National Research Council.

McDermott, L. (1996). *Physics by inquiry.* New York: Wiley.

Payne, D. A. (1997). *Applied educational assessment.* Belmont, CA: Wadsworth.

Slavin, R. E. (1995). *Cooperative learning.* Boston: Allyn & Bacon.

Roth, K. J. (1991). Learning to be comfortable in the neighborhood of science. In W. Saul & S. A. Jagusch (Eds.), *Vital connections: Children and science books* (pp. 143–161). Portsmouth, NH: Heinemann.

*Resources to Consider*_____

Barman, C. R., Barman, N. S., Cox, M. L., Newhouse, K. B., & Goldston, M. J. (2000). Students' ideas about animals: Results from a national study. *Science & Children, 38*(1), 42–47.

This article describes a study of young children's understandings of classification and the implications of the study for elementary science teaching and learning. The authors emphasize the importance of assessing student's prior knowledge and the need for teachers to carefully examine and select appropriate science trade books.

Doran, R., Chan, F., & Tamir, P. (1998). *Science educator's guide to assessment.* Arlington, VA: National Science Teachers Association.

The authors discuss various assessment formats and the construction of authentic science assessment tasks. In addition, they present a variety of assessment examples along with the scoring rubrics.

Fischer, C. F., & King, R. M. (1995). *Authentic assessment: A guide to implementation.* Thousands Oaks, CA: Corwin Press.

The authors describe strategies for implementing authentic assessment in the elementary classroom. They also suggest ways that teachers might involve students, parents, and the community in assessment processes.

Lazear, D. (1999). *Multiple intelligence approaches to assessment: Solving the assessment conundrum.* Tucson, AZ: Zephyr Press.

A multiple-intelligence approach to assessment is illustrated in this book. The author contrasts a traditional assessment paradigm with the more recent multiple-intelligence paradigm. A variety of practical assessment ideas are included to correspond with the eight ways of knowing: logical-mathematical, visual-spatial, musical-rhythmic, bodily-kinesthetic, naturalist, interpersonal, intrapersonal, and verbal-linguistic.

Martin, D. J. (2000). *Elementary science methods: A constructivist approach.* Belmont, CA: Wadsworth.

Chapter 7 presents an overview of authentic assessment in elementary science and discusses how to use several authentic assessment techniques, including portfolios and journals, to help children understand and benefit from their science learning experiences.

Mayer, D. A. (1995). How can we best use children's literature in teaching science concepts? *Science and Children, 32*(6), 16–19.

This article explores connections between the use of literature and the development of science conceptual understandings in young children.

Changing Contexts for Science Teaching and Learning

The *National Science Education Standards* (National Research Council, 1996) present a vision for science teaching and learning which emphasizes the need for situating science education in meaningful settings within the community. If students and teachers are to take seriously their role as part of the community, they must have opportunities and experiences through which they come to view the community as a minilaboratory for scientific inquiry. Many elementary schools operate on the assumption that science knowledge is best constructed within the four walls of the classroom. Yet in the ecology of child development, there is plenty of evidence to suggest that informal science education can play an important part in the process of schooling, in terms of both instructional value and the opportunity for students to make sense of science in the context of their own lived experiences. Every community offers a multiplicity of resources and settings through which students' thinking can be connected with experiences beyond the classroom.

In this chapter, we look at different community contexts through which children develop and learn science. In the first case, "El Secreto de las Ninas," science educator Angie Barton and fourth grade students Cynthia and Jessica discuss a dilemma that centers on the meaning of access to science in school. Cynthia and Jessica are immigrant girls who live in a community homeless shelter. Their story sheds light on the importance of understanding the communities where students live. An after-school science program designed to help diverse groups of elementary students feel able and enthusiastic about science is the setting for Chris Burke's case "Challenging the High-Tech Tapestry by Adding Diverse Threads from the Lives of Children." In this case, Chris introduces the computer as a tool to facilitate students' investigations about sound and music. Unexpected outcomes lead Chris to question whether computers might actually hinder the participation of diverse learners in science. The third case in this chapter is the story of Anna Ramos, a fourth grade teacher who attempts to move science outside the four walls of the classroom. In "How Formal Should Informal Education Be?," science educator Judith Sweeney describes Anna's plan to incorporate science learning experiences in the context of a nearby natural history museum and planetarium. As the case unfolds, Anna begins to question the value of informal science education learning opportunities in light of the need to cover the science curriculum.

The three cases in this chapter illuminate issues of science teaching and learning that take place in diverse learning communities. As these cases suggest, efforts to create science learning opportunities within diverse communities will require fundamental changes in the culture of schooling. The cases provide considerable support for viewing learning as a process of constructing meaning that can and should extend the boundaries of the school community.

■ C A S E 8 . 1 ■

El Secreto de las Niñas

Cynthia, Jessica, and Angela Calabrese Barton

■ *This story is written by Cynthia and Jessica, two fourth grade Mexican American girls, together with Angie, an adult white science teacher educator. As elementary students in an urban center in the southwest, Cynthia and Jessica are surrounded by many peers with life stories like their own. In this open case, Cynthia and Jessica, both children of immigrant parents and poor, tell the secret story (with Angie's help) of why they do not like science in school even though their teacher engages the class in many fun, student-centered projects. Cynthia and Jessica's story raises questions about what exactly access to science in school really means, especially for poor, immigrant girls. This case is followed by a possible solution to the dilemma by Claire Hamilton, a former teacher and elementary education professor who works through a community service program to provide support for homeless children and their families.*

My name is Cynthia, and I am nine years old. I am in the fourth grade. I have lived with my family in Austin, Texas, for five years. Before moving to Austin, I lived in Mexico. Most of my family still lives in Mexico, but some of my family lives here in Texas with me. Right now, my family lives in a homeless shelter. We have lived here for one year. Although I have lots of friends to play with here, I don't like living here when it gets dark outside. It is not safe. I also do not like it when boys think they are better than me or when they think I cannot do all of the same things as them!

My name is Jessica, and I am eight years old. Cynthia is my best friend. I also go to school in Austin, Texas. My parents are originally from Mexico, but from a different part of Mexico than Cynthia's family. I live in the same homeless shelter as Cynthia. Our families moved into the shelter at about the same time. I really like spending time over at my friends' places, but I don't it like when people fight, especially when people fight in my face! I also don't like it when boys try to show me up. I can run as fast as any of the boys around here! I also don't like going outside at night because it is not safe around here!

My name is Angie and I am a science teacher educator in the same city where Cynthia and Jessica live. I have known Jessica and Cynthia since the beginning of the school year (it is now December) because I teach and do research at the shelter where they live. We came to write this story together because these two girls were always particularly active and interested in our after-school science program, and I was interested to learn more about why. Well, I certainly got more than I bargained for when the direction of our writing was not about why they liked science but why they did not like science!

We want to tell about learning science in school. Actually, when Angie asked us to write this story with her, we did not want to do it at first because it was about science in our school. The truth is, we really do not like science. Our favorite subjects are math and reading.

We called our story *El Secreto de las Ninas* because the reason we do not like science is that we are not used to science! Sometimes when we complain about science in school, people think we don't like it because we are girls, and that is not true. They tell us we can be anything we want to be. We know that, sort of. We are just as good as boys, we just don't want to explain our reasons. It is our secret.

I told the girls that I thought their secret was interesting but that I was not sure exactly what they meant. What did it mean to be used to something, anyway? Did it mean that their schoolteacher never teaches science at all, and so they were not used to having science class at all? Did it mean that their teacher did teach science but the girls were not used to the topics, the content, or the pedagogical methods the teacher used to teach science? Finally, I wondered, did it mean that they were not used to the language or the skills the teacher required them to use? I asked the girls to explain their secret to me.

Okay. Let us tell you a story about what happened in school to show you what we mean.

Our teacher told us we were going to start a unit on movie making. We both thought this would be really cool because we love to go see the movies! One of the first activities we were going to do was make a shoebox camera. We would make this camera out of a shoebox, and it would take real pictures. And then we would be able to keep the camera and take whatever pictures we wanted! At the beginning, we were really excited about this project because neither of us have ever owned a camera before. We remember only one time when we were able to use a disposable camera because Cynthia's mother bought her one from the store for her birthday.

The day before we were to start the camera project, our teacher asked each student to bring in an empty shoebox. Well, where are we going to get empty shoeboxes? I told my teacher I didn't have an empty shoebox, so then she said to the whole class, "If you don't have a shoebox, you can ask your mother or an older brother or sister to take you to a discount shoe store and ask for a shoebox. They will give you one for free." Then she said, "For those of you who cannot get your own shoebox, you can bring in fifty cents and buy one from me." She then told us that we are getting older now, and we have to learn to become more responsible for our own education. Well, we are still like, where are we going to get a shoebox? My mother cannot take me to the shoe store! She doesn't even have a car, and she cannot speak English that well, and she has to watch my baby brother. And then we are also like, where are we going to get the fifty cents? So the next day we went to school without our shoeboxes and without fifty cents.

Your story so far reminds me of how easy it is to link what children are able to bring to school with them (whether it be cultural capital, material items, or feelings of power or belonging) to their "success" in science class. In other words, it seems that your teacher is tying your own ability to succeed in her class (or at least to develop positive feelings of belonging in science) to the kinds of things you might have access to at home. Did she understand how your situations at home affected how you might be able to participate in school science? What happened next?

Well, at the beginning of the day, the teacher collected the shoeboxes. A couple of other students in the class did not have shoeboxes or money either. Our teacher gave the class a lecture about being responsible. So we told her in private right before recess that our mothers could not take us to the store and we did not have any money, and that is why we did not have a shoebox. She asked us why we didn't tell her earlier. She also told us it was okay and that she understood. She told us we could help clean the erasers during recess to "earn" the shoebox and that it would be "our secret." Well, we both decided to go to recess because we were mad at her, and we didn't want to share a secret with her. When it came time for science, our teacher said nothing to us but gave us shoeboxes anyway so we could make our camera. But we were the last ones to get shoeboxes, and they were ugly. By that time, we did not want to make cameras anymore, and we just sat there and poked at our boxes.

FOR REFLECTION AND DISCUSSION

1. What did the girls really mean when they said they are not used to science?
2. What should the teacher have done once the girls disengaged from the project?
3. Doing projects in science class is often difficult because the supplies budget is often small. How should the teacher have handled the situation at the beginning? How should the teacher have handled the situation once the girls decided to go out for recess anyway?

■ C O M M E N T A R Y

Homeless Children in Our Classrooms

Claire E. Hamilton

For the last six years, I have been involved in a community program that provides subsidized child care services for homeless children and their families. A critical component of this program is educating child care providers in how to support homeless children in community-based child care centers and after-school programs. Cynthia and Jessica's story illustrates for me the challenges early childhood educators face in meeting the needs of children experiencing homelessness.

Too often, our image of homelessness is of ill-kept vagrants, usually men, panhandling on city streets or shuffling through lines in soup kitchens. We don't see homelessness as an issue confronting children in our classrooms, particularly if we teach in nonurban settings. The reality of homelessness is quite different. Homes for the Homeless (2000), an advocacy group, estimates that more than one million children each night have no home. Although homeless children in urban areas, like Cynthia and Jessica, may live temporarily in homeless shelters, homeless children in suburban or rural areas may be less easy to identify. For these children, being homeless may mean living in substandard housing with no running water or electricity, living in overcrowded trailers or apartments, or having no home at all and moving from one temporary situation to another. It has always been difficult to estimate the numbers of homeless people, but trends indicate that the fastest-growing segment of the homeless population is families (National Coalition for the Homeless, 1999). The typical homeless person in the United States is a child (Homes for the Homeless, 2000). As educators, we are increasingly likely to have children experiencing homelessness in our classrooms who may never share with us the "secret" that they are homeless.

Cynthia and Jessica's science teacher made a simple request: She asked that all of the children in her science class bring in a shoebox or, lacking the shoebox, fifty cents. This task, which might be so easy for most of the students, was impossible for Cynthia and Jessica, and this simple request in many ways undermined what Angie had seen as their enthusiasm and love for science. This science teacher was not intentionally singling these girls out, but she likely had no idea of what being homeless might mean for her students; her later effort to help only made the girls feel more alienated. To support students in our classrooms, we need to have some understanding of the complexity of what it might mean to be homeless.

> *Amber is staying in the women's dorm of a homeless shelter with her mother and older sister. Her father and teenage brother are staying across the street in the men's shelter. In the evenings, volunteers, residents, and shelter staff come and go through the common area; residents often argue; and the television is on loudly until lights out at 11:30. Amber has trouble finishing her homework and getting enough sleep.*

Like Cynthia and Jessica, Amber is living in a shelter. She probably shares with them a concern about safety. Almost half of all homeless children have been either a victim of or a witness to violence (Homes for the Homeless, 2000). Unlike Cynthia and Jessica, Amber has lost family members as well as her home. Homeless children are often separated from family members as they move from place to place because of foster care situations or because of shelter policies. Amber's teachers are worried that she nods off in class and never seems quite "with it." Amber, like many homeless children, is not performing at grade level and may be referred for special education services.

> *Nikoli's family has been moving from place to place for the last six months. They lived first with his cousins and then with a friend of his mother. They are now staying in an emergency shelter. Families can remain in the shelter only at night; during the day, they have to leave. Last week-end was a rainy three-day holiday. Nikoli, his mother, and his two younger sisters spent Saturday in the library. Nikoli got most of his homework done. On Sunday, Nikoli's family hung out in the hospital emergency waiting room. On Monday, they wandered through a shopping mall.*

Perhaps one of the most difficult aspects of homelessness for children is the lack of stability they face. Cynthia and Jessica are fortunate to be housed in a long-term shelter. Nikoli and other homeless children might not know where they will sleep, or eat, or simply be on any day. To his teachers, Nikoli appears anxious and somewhat of a troublemaker. He has missed a lot of school this year, and his teachers have had difficulty scheduling parent conferences.

Like Cynthia and Jessica's teacher, we might not know that a child in our classroom is homeless. Cynthia and Jessica did tell their teacher, but other homeless children might not feel comfortable sharing such a secret. How can we begin to support the needs of homeless children if we don't even know who may be homeless? A first step is recognizing that children and families are a large part of the homeless population and that being homeless may mean living in a shelter, living in a welfare hotel or inadequate substandard housing, or having no stable housing at all. The second step is rethinking how we structure our classrooms and expectations so that all children can be responsible and successful. When we need materials in our classrooms, how can we involve children in accessing those materials? Can we ask students to work in teams or brainstorm alternatives for finding the materials we need? Cynthia and Jessica's teacher provided an alternative—cleaning erasers to earn shoeboxes—but it was not a meaningful alternative. What alternatives can we provide for students that allow them to responsibly participate? We also need to think about the structure of our assignments. Nikoli finished his homework one weekend, but he might not have been successful completing or even keeping track of a project-based assignment. How can we support his learning and incorporate project learning in class? Amber rarely gets her homework done and is not attentive in class, but she is overwhelmed, not irresponsible. What expectations and attitudes do we have about children and their class participation? How do those expectations influence students' motivation and success? I hope that as we begin to consider what it means for a child to be homeless, we can help all the Cynthias, Jessicas, Ambers, and Nikolis that may be in our classroom enjoy learning.

■ C A S E 8 . 2 ■

Challenging the High-Tech Tapestry by Adding Diverse Threads from the Lives of Children

Christopher Burke

■ *I have been working in an after-school science program, Science Playground, with fifth and sixth graders for two years now. The Materials Research Laboratory at the University of*

Illinois funds the program. The long-term goal of the program is to help increase the number of minority members represented in the sciences. To this end, Science Playground hired undergraduate minority students with science majors to act as mentors for minority elementary students in the after-school program. The program's focus was student-initiated inquiry, building on the belief that students learn science best when it emerges from their experiences and values their perceptions and ideas about how the world works. This semester, we studied the science of music. A dilemma arose when the students began using computers as tools for further inquiry. The introduction of the computer as a tool into our classroom marginalized the students' understandings and work exploring the science of music and further distanced them from formal science. The case is followed by commentary from David Jackson, a science teacher educator with much experience using technology to enhance science instruction.

The semester started with the students making instruments such as shoebox guitars and PVC xylophones. We collected materials from around the park outside the school. I contacted a local plumber and brought in old pipes. The students brought in newspapers, boxes, and other potentially relevant things from home. Using these materials, we made instruments that we could play along with the music brought in by the students. In the beginning, the students made percussion instruments by tying whatever they could find together and striking it with their hand or a stick. I usually watched and waited until they solicited my advice, and occasionally I would suggest alternative ways to connect materials. After a while, I decided that I would add to the music by making my own instrument. Using a drinking straw and my pocketknife, I made a straw flute. This encouraged students to work on other kinds of instruments. Modupe, whose family had immigrated from Guinea in the middle of the year, was the first to make a different kind of instrument. She collected soft drink bottles and made a bottle organ. Watching and working with Modupe, Franchesca decided that she wanted to build a xylophone and collected the steel pipes that I had brought in and began to put these together. Kah decided that he wanted to make a guitar, and working with Charles, one of the mentors, he created a plan to make guitars out of shoeboxes. They were able to get a local shoe store to donate twenty shoeboxes, and Kah led the class in making a set of shoebox guitars.

After a few weeks of making instruments, the students began to borrow my tape recorder to record their own music. At first, the students were playing on their instruments and recording their music. Then they would rewind the tape and play it back, discuss (argue about) how to play the song differently, and record it again. This activity slowly evolved, and with the advent of an early spring, the students took the tape recorders outside and used them to record sounds in the park. They were not passively recording sounds that could be heard in the park but worked to actively orchestrate sounds by swinging on the swing, banging on the slide with different objects, playing their instruments, and singing. The result was a series of songs that sounded like a mix of gospel, industrial, and hip-hop. Embedded in this composition was a dynamic science that reflected the students' growing understanding of experimentation in which they developed theories, tested hypotheses, and manipulated variables. The students also developed an intuitive feel for the variety of properties different materials possess and how these properties affected the sounds they produced, in addition to a complex construction of the relationship between rhythm, pitch, frequency, and volume.

As we approached the final weeks of the semester, I suggested that we could digitize some of the music we had made and work at manipulating the sounds with the computers in the room. We worked in small groups on three computers in one of the rooms down the hall. We searched the Internet for shareware sound utilities that we could use on our computers. We found two that seemed to work, *SoundHandle* and *SoundView.* Both of the programs allowed the students to record sounds and music on the computers, and *SoundHandle* allowed them to manipulate the music by adding echo and reverb. After some quick instruction on where to plug in the microphone and how to activate the recording program, the students started recording their own music. Developing the ability to record and play their own music on the computer further encouraged the students to try new things. It was when the students started to edit and alter their music that we ran into problems.

The programs that we were using represented the sound in terms of frequency, amplitude, and time, but the students talked about the music in terms of rhythm and narrative. Each of these frameworks describes different components of the music that the students were recording. The ideas are closely intertwined, with the rhythm usually defined by repetitive low frequencies and the narrative conveyed in the varying frequencies of the vocals and the melody. On the computers, visual representation of the sound rhythm could usually be seen as the regular spikes in the low-frequency band. Because the vocals were typically the loudest part of the song, lyrics stood out as well, as the highest peaks in the graph. It was this similarity that led to the confusion and resulting frustration that the students experienced in working with the computers.

Rose's experience with the computer most clearly illustrates the difficulty. She was trying to edit a song that she had recorded. She was working in *SoundHandle* and wanted to put echo in one work. First she selected the whole thing and added the echo; this didn't create the effect that she desired. She closed the window, deleting the file, and started over again.

"HEY, YEAH LISTEN UP I GOT SOMETHING TO SAY, YOU REALLY SHOULDN'T," she started off.

When she was done, she went back to the amplitude time graph, selected the area around the peak on the time versus amplitude with the mouse, and added echo to that section. This caused the last syllable of the work "SOMETHING" to echo. Rose angrily closed the program and recorded her song again. This time, she selected the eleventh peak in the graph and added echo to that section that caused the word "TO" to echo. Rose started again. She continued to count the words in the song and assumed that each peak represented a word. She would count the words and then select a peak in the graph and add echo, but it wouldn't be the right word. She was running into several problems. First, she was changing the way she said words, and the change in emphasis caused the computer to recognize different words as either one or two syllables. This was particularly problematic. The first time through, she would say it quickly, and it would generate one loud peak; the next time through, she would slow down, and there would be two peaks representing two distinct syllables. I tried to have her watch the progress bar as it ran across the graph when the music was played, but this didn't help. Rose continued to demarcate words by the beginning and end of peaks based on the volume of noise in the room at any given time.

In talking to Rose and other students, I found that they were using a very different paradigm to think about the music and its representation than I did or than was embedded in the computer program. Their understandings and explanations continually shifted as they tried to do different things and create the sounds that they wanted to create. Each new failure provided a new explanation of what was going on, but there appeared to be very little convergence between the students' ideas and the operation of the computer program. The students' constructions focused on the importance of the whole song, examining it in terms of rhythm and narrative. In contrast, the computer program reduced the song to component sounds and represented it in terms of frequency, amplitude, and time. I tried to bridge this gap and help the students make connections between their understanding of the music and the program's representation by talking about different ways of representing sound and music.

"Chris, our drawings are not science, they're just our drawings," Tayana interjected. "I don't understand why you make such a big deal about this stuff, calling our dancing representing music with our bodies and calling our paintings representing music with pen and paper. They're just our drawings. This is not science, it is music or art."

Tayana went on to explain that science was the study of chemicals, plants, the earth, and the other stuff that they learned in their class. "We were doing science when we made the speakers with the magnets and the wires. That had to do with electricity." Other students agreed with her, and several said that we had not done science this semester.

What was even more disturbing to me was Franchesca's comment: "Our drawings are not scientific. The images on the computer are scientific. Computers generate scientific representations of the music, and that's why scientists use computers."

Using the computer as part of our inquiry created an awkward tension in the program. We had spent the semester valuing and centering students' ideas. These ideas became the foundation for our inquiry. When we moved to the computers and began our work there, we experienced a conflict between the students' ideas and the computers' representations. Instead of recognizing that each of the ways of thinking about music was valuable, the students saw their ideas as nonscientific and less valuable.

Computers occupy a strange place in the classroom. Because of their expense, they are carefully protected with their own area and special rules for their use posted prominently on the wall above them. They have the ability to efficiently produce clean graphics and slick representations of multiple and complex data. The complexity of the understanding and the assumptions made by the programmer about these data are hidden behind the beige casing and the graphic design of the program interface. These characteristics provide the representations they create and the ideas they present with a level of authority. As a result of this authority and the students' difficulty in using computers, computers served to create a greater space between the students and science. The computer became an authority in the classroom, defining what was and what was not science. By moving our work from the eclectic material that we were able to find around the community and the school to the computer, we added a layer of formality to our inquiry.

FOR REFLECTION AND DISCUSSION

1. Why was what the students were doing science? Why were the students' drawings more than just drawings and their dancing more than just dancing?

2. What was it that made the students' representations of the music and sound science in the same way that the representation of the music on the computer was science?

3. How could Chris have helped the students to bridge the gap between their informal knowledge of science and the formal institution of science embodied in the computer?

■ **COMMENTARY**

The Computer as Formalizer of Inquiry: Valuable Tool, Oppressive Limitation, or All in the Hands of the Teacher?

David F. Jackson

In reading the case "Challenging the High-Tech Tapestry," I was struck by its parallel to many other stories I hear or observe involving the use of technology in teaching. The common thread in these diverse experiences is that the most critically important issues have very little to do with technology itself, or even the procedures and contexts of its use, and everything to do with broader issues (both practical and theoretical) in education. In this case, the crucial question is "What counts as science?," and the possibly interesting questions "What technology is appropriate for this application?" and "What is the interaction between software capabilities, students' prior understanding, and the role of the teacher?" will follow only if they are relevant in light of the broader view taken or implied.

As was stated in the case, the focus of the Science Playground program was student-initiated inquiry, and Chris placed a premium on valuing students' perceptions and ideas so as not to risk marginalizing these understandings or distancing them from formal science. The use of *SoundHandle* was problematic in this context primarily because Chris clearly questions the traditionally accepted views that (1) not all inquiry is scientific and (2) formality—specifically, reductionism—is a central aspect of science. This point of view is appropriately highlighted by the first two questions. Given a completely unbending version of this stance, the use of this particular technological resource, which I agree embodied the formal institution of science, was clearly inappropriate, and our own inquiry should stop here.

As reflected in the third question, however, Chris, as a scientist, *did* care not only that science emerge from students' experiences, but also about bridging the gap between informal, intuitive, opportunistic, and holistic perceptions and experiences and the more formal, abstract, systematic, reductionistic views of institutionalized science. I would suggest that it might be possible to help students toward a view of the worlds of nature and of design that accepts that some ways of thinking about science- and engineering-related phenomena can meaningfully be called nonscientific without implying that they are inherently less valuable.

The students may, indeed, have been spontaneously developing theories, testing hypotheses, manipulating variables, and so forth, but a formal scientific view would place a great emphasis on making these actions conscious and at least somewhat systematic (in the words of the canonical literature, "teaching integrated process skills"). I have no doubt that the students did indeed have a highly complex construction of the relationship between rhythm, pitch, volume, and the like—probably so complex as to be incomprehensible and unmanageable. The value of taking a more formal scientific view would be to empower the students by temporarily reducing this complexity to more manageable and interpretable aspects before putting them together again to reconstruct an equally complex but more understandable view.

Therefore, it seems worthwhile to search for a workable middle ground and to consider some practical, technology-specific issues and considerations that might facilitate this understanding.

If the primary goal of the use of technology is to encourage the students to try new things by developing the ability to record and play their own music, there are common technologies that are much simpler, more user-friendly, and already culturally embedded in the students' familiar community: the cassette tape recorders previously used by the students early in the project or (perhaps richer and therefore better still) an analogue videocamera.

The specific and highly frustrating problems encountered by Rose seem to be caused not by the design of the software but by three crucial missing pieces of prior knowledge: first, the distinction between a word and a syllable; second, the ability of any computer operating system to save and retrieve initial and/or modified versions of application files (versus starting over again); and third, the power of changing only one variable at a time between successive iterations of analysis or modification (versus recording entirely new, nonidentical data).

Finally, in considering the software itself, are its formal representations and functions really so totally distanced from intuitive thought, or are they particularly suited to bridging the gap in any specific ways? A computer program that represented these holistically valuable songs as, for instance, successive sets of three numeric parameters—meaningless without an understanding of their abstract labels (e.g., frequency, amplitude, waveform)—would be quite useless in this context. I would suggest that the analogue graphic display provided by *Sound-Handle* is actually an excellent potential bridge between the informal and formal worlds in this case. This is especially true given the ability to simultaneously play back the recorded sound and dynamically highlight the corresponding part of the display. For instance, in the case of the (program default) time versus amplitude plot, one need not either have heard any of the aforementioned terms or have any indication of the numeric calibration of the vertical scale on the display to get an intuitive feel for the distribution of sound pulses and their accent pattern as the narrative progresses. From the case description, it seems that Rose, and very likely all of the other students, understood this correspondence immediately.

In short, it seems likely that if Chris had devoted more time to demonstrating one or more concrete sample cycles of recording, interpreting, editing, reinterpreting, and re-editing (versus only some quick instruction on where to plug in the microphone and how to activate the recording program), a productive bridge might have been built and much frustration and alienation might have been avoided.

■ **CASE 8.3** ■

How Formal Should Informal Education Be?

Judith K. Sweeney

■ *In this closed case, Judith tells the story of Anna Ramos, an elementary teacher, who has found the local natural history museum and planetarium to be an excellent community resource for her fourth grade students. Consistent with Anna's belief that educational excursions should be well integrated with the school curriculum, the field trip that she leads to this venue each year is coordinated to support and reinforce the fourth grade astronomy unit taught in the spring. But this year, Anna decides to have students interact with the museum's new exhibit on the skeletal system in addition to the planetarium experience. Her decision brings with it questions and concerns about the appropriateness and value of engaging students in an informal educational opportunity that is not directly related to the school science curriculum. Anna Ramos is a composite of teachers with whom Judith has worked in the past as the education curator of a museum of natural history. The case is followed by commentary from Anne Shenk, an educational director at a state botanical garden and strong advocate of informal science learning opportunities for children.*

Anna Ramos is the teacher of thirty-two fourth graders in a large elementary school located in an urban school district. She is responsible for teaching all subjects except physical education and art. The parents of Anna's students are part of the diverse working class of their large urban community, and it is likely that most of Anna's students will not attend college.

There is a natural history museum and planetarium nearby, and Anna's school has traditionally organized a field trip during the spring for all fourth graders. This is the only supported field trip for fourth grade students during the year. Anna values the use of informal community resources and believes that they can reinforce classroom instruction in ways not possible within traditional school settings. Consequently, Anna makes every effort to take advantage of informal learning venues whenever appropriate, as a means to enhance her classroom instruction. Because this field trip is always scheduled by the school administration in the spring, Anna usually teaches the fourth grade astronomy unit in April to coincide with the visit to the natural history museum and planetarium. Before the trip, Anna discusses with students what they will see and do on the trip, how the trip is related to what they are doing in science, and what they are expected to learn as a result of the field trip.

During the science lessons before the trip, Anna's students learn all about the solar system. They study details about each of the planets, including their orbits, environments, relative sizes, and distances from the sun. One of Anna's favorite activities is to have students develop a scale model of the solar system on the athletic field behind the school. This provides the students with a very concrete idea of the relative distances between the planets. Her students are always amazed at how these distances appear relative to the poster on their classroom wall. The planetarium program that fourth graders see also includes this information but presents it in a much more visually dramatic way. Anna knows the value of students' being given a variety of representations of whatever they are being asked to learn.

One week before the field trip, Anna takes some time in class to discuss the logistics of the trip. Although the students have been anticipating the trip all year, Anna knows that they need to be well aware of important procedures, such as how they are expected to behave, the role of chaperones, and, of course, where and when they will eat lunch. Anna also provides each student with a permission slip to be signed by a parent or guardian. As part of this orientation, Anna asks about students' personal experiences at the museum and planetarium that they will soon visit as a class.

"Has anyone ever been to the planetarium in the city park?"

"No, but I went to one when I visited my grandmother last summer," answers Bobby. "It was really cool. We got to look through a telescope, and I saw planets and stars."

"Wow, you mean you could see all that in the sky during the daytime?" Sally marvels.

"Ms. Ramos, how are we going to see anything during the daytime except blue?" asks Ginger in a quizzical tone.

"I think you may get a chance to see a telescope, but what you see in a planetarium is not the real sky," Anna replies. "A planetarium is more like a movie theater where the screen is on the ceiling. The planets and stars are projected onto the ceiling by a very special projector."

"So does that mean we will be looking at a movie of the sky made at night?" asks Jim.

"Not exactly a movie," answers Anna with a smile, "but a recreation of what the sky would look like if you looked at night."

Satisfied that the students understand the logistics of the trip and are really excited about what they will see, Anna spends the next few days helping students to develop the appropriate foundational knowledge needed to establish a coherent mesh between the planetarium exhibits and classroom activities. She views the planetarium as an important supplement to her classroom instruction, not as a substitute.

Anna knows that her fourth graders will have an opportunity to take part in an interactive demonstration at the planetarium during which a model of a comet is created. In an effort to focus their attention, Anna creates a worksheet for her students to complete while they are at the planetarium. Her students know that these worksheets are to be completed while they are on the trip and will be collected as they board the bus to return to school. The next day, Anna will use these worksheets as a springboard for a review of the trip and a discussion of what the students learned. She and her students will also discuss how the planetarium offers a different presentation of the subject matter being discussed in school. As an assessment, she will have students work in groups of three to design a storyboard for their own planetarium show about the solar system.

A few days before the field trip, Anna receives a flyer from the museum announcing the opening of a new exhibit about skeletons. She knows that it is unlikely that her students will get to see this exhibit on their own and thinks that it would be a unique learning experience for them to have. Because the planetarium is inside the museum, it would be easy for her students to visit both sites while they are on their field trip. However, neither vertebrates nor skeletal anatomy is part of the fourth grade science curriculum, and so Anna cannot make an instructional link to her science curriculum. Anna is also concerned that this diversion will interfere with her main objectives for the trip. She doesn't want the skeleton exhibit to distract her students' attention and dilute the informal learning benefits for the astronomy unit. After visiting the exhibit on her own, Anna eventually decides to include the museum exhibit in her field trip.

After a class discussion of the astronomy they learned at the planetarium, Anna engages her students in a discussion about the skeletal system exhibit. The students thoroughly enjoyed the exhibit and ask numerous questions that Anna is able to relate to the concept of form and function. Form and function is not a concept included in the fourth grade science curriculum, but Anna believes that the discussion is worthwhile. She is pleased that the students enjoyed the unplanned portion of their field trip, but she still wonders whether it compromised in any way what the students learned at the planetarium about the solar system. Anna chooses not to assess what students learned about the skeletal system in any formal manner because what they learned was not part of the fourth grade science curriculum. During the weekend, Anna carefully reflects on the field trip and her decision to have the students also visit the museum exhibit. She still isn't sure that her decision to include the exhibit as part of the field trip was a good one and wants to be clear about her thinking before planning for next year's field trip.

FOR REFLECTION AND DISCUSSION

1. Should all aspects of informal venues be used, regardless of their relationship to the science curriculum?

2. Is there value in learning experiences that are simply interesting and enjoyable to students without any regard for cognitive outcomes?

3. Does time spent on unplanned learning experiences, or those not directly associated with the curriculum, dilute the learning specified by the science curriculum?

4. Is the primary role of informal settings to support school-based instruction?

5. Should all activities on which time is spent be formally assessed? Does Anna really know what students learned related to the skeletal system exhibit?

■ **COMMENTARY**

You Never Know Who Might Be the Next Leading Skeleton Expert

Anne M. Shenk

Having worked as an informal science educator for over twenty years, I am always happy to meet and work with a teacher like Anna Ramos. I appreciate her commitment to making field trip experiences as meaningful as possible for her students. Although the solar system program is the primary reason for her museum visit, I would welcome the opportunity to aid in her efforts to link the new skeleton exhibit to some aspect of her fourth grade curricular requirements. In the process, my museum program would become more relevant not only to her class but also to other formal audiences.

If Anna teaches in a self-contained classroom, she may be able to link the skeleton exhibit to her curricular requirements in language arts. Could students be given a creative writing assignment? Or could they focus on using appropriate adjectives or verbs in an essay about skeletons? Perhaps some students could write about the importance of bones to the human body. Other students may be interested in writing about the skeletons of runners or other athletes. More adventurous students might write about skeletons in space!

Do the students at Anna's school participate in a science fair? If so, the museum visit can provide the opportunity for students to generate research questions (related to the skeletal and solar systems) for the fair. This would provide Anna with further justification and curricular links for the museum visit. I have had teachers visit the botanical garden where I work just for that purpose. After participating in a data collection exercise, such as observing insect visitors on flowers, students are given the opportunity to prepare "I wonder" questions about the insects. Some responses include "I wonder if pink flowers attract more insect visitors than blue flowers," "I wonder if more insects visit the flowers in the morning or in the afternoon," and

"I wonder why we didn't see any insect visitors on our flowers." These "I wonder" questions can provide launching points for hypotheses for science experiments.

By visiting the exhibit before the students' field trip, Ms. Ramos could develop additional questions (extra credit or language arts) for her field trip worksheet that relate to the skeleton exhibit. If she planned to have lunch at the museum, her students could view the solar system exhibit before lunch and the skeleton exhibit after lunch. The break between the two museum exhibits might lessen the possibility that the skeleton exhibit would dilute the benefits of the astronomy unit.

In this day of ever-increasing accountability, it is important for Anna to justify the time she spends at the museum. Although supporting school-based instruction is a goal of most informal science institutions, it is rarely the primary goal. A critical audience of many informal science institutions is the casual visitor. Consequently, key goals of many informal institutions include the following:

- To stimulate curiosity about the natural world
- To develop an interest in lifelong learning related to science
- To encourage positive attitudes toward science
- To enhance visitor understanding of science processes

Most state and local curricular requirements refer to similar goals. Would it be possible for Ms. Ramos to address these more elusive goals rather than her specific learning objectives as she justifies her students' visit to the skeletal exhibit? Goals related to lifelong learning and positive attitudes toward science are especially relevant to Ms. Ramos students, as many of them are not likely to attend college.

I support Ms. Ramos's decision to include the skeletal system exhibit as part of her museum visit. If she sees an opportunity to link this unit to other components of her fourth grade curricula, I would encourage her to share this information with the museum staff. This curricular correlation would assist the natural history museum in its efforts to successfully serve other school groups. If not, a simple follow-up discussion is fine. Of course, Ms. Ramos might never know whether her decision to include the skeleton exhibit stimulated one of her students to pursue a career in medicine and become a leading expert on the skeletal system. The outcomes of the informal learning experience can be far-reaching and exciting.

References

Homes for the Homeless. (2000). *Facts about homelessness* [On-line]. Available at: http://www2.Homesforthe Homeless.com/hfh/facts.html.

National Coalition for the Homeless. (1999, June). *NCH Fact Sheet #10: Education of homeless children and youth* [On-line]. Available: http://nch.ari.net/edchild.html.

National Research Council. (1996). *National science education standards.* Washington, DC: National Academy Press.

Resources to Consider

Barton, A. C. (2000). Crafting multicultural science education with preservice teachers through service learning: A case study. *Journal of Curriculum Studies, 50*(4), 303–312.

This article explores the concept of service learning as a tool for investigating science teaching and learning in diverse community contexts.

Bourne, B. (2000). (Ed.). *Taking inquiry outdoors: Reading, writing, and science beyond the classroom walls.* York, ME: Stenhouse Publishers.

The natural world as a setting for student and teacher learning is illustrated through the stories of educators who have used child-centered practices in outdoor learning environments.

Britton, E., Huntley, M. A., Jacobs, G., & Weinberg, A. S. (1999). *Connecting mathematics and science to workplace contexts: A guide to curriculum materials.* Thousand Oaks, CA: Corwin Press.

This book is designed as a guide for educators seeking to link academic subject matter with workplace and real-world contexts for learning. The book includes a description and analysis for more than 200 curriculum materials that emphasize connections between science, mathematics and real-world contexts.

Buck, G. A. (2000). [On-line]. *Teaching science to English-as-second language learners.* National Science Teachers Association. Available at: http://www.nsta.org.pub/sc/article1.asp

Also published in the November 2000 issues of *Science and Children,* the article presents ideas for teaching and assessing ESL students. This electronic version of the article is linked to a number of on-line resources and a discussion group for sharing ideas about teaching science to students whose first language is not English.

Eisenhower National Clearinghouse. [On-line]. *Informal Education.* Available at: http://www.enc.org/topics/informaled

This site provides a wealth of information about science education in informal settings and links to dozens of informal science education resources including zoos, museums and science centers, aquariums, and national parks.

9

Controversial Issues in the Science Classroom

Science is a social activity, which by its very nature is value laden and draws on different viewpoints. Likewise, teaching is not a neutral or objective process; it is a reflection of individual values and beliefs, which are played out in the classroom. Good elementary science teaching involves the attempt to help children derive meaning from their experience. In this context, it is imperative for teachers to recognize and acknowledge that varying cultural perspectives among learners will evoke discussions about topics that might be viewed as controversial. Controversy often emerges when learners' prior experiences come into conflict with new ideas, creating a sense of personal dissonance. The dissonance that is produced when student experience interacts with information from the discipline of science can lead to conceptual thinking under the guidance of a skillful teacher. Indeed, throughout history, science has been moved by controversy and dissonance in the search for explanations.

The diverse backgrounds and perspectives of learners can be an instructional resource and a powerful context for cultivating student understanding of controversial issues. Although it might seem that emotionally charged issues should be the purview of secondary science classrooms, it is important for processes that transcend concrete and formal thinking to begin while children are still young. Teachers have a critical role to play in fostering an environment in which students are empowered to question how science interfaces with their world.

In the elementary classroom, controversial issues are usually overarching and involve the integration of ideas across disciplines. Situations that involve controversy may reflect global (e.g., energy resources, poverty), national (e.g., water use, health care), local (e.g., recycling, waste disposal), or personal (e.g., recreation, utilities) kinds of issues. Controversial issues are embedded in the study of rainforests, dinosaurs, or solar systems, but concepts associated with these topics may be too abstract or removed from students' personal experience. The situations and problems that students encounter in their daily lives are perhaps more personally meaningful and best discussed in relation to teachers' and students' own communities. Research suggests that students need "critical spaces" in which to discuss controversial issues where their questions and beliefs are "shaped in ongoing interactions that include both the teacher and the students" (Bransford et al., 1999, p. 171). Rosebury et al. (1992) emphasize the need to build communities of scientific practice that engage young children in opportunities to negotiate conflicts in belief and evidence and discuss alternative interpretations.

The cases in this chapter portray situations in which science learning in elementary classrooms is influenced by diverse value systems. In "The Day the Lobster Died," Joe Riley discusses a dilemma that emerges when students' beliefs and values about animals conflict with the teacher's attempt to develop a culturally responsive science curriculum. When her students' discussion of ancient Egyptian embalming techniques moves in an unpredictable direction, first grade teacher Amanda Neff is faced with a dilemma at the interface of science and religion. Her case, "The Egyptian Exhibit," explores the role of controversy in early childhood classrooms. In their case "What Happened to Bunny?," Lynn Bryan and Yuki Nakagawa explore the way in which Japanese cultural beliefs and values mediate science teaching and learning in a first grade classroom. The chapter concludes with David Whitney's case "Integrating Technology into Science Research Projects: Cutting and Pasting Made Difficult." In this case, David's efforts to introduce the computer as a learning tool for science projects leads to questions about the authenticity of student work.

■ **C A S E 9 . 1** ■

The Day the Lobster Died

Joseph P. Riley

■ *This open case raises questions about the ethical treatment of animals in the elementary classroom. Stan, an experienced fifth grade teacher, faces a number of dilemmas when the lobster cookout he has planned for the end of his oceanography unit takes an unexpected turn. Stan is left wondering how he got into the dilemma and how he might find a way out. Questions of life and death, the issue of animals as a source of food and clothing, ethical questions about animal rights, and the treatment of these issues with elementary students all come into sharp focus for Stan on the day the lobster died. Some thoughts on Stan's dilemma are provided by science teacher educator Merton Glass after the case.*

Stan noticed the sudden change on Erin's face. Her expression registered shock, as if she had just become aware of some awful truth. He would never forget the panic in her eyes. He stood transfixed as Erin's emotions plummeted from engaged curiosity to anxiety, then fear. Her chair crashed to the floor as she ran to the classroom door and out into the hall. "Oh no! You're going to kill it!" she shrieked in disbelief. Stan stood motionless in front of the class. A look of astonishment swept over him as another student ran from the room in tears. Pandemonium broke loose as some students hooted, hollered, and laughed while others sat in stunned silence.

Stan thought his idea to end the oceanography unit with a "lobster cookout" deserved a self-congratulatory pat on the back. He knew that lobster was not readily available and that most of his students would not have had an opportunity to see or taste this "Down East" treat. He thought the activity would give the class an opportunity to learn not only about lobsters but also about how a marine animal can shape the economy, life, and identity of a region. It reflected the interdisciplinary approach to teaching he favored. He had searched his kitchen to find lobster artifacts collected over the years—everything from a bib with the saying "The lobster you eat today spent the night in Casco Bay" to the mallets, shell cracker, and tiny forks for getting at the lobster claw meat. His enthusiasm was high enough to sustain the two-hour drive to Atlanta where he could buy live lobsters.

Stan was a fifth grade teacher in a small university town in the southeastern United States. He was born and raised in New England and, before coming to this rural school, had taught in a suburban school district outside of Boston for four years. He had come south to enroll in the graduate program of the nearby university. To establish residency, he had decided to teach in the local school system while taking evening classes. He had a master's degree in elementary education with an emphasis in science education.

Stan had started the lesson by showing the class a carefully wrapped box with ribbons and a bow and saying, "I would like you to make some observations about the box." He had placed the lobster in the box and wrapped it before the class arrived. He wanted to reinforce students' inquiry skills in making distinctions between observations and inferences. Stan believed that the basic process skill of observing was central to teaching science at this level. He wanted students to be able to distinguish between observed and inferred information. Student attention focused on the shoe size box wrapped in gift paper. Enthusiastic student responses followed one after another: "There is a toy present inside!" "It has a red ribbon around it!" "It is about the same size as a shoe box." "I can hear something moving inside!" Stan wrote the students' responses on the board. After the class discussed differences between observations and inferences, he asked whether anyone could now identify which statements on the board were observations. Students were quick to eliminate the guesses and identify the observations. Stan then asked them for some inferences about what might be in the box. To make it more challenging, he told the class they could ask only questions that he could answer with a yes or no. "Is it a plant?" "No," Stan replied, "It's not a plant." The class excitement began to build again after he answered "Yes" to "Is it an animal?" The next series of questions were wild inferences about what it could be based on the size of the box. Finally a student asked, "Does it have a backbone?" "No, it doesn't, but that is a great question," Stan responded. He was pleased with the level of questions that followed. After exhausting all of the students' questions, Stan slowly unwrapped the gift box, opened it, and held up the lobster. "Oh, it's a lobster! But I thought lobsters were red. This one is green!" one student exclaimed. "What's its name!" With a smile, Stan responded, "We don't name our food, Erin."

The door slammed shut after the second student dashed from the room following Erin's lead. The loud sound snapped Stan out of his stunned silence and brought a momentary lull to the classroom commotion triggered by Erin's exit. This, he thought, cannot be happening. "All right, enough!" His voice commanded attention with volume and a somewhat businesslike tone. As things in the room calmed down, Stan quickly reviewed his options. Should he continue with the class as planned? Should he run after the students who had fled the room? "I want you to take out your paper and pens and write a thank you letter to Mrs. Carson." Emily Carson, a marine biologist with the university, had visited the class the day before.

This task bought Stan the time to follow the two students who had run from the room. He found them both in the hall crying. Erin sobbed inconsolably. Gretchen appeared more composed. Stan suggested that Gretchen accompany Erin to the restroom and return with her to the classroom after they settled down. Stan reentered the classroom and was relieved to see that the students were diligently working on their letters. The water in the lobster pot, hidden out of sight in the back of the room, boiled. Okay Stan, he thought to himself, what now?

FOR REFLECTION AND DISCUSSION

1. Should Stan continue with the lobster cookout?
2. What is the message if he stops? What is the message if he continues?
3. How might the lesson be changed to avoid or soften the issues raised by the children's unexpected behavior?
4. How should animals be treated in a science classroom?
5. Should fifth graders be protected from such life experiences?

■ COMMENTARY

The Lobster's Bad Day?

Merton L. Glass

The idea of cooking a live lobster in front of the class has some merit. Ethnic foods have been used in a number of educational settings to great effect. Using ethnic foods does provide students with a significant sense of the larger world—a world that is different from the one most students have been exposed to in their local communities. Once in a Southern middle school, I had the pleasure of tasting *ga xao xa ot* (chicken in lemon grass and chili) as part of the school's ethnic awareness program. The school's population was about 20 percent Vietnamese. The use of ethnic foods did seem to play some part in unifying the diverse student population. It clearly provided a larger world view for the non-Vietnamese students.

However, there are significant problems with cooking the lobster in the classroom. First, it is based on the premise that Stan was going to have his students taste the cooked lobster. In some communities, the health department has stringent regulations about foods being prepared in inappropriate facilities. The regulations are based on health and safety concerns. Basically, any foods that are to be consumed by students must be prepared in an inspected and approved facility, such as the school's cafeteria.

A second problem can be broadly characterized as psychological or emotional. That is, many younger students are very squeamish about harming any organism, particularly ones they have seen in animated films or cartoons. In a popular animated film, the crab's name is Sebastian. Students who have seen this film could perhaps have an emotional attachment to crustaceans. The power of these emotional attachments can be extremely strong. For example, when I taught high school chemistry, I used a plastic mole named Avogadro several times in class. The mole was a toy derived from an animated character in a children's television show. One day, I started a lesson on making solutions and demonstrated making a one-molar solution by dropping Avogadro into a liter of water. One of my students cried out that Avogadro was drowning! I was able to quickly "rescue" Avogadro with some tongs. If a high school student can get upset over the use of a plastic toy, it is little wonder that fifth grade students would become distraught at the prospect of cooking the live lobster.

A third problem can broadly be classified as ethical. That is, there are a number of organizations, and consequently communities, that are vigorously opposed to harming any animal. This has led to some strict restrictions on the use of animals in the classroom. These restrictions can range from limiting dissections to eliminating or restricting the use of animals or animal components in the classroom. In schools that do allow the use of animals, there are often restrictions on the type of animal. Some schools restrict the use of mammals, other animals with backbones, and the like. As an example of how extreme some group's ethical concerns have become, at least one national organization advocates the closure of pet shops, viewing them as unethical. The National Science Teachers Association has addressed the issue of the ethical treatment of animals in a set of guidelines. Teachers should also examine the organism guidelines provided by the International Science and Engineering Fair organization for guidance regarding classroom use.

Still, the use of the lobster does suggest some possibilities for learning in the classroom environment. First, just having the lobster as an example organism has advantages. In other words, just showing the lobster and doing the lesson as described (without harming the lobster) might be better than not bringing in anything. Then, without threatening harm to the lobster, use the lobster to summarize the whole unit. If Stan still wanted his students to taste lobster, he could provide previously prepared samples.

A second possibility is to use the live lobster as part of an engagement activity for the unit, in which the live lobster could be used to activate student curiosity. I can see, for example, developing a chart that asks students, "What do you know?," "What did you learn?," and "What do you want to know?" after they have had a chance to observe the live lobster in an aquarium. Different teams could be formed to explore the components of the unit's lessons— from writing lobster stories, to exploring the anatomy of lobsters, to the economic importance of lobsters, even to recipes for lobster Newburg.

Stan could have also used the live lobster as the starting point for a science–technology–society lesson. One component of the lesson could involve students in determining the amount of energy required to get the lobster from New England waters to their community's school. In the final analysis, I would strongly discourage cooking the lobster but would recommend using the lobster in some other educationally sound manner. There are many exciting possibilities.

■ C A S E   9 . 2 ■

The Egyptian Exhibit

Amanda P. Neff

■ *As part of an integrated science and social studies lesson, Amanda encourages a gifted first grade student to share remembrances of a special field trip to see an Egyptian exhibit. The student has had great difficulty in developing positive relationships and making connections with the other students in the class. Amanda sees this as an opportunity for the student to develop a more positive rapport with her classmates. Much to Amanda's surprise, the discussion takes a decidedly religious turn. Later that day, Amanda shares what she believes to have been a wonderful experience with the child's mother and is very surprised by the reaction that she receives. One possible solution to the dilemma is discussed by Judith Reiff, an elementary teacher educator and former classroom teacher with much experience helping parents and children recognize the benefits of diverse educational experiences.*

It was the last ten minutes of the school day. My first grade class had just come in from the playground. It was that time of the day when everyone is ready to gather his or her things and prepare to go home. Emily came in from her enrichment class with an armload of stuff that she had made as part of an integrated science and social studies unit about Egypt. "Can I show the class what I made and tell them about my trip to see the mummies?" she asked as the other children were gathering their bookbags.

"Sure," I replied, and I called for the class's attention. I was pleased that Emily wanted to talk about her trip and saw her request to share as a way of allowing her to bond with the class.

"Emily has some things that she'd like to share with everyone," I announced. "Her enrichment class took a trip to a museum last week. They have been learning about the Nile River and desert habitat in the country of Egypt. Emily, tell us about some of the things that you saw at the museum."

"Well, we saw a cartouche."

"Explain to the class what a cartouche is," I interrupted.

"It's a tablet that has some really old writing on it," she explained.

"Does the writing look like our writing?" I probed.

"No," she replied. "It looks like little pictures. They called them hieroglyphics."

"Very good. That's a hard word to remember. What else did you see?" I urged.

"We saw mummies!" she said with delight.

By the very awed expressions on the faces of her classmates, I knew that she had their undivided attention.

"What did the mummies look like?" I asked.

"Well, they were all wrapped up, kinda like in swaddling cloth," she described.

"Were they dead?" asked another child in the room.

"Yeah," giggled Emily.

The rest of the class oohed and ahhed again, as if on cue. Thinking at this point that the discussion was turning into a perfect teachable moment, I decided to facilitate the discussion so that Emily would give the class a little more information.

"So the mummies were wrapped in cloth," I said.

"Yes," she replied. "But don't ask me to tell them about what they did with their brains."

I could tell by her tone that she really did want me to ask. So I said, "Explain to the class how the ancient Egyptians made the mummies, Emily." I wanted the class to understand more about the preservation of the body.

"After the person died," she explained, "they would take out all of his insides and put this stuff inside of him."

"Go ahead and tell them how they removed the person's brain," I encouraged.

"They stuck this wire up the person's nose and pulled the brains out!" she exclaimed. The class responded with the appropriate, but not unexpected, gasps and noises of disgust.

"Well, Emily, why did the ancient Egyptians do all of this to the person's body after they were dead?" I asked.

Emily looked at me blankly, and since we were short on time, I explained to the class that these techniques made the body last longer. "You know, after you are dead for a while, your body and skin dry out, and all that is left are your bones," I told them. I reminded the class that we had touched on this subject back at Halloween when someone had asked me about skeletons.

"Emily, did you see anything else that would have been buried with the mummies?" I asked.

"Yes, we saw some pottery and some jewelry and statues and stuff," she replied.

"Why did they bury those things with the person who had died?" I questioned.

"Because they thought that the person who had died would need those things. They believed in an afterlife, but not like we believe in an afterlife," she explained.

I knew that we were beginning to tread on some shaky ground. Emily had been exposed to a very fundamentalist Christian upbringing. Her strong beliefs and intolerance of those who believed differently had been a source of difficulty in many of her social relationships. Instead of commenting about the belief in an afterlife, I just nodded my head in agreement and pushed the conversation along.

"So the ancient Egyptians believed that preserving the body was important. They believed that doing these things would keep the body from turning to bones as quickly."

"Yes. On some of the mummies, you could still see some of their skin and hair. It was all brown," she responded, crinkling up her nose.

"Yes, their techniques did work very well," I agreed, "but eventually the mummies would turn to bones. And a very long time after that, the bones would just turn to dust. That is why sometimes when you go to a funeral, you might hear someone say, "Ashes to ashes and dust to dust.""

"Yeah," Emily's eyes lit up, "because God made us from dust, and we turn back into dust when we die."

The Christian in me felt a little proud of her for making that connection, but I decided that the most appropriate response was just to nod my head.

"Oh, Mrs. Neff," Timara, an African American student exclaimed, "is that why your skin is so light, because God made you out of sand?"

The light in Timara's eye was just as bright. I somehow got the feeling that a really big question had just been answered for her. I tried to hide my amusement. I had just begun a brief explanation of how our skin color actually had a lot to do with the places from which our ancestors came when the bell (rather fortunately) saved me. It was time for everyone to leave. Emily looked very pleased with herself, and I felt good about the experience. The other children had seemed very interested, and although I knew we had touched on some sensitive issues relating to religion and science, I felt that I had not overstepped any boundaries and had provided Emily with an opportunity to shine. I decided that this might be a good experience to share with her parents. I liked them. Her mother and father were both well educated, and each had a pretty clear picture of their child. They understood that Emily was strong-minded and had been very concerned about the difficulties she was having in class. I also thought that they would be proud of the way she had discussed and related her own beliefs in relationship to what she had seen at the museum.

That night, I phoned Emily's mother and related to her the story of the discussion that Emily had led earlier in the day. As I was wrapping up my tale, I noticed that Emily's mother was not as amused by the story as I. She chuckled a bit, but then her voice took on a decidedly different tone. "I've been meaning to talk to you about Emily's enrichment class," she began. "She hates it. And quite frankly, my husband and I were very upset when we saw some of the things that she brought home today. Did you realize that they have been studying about the various gods that the Egyptians believed in, and that the enrichment teacher has been making them memorize what each god stood for? I just don't see any need for young children to be exposed to that information. When we signed the permission slip for her to go on the field trip to the museum, we thought that it was to see the art museum. If we had known what kind of exhibit they were going to see, we'd never have let her go."

My heart dropped to my stomach. I was stunned. I was totally unprepared for that type of reaction. With every complaint, I felt myself become angrier. I sincerely believed that I was doing my best to respect her family's beliefs and to encourage Emily to feel free to express her beliefs as well. I was overcome by the feeling that, because I, too, had a daughter who went on this field trip and because I was a Christian, Emily's mother expected me to agree with her. The best response I could muster was to advise her to speak to the enrichment teacher about her concerns. At this point, all I could think about was how to end this discussion. I made an excuse and ended the telephone conversation as quickly as I could.

FOR REFLECTION AND DISCUSSION

1. Was Amanda right to encourage a discussion of ancient embalming techniques with children in first grade?

2. Were Amanda's responses to the religious questions and responses of the children appropriate?

3. Were Amanda's beliefs evident in her discussion with the children?

4. Should Amanda have shared the experience with Emily's mother?

5. Could Amanda have responded to the mother's concerns in a different way?

6. What other science topics might lead to discussions of religious beliefs?

■ COMMENTARY

Extracting a Teachable Moment from Emily's Story

Judith C. Reiff

Amanda should get credit for being spontaneous and for responding to the interests of her first grade students because she did facilitate a teachable moment. Teachers have to make approximately "130 decisions per hour in a 6-hour teaching day" (Kauchak & Eggen, 1998, p. 19). They make these impromptu and split-second decisions throughout the day while considering children's needs, time, curriculum, and many other factors. In this case, Amanda illustrates the difficulty and yet the importance of teaching to all aspects of child development. Immediately, Amanda knew that she had to consider the social, emotional, and intellectual development of Emily and the other children as she made decisions throughout this situation.

When Emily asked whether she could share her experiences from the museum field trip, Amanda provided an opportunity for her students to learn from a child who was not connecting with the other children in the classroom. Emily's enthusiasm and knowledge about the Egyptian exhibit were evident. Amanda would have been remiss had she dismissed or ignored that particular moment for Emily.

To support Amanda's decision making, we can refer to the research summarized by Westmoreland (1996) about the perceptions of children regarding death depending on their ages and developmental levels. Children from ages three to five do not have a true concept of time and permanence. They may view death as temporary, like sleeping. Six- to eight-year olds begin to understand the permanence of death, and they are interested in what happens to the body afterward. They also view death as what happens to someone else, not to themselves. Thus, Amanda's students, not unexpectedly, responded with curiosity and interest to the mummy discussion.

Furthermore, it was appropriate for Amanda to clarify the terms and to encourage the questioning and discussion. One suggestion might be that when Emily recognized that the Egyptians believed in a different afterlife than "we" did, Amanda might have reaffirmed that people do have different beliefs about a variety of things, such as what we like to eat and what we like best in school.

In my opinion, there tends not to be enough unstructured discussion in classrooms based on children's experiences. Unfortunately, owing to time and curriculum constraints, teachers are limited in how much they can deviate from the mandated curriculum throughout the day. Amanda only had ten minutes left in the school day, and she chose to conclude with a brief discussion based on a child's interest. According to Kauchak and Eggen (1998), effective questioning includes being "flexible and sensitive to student's needs" (p. 154). As far as the children are concerned, especially Emily, Amanda would probably receive an A for her openness and flexibility.

When Emily's mother did not react positively during the telephone discussion, Amanda questioned her own decision-making abilities in the classroom and her advice to this parent. I do not believe that Emily's mother was upset with Amanda in particular; it appears that she and her husband were already distressed by the activities in the enrichment class. It was appropriate for Amanda to recommend that Emily's parents contact the enrichment teacher to discuss their concerns. Amanda should not put herself in the middle of any assignment from another teacher. However, Amanda could have mentioned that Emily might be learning about other religions as she progresses through her schooling.

Another approach Amanda could have used with Emily's mother would be to explain that in her professional view, aspects of death should be discussed with children before an actual event occurs. Because death is a part of life, it cannot and should not be ignored. By discussing the preparation of mummies, the class was able to talk about a difficult subject in a safe way. According to the age and developmental levels of the children in Amanda's class, she was correct in realizing the appropriateness yet sensitive nature of the discussion about the Egyptian mummies.

■ **CASE 9.3** ■

What Happened to Bunny?

Lynn Bryan and Yuki Nakagawa

■ *In this open case, Lynn and Yuki tell the story of Miss Murata and her first grade students in Japan. On entering the classroom one morning, Miss Murata finds her students in tears because their classroom pet, Bunny, has died. The death of Bunny leads the students to question*

Miss Murata and each other about death and the afterlife. The class discussion highlights tensions associated with the influence of community and culture on science teaching and learning. The case is followed by a response prepared jointly by an American and a Japanese science educator, Jamie Calkin and Kiyoyuki Ohshika.

Early one morning, I walked into my first grade classroom to see all of my thirty-two students huddled near the corner of the room. I knew that something was wrong because this was the corner where we kept our rabbit, Bunny. Usually, when I come into our classroom each day, the children are attending to their morning duties, such as cleaning the boards, wiping the desktops, reshelving books, taking attendance, and even feeding Bunny. All of the students are responsible for morning duties that they complete before the first bell. When I walked in on this particular morning, however, I could see tears welling up in the eyes of a few and hear sad whispers from some others. The mood was quite somber for a class that was normally buzzing with cheerful energy.

"What is wrong?" I asked.

"Murata-sensei, Bunny has died!" the children shouted.

"Oh, I am so sorry, my children. What do you think happened to Bunny?"

Bunny's death came as a shock to all of us. The children have been caring for Bunny since the first day of Seikatsuka. They have been observing Bunny and learning about rabbit habitats for nearly six months. Each day has brought new excitement to the children; they find more patterns, ask more questions, and think of more aspects of Bunny's life to explore. But today's observation will bring an unexpected aspect of Bunny's life for us to explore.

OUR COURSE, SEIKATSUKA

My name is Miss Murata, and my students call me "Murata-sensei," which is a respectful title that literally means "Murata-teacher." I am a second-year first grade teacher in a Japanese public elementary school located about thirty miles from Tokyo. My students enjoy a course that is part of the national curriculum for first grade, called *Seikatsuka*.

Seikatsuka, which means social living or life, was introduced in the Japanese national course of study in 1989. This course replaces science and social studies for the first and second grades. In this course, activities address both science and social living. We focus on the relationship between one's self, community, and nature, shown in Figure 9.1. The relationships

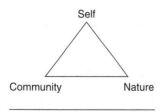

FIGURE 9.1

shown in this triangle are important in Seikatsuka. Students must be aware of and interested in the relationships between themselves, the people around them, the community, and the natural environment. They must also learn customs and skills for everyday life in Japan and build a strong foundation for independence, as they think about themselves in everyday life. They must learn what their roles will be in a community and how their actions affect plants, animals, and the nature around them.

The Seikatsuka curriculum has many goals. Children learn how to be creative and expressive through drawing, writing, acting, and speaking. They are encouraged to explore their feelings, beliefs, and knowledge about themselves and the world around them. They develop skills for how to play and enjoy living. Children also learn to appreciate and take care of their surroundings. For example, last year, my students worked on a project that lasted the whole year. They chose plots of land in the community and took pictures of their plots during the fall, winter, spring, and summer. As the seasons changed, the children brought in their pictures and compared what happened to their community plots. The children noticed many things about the community that they had never realized before this project. They observed how the seasons affect the plants and animals that they will see. Some kept track of the weather. Others noticed the coming and going of birds, squirrels, and insects. As part of the project, we used some of the fallen leaves and local plants to make dyes for *happi,* the clothing for our fall festival.

This year in Seikatsuka, my students have been raising a rabbit from the time she was born. They have been learning about caring for nature but also watching the rabbit grow and change. They are learning about their own lives. They are curious about their own lives, how they grow up, how they build relationships with others. So it was not unusual for our class to have a very interesting discussion the day that Bunny died.

DEATH AND RELIGION IN A FIRST GRADE CLASSROOM

"What happened to Bunny?" cried Hideki. "Did you feed her yesterday before we left?"

"Yes, I did! I put in more pellets and changed the water. Maybe Miho needed to clean the cage yesterday!" Satoshi exclaimed as he pointed to Miho.

The children were trying to make sense of what they observed. Why would Bunny die so young? Was she starved? Was she thirsty? Did somebody hurt her? Was she sick with a disease? Wouldn't we know if she had been sick for a long time? Was she lonely? What could we have done? *Why did she die?*

"My baby brother died when he was only three months old," murmured Setsuko. "Before he was born, God asked him if he wanted to be born, even though he could only live for three months. He answered to God, 'Yes, I want to be born to this family. I don't mind living for only three months.' So then he was born, and my family was very happy for three months. Maybe God asked Bunny if she wanted to live with us for these months, and Bunny said, 'Yes' . . . even if her life will be short."

"Did you have a funeral for your brother?" asked Koki.

"Yes," Setsuko replied.

"We should have a funeral for Bunny!" cried the children.

"Yes. We can make a grave by the butterfly garden on the playground. Do you remember when we took her to the playground and she liked to sniff the flowers?" Koki asked his classmates.

"Yes. And I can pick some flowers and write a letter for her grave, too, so she can go to heaven with them," added Sachiko.

"And when she gets to heaven, she can hop around anywhere she wants to and not get lost, because God will always be with her!" smiled Koki.

"But when will she come back?" Hideki asked.

"I hope she will come back as a person next time so that I can talk with her," Satoshi said as he looked longingly at the motionless bundle in the cage.

"No, animals come back as animals again," Miho corrected Satoshi.

"No, everybody can be *anything* when they are reborn," Satoshi retorted.

Miho insisted, "No, only people come back as people!"

"No."

"Yes."

"No!"

"Isn't that right, Sensei? Only people come back as people? Can Bunny really come back to life as anything?"

WHAT IS APPROPRIATE TO DISCUSS?

In Japan, we have several different religions. However, in today's everyday life of a Japanese person, religion is not very important. Most Japanese consider themselves Shintoists, Buddhists, or Shinto-Buddhists. Approximately 1 percent of Japanese people are Christian. But no matter what their religion, children and teachers are allowed to discuss their beliefs openly in the classroom. Children are encouraged to ask questions and explore religious and moral issues about God, heaven, and reincarnation, just as my class did. This is one of the cultural aspects of Seikatsuka.

FOR REFLECTION AND DISCUSSION

1. If you were in Miss Murata's classroom on this day, how would you respond to Miho's question?

2. How might a teacher from a Western culture, such as in the United States, respond to Miho's questions?

3. How would you continue the class discussion? Where would you direct the life lesson that Bunny brought to the class?

4. What cultural expectations might affect the ways in which science teachers in Japan and the United States react to children's questions about life and death?

5. What science understandings might be explored through the death of any classroom pet?

Bunny's Dead: Thinking about the Value of Life

James B. Calkin and Kiyoyuki Ohshika

I (Jamie) am an American science educator with five years of teaching experience in public schools and three years of experience as a full-time graduate student in science education. Dr. Kiyoyuki Ohshika is a professor in the Science Education Department at Hiroshima University in Japan. He is in the United States to study American science education as a visiting professor. After reading the story of Bunny, we came together to discuss some of the issues that were central to the case. We began our discussion by sharing some of the similarities and differences in our two cultures, particularly in relation to beliefs about the role of animals and religion in the elementary science classroom. We've listed some relevant comparisons between our cultures in Table 9.1.

Although the case authors approach the story of Bunny from the perspective of religious issues surrounding death, we will focus first on the value of life and its place in Japanese and American education. We first identify a common problem, then describe its possible roots and outcomes, and finally examine how the death of a classroom pet provides an opportunity to address this problem.

TABLE 9.1

Similarities between Japan and U.S.	*Differences between Japan and U.S.*
The value of life is deemphasized in mass media, especially in video games, cartoons, and comics. (Comics are even more popular in Japan than in the U.S.)	Teachers are ultimately responsible for classrooms (and pets) in the U.S.; students are ultimately responsible for classrooms and pets in Japan.
Animals can be seen either as pets to be cared for or meat to be eaten.	Few children in Japan keep pets at home; many U.S. children have various pets.
Industrialization and postmodern societies have put death outside the daily experience of most children.	The dominant culture in the U.S. has historical roots in the domination and control of nature; Japanese historical roots lie in humans as part of nature.
Family time is down, consumerism is up, and there is an increased reliance on schools to teach values and discipline.	There is a high level of diversity in children, classrooms, and teaching in the U.S. compared with the homogenous culture and education of Japanese students

IDENTIFYING THE PROBLEM

In both Japan and the United States, we take life for granted. Similarly, death has become re-mote to most young people in both cultures. Most Japanese and American children are insulated from death in the real world, owing to modern medicine and the conveniences of postmodern societies. In addition, children of both cultures play video games at unique levels compared with other children around the world. Even before first grade, many children in both societies take part in make-believe yet interactive violence. Furthermore, violence and make-believe death are common themes in cartoons and movies. Compounding the problem, parents in both Japan and the United States spend less time with their children than parents did in the past. In fact, Japan-ese parents in the 1990s essentially told the teachers to teach discipline and morals. Certainly, schools in both nations find themselves addressing values and moral education.

OUTCOMES OF THE PROBLEM

This double-edged sword of increased exposure to violence in the media and decreased real-life experience with death has many potentially detrimental impacts on children and their so-cieties. Indeed, this is a large-scale sociological problem that affects many facets of society. In this context, violence will undoubtedly continue to increase. Community awareness and em-pathy will likely continue to decline.

IDENTIFYING A SOLUTION

The goals of Seikatsuka relate directly to addressing the issues described above. The relation-ships between one's self, the community, and nature are exactly what is at stake. We believe that the death of Bunny provides an important opportunity for teaching lessons in the value of life in the real world and the relevance of death. If we were Miss Murata, we would take a few weeks to address the following goals:

1. Students will learn about the value of life and the meaning of death.
2. Students will learn about the difference between death (and violence) in the media and death (and violence) in the real world.

There are probably as many ways to try to meet these goals as there are classroom rabbits. We propose discussions and activities surrounding (1) the physical death of Bunny and the student-led funeral, (2) the emotions related to death, and (3) the similarities and differences in the death of Bunny and death in the media.

Discussion of Physical Death and the Funeral

We would start our unit with the difficult task of describing the death of a living thing. As hard as it would be, we believe that at this point, the children have a unique chance to observe and understand more about physical death. If willing, the children should be allowed to touch Bunny and use their senses to make observations.

  Following a student-led funeral, we would lead a brainstorming session on the physical death of Bunny. We might ask, "What can you say using your five senses about Bunny when she died?" We would expect answers such as "motionless" and "cold." We would then share with them the true story of a Japanese boy and his pet beetle. When the beetle stopped moving, the boy went to his father and asked him to replace the batteries in the beetle. We would ask students to give input, possibly comparing and contrasting battery-powered toys with Bunny and the beetle. The students could then work in groups to generate a list of the characteristics of life.

Discussion of the Emotions of Loss and Death

For the next few days, we would do activities related to the emotions of death. "How did it feel when you found out Bunny had died?" "What memories do you have of Bunny?" "How might those memories be important or valuable?" "How did you deal with your feeling?" Sensitive discussion and feedback are crucial during these activities. We would model and clarify appropriate listening and responses. One of our major objectives here would be to help the students see that although Bunny and all living things return to nature after death, they can live forever in our memories.

At this point, we believe that students will have divided themselves into two groups: a group that wants to rush out and get another rabbit and a group that doesn't want another rabbit because Bunny's death hurt or because they would be disloyal to Bunny. We believe that both groups need time to think about what happened. The first group especially needs to think about what death means to them. They need to know that dead things cannot be revived or perfectly replaced like broken toys. This need derives, in part, from the students' cultures of consumerism, in which things are quickly worn out and replaced.

Discussion of Real Death versus Death in the Media

In the last few days of the unit, we would ask the students to investigate how Bunny's death is different from the death and violence most of them witness everyday in cartoons and video games. Video clips or even video games could be shown at this point. In doing so, we would try to lead the students to come to a personal understanding that death and violence in the media are different from death and violence in the real world. We hope they would find that death in the real world hurts and that life is not to be taken for granted. We would conclude our unit by leading students in a discussion about how we should treat life—other people and other living things. Here, we would reinforce the core goals of Seikatsuka. In addition, we would have the class generate guidelines for the ethical treatment of people and other living things. These guidelines would be posted in the classroom.

CONCLUSION

These lessons would be hard—for the students and their teachers. We believe that these lessons are important, not just for fulfilling the goals of the curriculum, but also in helping to develop more humane and sensitive people. Bunny's death provides a challenging yet unique opportunity for these lessons in the connections between the value of life and the reality of death.

■ C A S E 9 . 4 ■

Integrating Technology into Science Research Projects: Cutting and Pasting Made Difficult

David Whitney

■ *In trying to integrate technology into his students' fifth grade science curriculum, David decides to have his students use the World Wide Web, e-mail, and multimedia encyclopedias to enhance the quality of their science reports. After being extremely pleased with his students' final projects, he comes to realize that maybe the work of one of his students was a little "too good." In this closed case, David describes how he dealt with this dilemma. The case is followed by a response from science teacher educator Kim Nichols.*

Each year in the springtime, David, a fifth grade teacher, likes to have his students work on science research reports to gain an in-depth understanding of topics in which they have become particularly interested over the course of the school year. In recent years, his school has acquired a significant amount of modern technology, including computers with Internet access, digital cameras, and plenty of software. Having been strongly encouraged by his principal to start "getting our money's worth" out of the available technology, David began to think of ways to get his students to use the computers to improve the quality of their science projects. Initially, his students worked for four weeks learning how to conduct searches on the Internet, send and receive e-mail, and use multimedia encyclopedia software.

Once his students had shown an ability to utilize the available technology, David thought that they were ready to begin work on their end-of-the-year science reports. As they began to explore the topics of their reports, students used various search engines on the Internet to find the most up-to-date information. In addition to surfing the Internet, students e-mailed experts in their topic areas to get information, and they read articles from multimedia encyclopedias. Once his students had accumulated information about their topics, David showed them how to write outlines and use a word processor to compose their reports in a logical and professional-looking fashion. Students conferenced with David to learn how to put their new information into their own words. David's students then worked for one more week to get their reports into a final draft stage.

When the day came for these fifth grade students to turn in their science reports, David was very pleased with the results. Many students had turned in wonderful reports with elaborate graphs, pictures, and diagrams. The principal and the other teachers on his hall were excited to see the endless learning possibilities brought about by the use of the new computer technology. Students and parents alike were proud of the work that had been done by students in the class. Things could not have been much better.

David was anxious to read the students' reports in more detail, so after school, he bundled them up in his briefcase and prepared to spend several evening hours reading students' work. Sitting at his desk after dinner, he began to read, starting with Lisa's report and then going on to Joel's project. David was amazed at the ingenuity and skill students were demonstrating in their use of the computer as a learning tool. As David began to read Erin's report, he noticed something interesting. Erin, who usually was only an average writer with a below-average work ethic, had written a report that appeared as though it could have been written by a high school or college student. David's natural first response was to credit the technology with the improved work habits and final project of this student. However, when David bragged about Erin's report to a colleague the next day, it dawned on the other teacher that some of the wording sounded very familiar. After investigating the situation further, David learned that Erin had a computer at home and had used a different multimedia encyclopedia from the ones available at school. It appeared that Erin had simply cut and pasted information directly from the encyclopedia into her report. Through some additional inquiries, David learned that Erin had also cut and pasted information directly from the Internet and the e-mail responses from the topic expert. It appeared that virtually none of Erin's report was original work! As David pondered this issue, he reflected on the following questions:

> How can I be sure that my students are really learning something from doing this technology-based project?
>
> How can I be sure that future students will learn something from doing this project?
>
> How can I make sure my students don't plagiarize from multimedia encyclopedias, e-mail, and Internet sites outside of the classroom?
>
> How should I approach Erin and her parents about this situation?
>
> In the future, should I let my students work on their projects at home where I have no control over what they do?
>
> How fair is it that some of my students have computers at home with which to work while others do not?

After considering these questions, David decided to address the immediate situation by having students give oral reports about their projects. Although this did not help with the plagiarism problem, it gave an indication of how much the students had actually learned about their science topics as a result of conducting the research. David decided that in the future, the best way to prevent this scenario from repeating itself would be to have his students word their research questions in ways that could not be answered through cutting and pasting. Rather than writing strictly expository text, students would create portfolios about their topics in which they had to include fiction stories, poems, hand-drawn pictures, and letters to experts. Students would then learn how to use the school's scanner and create web pages by scanning the contents of the portfolio's contents and uploading it to the class web page.

FOR REFLECTION AND DISCUSSION

1. David avoided discussing his concern with Erin's parents. How should he have approached them about this problem? What should he have said to them?

2. How would you handle a situation involving plagiarism if it happened to you?

3. How can David ensure that his fifth grade students have equal access to computer technology for their science projects?

4. What are some ways in which David might nurture students' writing skills in science?

■ **COMMENTARY**

Strategies for Helping Students Develop High-Quality Science Projects Using the Internet

B. Kim Nichols

There are several important issues that need to be addressed in this case, including plagiarism and equitable access. The plagiarism issue is one that has plagued educators in the past and will continue to be a problem as long as students are required to write research reports. As students have more resources available, owing to increasing access to technology, the task of monitoring plagiarism becomes further complicated. Many of the strategies that teachers used in the past to deal with plagiarism involving traditional information sources, such as textbooks and magazines, will still prove effective in our increasingly technology-rich environments. However, additional strategies will need to be considered. The other issue, equitable access to technological resources, requires that teachers plan for and provide opportunities for all students to utilize technology. The disparity between those who have access at home and those who do not is a dilemma referred to as *the digital divide,* and there are ways in which teachers can minimize the disparity between the technology haves and have-nots.

David's first issue—preventing, detecting, and properly handling instances of plagiarism—is common to most teachers who require their students to collect information and write reports based on the information that they have gathered. In the past, when the information available to students was limited primarily to a few encyclopedias and the books found in the school or public library, the prevention and detection of plagiarism were easier. On-line books, journals, magazines, newspapers, and other Internet sites have greatly expanded the amount of information that is readily available to students. Encyclopedias and databases on CD-ROM are also common in schools, and many students also have access to these at home. Although this explosion in available information is exciting for students and teachers, it makes it virtually impossible for teachers to locate and read all of the possible information sources that students might use and quote. Therefore, documenting plagiarism is much more difficult. David is on the right track with his requirement that students must also discuss their reports with the class. This is similar to allowing science fair judges to talk with the project presenters. I have found discussions with students to be enlightening and beneficial when I have served as a science fair judge. I am better able to ascertain the presenter's level of understanding of the research design, implementation, results, and conclusions. In David's case, discussing the project with the students throughout the information-gathering and writing process, as well as during the presentation required at the conclusion, can also help David to gauge the students' levels of participation and understanding. Requiring that students cite their sources, as many teachers already do, is another important step. David might consider limiting his students to two or three on-line sources and requiring them to provide printed copies of these sources, such as web pages, along with their final reports. It might be sufficient to inform students and parents that he may ask students to produce their sources if there is any question about the authenticity of a report.

Finally, for many students, plagiarism is not an intentional act but results from a lack of understanding of proper research and writing techniques. It will be well worth David's time to teach his students good research and writing skills. David should conduct research practice sessions in which students read information and then summarize it in their own words. The time-tested method of using notecards might seem dated but is still very effective. David can teach students how to record only the facts, in list form, from a source onto notecards, and he can then require that students use only their notecards, not the original sources, when writing their practice reports. In many cases, simply working with students on the proper ways to use and cite sources will eliminate plagiarism problems.

David should have approached the parents of the student who plagiarized, but he might have been fearful of their response. It is difficult to discuss issues of this nature with parents, particularly when the implication is that their child has been less than honest. It is important in such instances to avoid putting the parents on the defensive; rather, David must let the parents know that they are on the same team, working toward a common goal: to help the child learn and grow as a person and a student. By discussing with the parents ways in which they can work with their child to ensure that she conducts research and writes papers properly, David conveys to the parents his desire for the student to learn from the situation. Rather that attacking the honesty of the child, David comes to the conference table with an attitude of caring. David might consider allowing the child to select another topic, conduct the research, and write another paper. David, the parents, and the child can discuss and develop strict guidelines that must be followed throughout the process, with all parties involved assessing the progress throughout the research-gathering and writing stages. This is less punitive than assigning a grade of zero, but it is still disciplinary in nature. The child must repeat the entire research and writing process, and the benefits from this activity are twofold: She will learn that there are consequences for her actions, and she will also learn proper methods for conducting research and writing reports.

David's second main concern, the one pertaining to equitable digital access, is shared by many. This concern is so prevalent that it has been the focus of extensive and ongoing federal research. The U.S. Department of Commerce's report entitled *Falling through the Net: Defining the Digital Divide* finds varying degrees of computer and Internet access among households based on demographic factors such as income level, geography, and race. So this is a very real and legitimate concern that David has to consider. One solution proposed in the case study is to limit students to conducting all research at school. By doing so, David can have greater control over what they do, and he will also make sure that no student has an unfair advantage regarding access to technology. Although this solution might seem appealing at first glance, there are some serious drawbacks to consider. First, the issue of control is better dealt with by teaching students good research and writing skills, making them accountable for documenting, and even providing their sources, if necessary. Second, this is a temporary fix to a long-term problem. As students enter middle and high school, class time is often limited to less than an hour per subject. It is not feasible to expect that all assignments will be completed in class. So, although this might work for lower elementary grades, it becomes less and less practical as students advance through the upper elementary, middle, and high school grades. Even in the fifth grade, this could prove quite difficult. In an already crowded curriculum, it is unlikely that adequate classroom time will be available for students to gather information, write, edit, and generate polished, finished products—all under David's strict supervision. This is especially true if David plans to require several research projects throughout the year. Students will need access to the media center, either individually or in small groups, during the day. David will not be able to monitor students strictly during these times. Some students will take advantage of the resources available at public libraries; by restricting students to classroom time, he will eliminate this opportunity. And although restricting students to classroom research might seem like an equitable solution, it begs the question: Is it better to restrict everyone to make circumstances fair, or should we seek to increase the opportunities for those with limited or no access? The latter seems like a much better solution, and by increasing opportunities for those without access at home, David's actions will be consistent with recommendations by those conducting research on the digital divide. *Falling through the Net* refers to alternative points of access as one possible solution to the problem of disparity among households. This report, based on Census Bureau data, finds that K–12 schools are the second most commonly used point of access for individuals who lack Internet connectivity at home. This is particularly evident in rural areas of the country. Therefore, David should find ways to increase computer and Internet access at school for those who do not have access at home. David can work with students before school, after school, or during study hall. David can increase opportunities for students to go to the media center throughout the school day, and he can make maximum use of the computer lab, if one is available at his school.

In summary, David can take steps both to diminish plagiarism and to ensure equitable access to technology resources. To deny access out of fear of the pitfalls is to do a disservice to his students. Technology is here to stay, and the resources that are available through the use of technology can and should enhance both the teaching process and the learning process.

References

Bransford, J. D., Brown, A. L., & Cocking, R. R. (1999). Effective teaching: Examples in history, mathematics and science. In J. D. Bransford, A. L. Brown & R. R. Cocking (Eds.), *How people learn: Brain, mind, experience and school* (pp. 143–177). Washington, DC: National Academy Press.

Kauchak, D., & Eggen, P. (1998). *Learning and teaching: Research-based methods.* Boston, MA: Allyn & Bacon.

Rosebury, A. S., Warren, B., & Conant, F. R. (1992). Appropriating scientific discourse: Findings from language minority classrooms. *The Journal of Learning Sciences, 2*(1), 61–94.

Westmoreland, P. (1996). Coping with death: Helping students grieve. *Childhood Education, 72*(3), 157–163.

Resources to Consider

Connolly, B., Gordon, M., & Shulof, C. (1998). *Prisoner or protected? A web quest exploring the humanity of zoos.* [On-line] Available at: http://www.richmond.edu/~ed344/webquest/zoos/
    Through this interactive web site, students take on the roles of animal rights activist, habitat expert, zoo evaluator, and zoologist to make planning decisions about zoos and the rights of animals. The students'

mission is to design an ideal zoo based on what they have learned. In addition to the various components necessary for students to carry out the mission, the site includes a teacher's page, a glossary, and other resources.

Grabe, M., & Grabe, C. (2000). *Integrating the Internet for meaningful learning.* New York: Houghton Mifflin. This book provides many suggestions for helping students use the Internet effectively when engaging in science research. Chapters focus on topic such as "Learning with Internet Inquiry Tools," "Integrating the Internet in to Inquiry-Based Projects," and "Responsible Use of the Internet."

Mason, C. (1998). *Everybody's somebody's lunch.* Gardiner, ME: Tilbury House.
The killing of a young girl's cat by a coyote serves as the backdrop for this story, from which children learn about predator–prey relationships in the living world. The teacher's guide that accompanies the book provides activity suggestions that emphasize respect and tolerance for life and the role of humans as predators.

10

Professional Development of Elementary Teachers in Science

Much of the focus of current research on educational reform, standards, and restructuring of schools is on the teacher, indicating why the role of the teacher is growing in responsibility and respect. Today, we are in the midst of science teacher education reform, and there are few who would argue against the need for the ongoing professional development of teachers. According to a Department of Education study (National Center for Education Statistics, 1999), most teachers (99 percent) receive some professional development each year. The most common topics of this professional development are curriculum and performance standards, educational technology, new teaching methods, and in-depth learning in the subject area. Nevertheless, most of this professional development appears not to be very intensive, characterized by one-shot workshops, and involves bringing outside expertise to teachers to increase their knowledge. The research base for the elements of effective teacher development programs indicates that short-term workshops, without the opportunity for teachers to meet with and observe other teachers' classrooms, do not produce significant growth for teachers or students.

Even though science teachers engage in several hundred interactions with children each day, little time is spent with colleagues discussing important educational issues. If teachers are to develop the knowledge, skills, and talents that are different from what they experienced as students and build on what they learned in their science teacher preparation programs, then they need opportunities to study and reflect collaboratively with other teachers over the course of their careers. Teachers can help one another function as career-long learners by collaborating with each other as they work with students, studying their own and each other's teaching, and sharing new ideas. Collaboration among teachers allows them to build a community of learners in which they can think about their teaching in ways they can't when they work alone. Professional development is a vital component of education in general and of science education in particular.

Many national professional organizations are involved in extensive and effective initiatives to develop performance-based standards for teachers, including the National Education Goals, the National Board for Professional Teaching Standards, Interstate New Teacher Assessment and Support Consortium, the National Council for Accreditation of Teacher Education, and the National Research Council, to name only a few. All of these standards view teaching as an intellectual activity involving collegial work.

We know that when teachers engage in continuous, collaborative professional development, they become empowered professionals. Developing habits of continual growth and improvement requires self-reflection. Reflective teachers ask important questions and seek out alternative answers about how they can improve classroom events and children's lives. Reflective teachers develop problem-solving orientations by becoming involved in teacher research, school-based inquiry, and inquiry into students' experiences (Darling-Hammond, 1996).

A relatively new collaboration in which public schools and universities work together in partnerships benefits both prospective and practicing teachers in their professional development. Certainly for prospective teachers, learning "to become a teacher" is more contextualized in the school than it has been in the past. School-university partnerships aim to provide sites for best practice that support the preparation of new teachers, expand the professional development of practicing teachers, and support collaborative research and inquiry (Darling-Hammond, 1996).

The three cases in this chapter provide a glimpse of the dilemmas faced by elementary teachers as they attempt to improve their science teaching through various types of professional development. The first case, "Of Love and Other Demons in Science Teaching" by Michalinos Zemblyas, illustrates how Catherine, a twenty-five-year veteran elementary school teacher, uses the process of self-reflection to justify her beliefs about the role of emotions and intuitions in her science teaching. The second case, "Teaching Science the Right Way" by Melissa

George and Sandra Abell, focuses on the teacher's expectations for science teaching and learning. In this closed case, Emily, a veteran second grade teacher, struggles with her lack of science content knowledge as she attempts to reform her approaches to teaching science to bring
them in line with the *National Science Education Standards* (National Research Council,
1996). In the final case, "Partnering for Progress in Elementary Science," Janet Powell and
Linda Block-Gandy use layers of commentary to highlight the many challenges and obstacles
they encountered as a school–university partnership evolved over time.

■ C A S E 1 0 . 1 ■

Of Love and Other Demons in Science Teaching

Michalinos Zembylas

■ *Self-reflection is an important aspect of teachers' professional growth and serves multiple
purposes, from shaping to rationalizing practice. The process of reflecting on one's own practice has usually been described as a rational, intellectual process. Other ways of reflecting on
teaching, such as using one's emotions or intuitions, have been dismissed as invalid and inappropriate. In this closed case, Michalinos Zemblyas, a university researcher, describes the
journey of Catherine, a twenty-five-year veteran elementary schoolteacher who wrestles with
the dilemma of justifying her beliefs about the role of emotions in science teaching. Such a
dilemma is not resolved except in the act of self-reflection itself, an act that, for Catherine, involves as much emotion as her teaching itself. The case is followed by commentary from science educator Megan Boler.*

Many years later, as she was talking about her earlier teaching experiences, Catherine remembered that distant morning when her principal called her into his office. "Ms. Myers," he
said in a serious voice filled with a striking determination, "it has come to my attention that
you frequently spend time in your science class talking to the students about *how* you feel and
that you also waste time asking them to share their feelings. Didn't they teach you, Ms. Myers,
that teachers should leave their feelings outside the classroom? Teach them the facts, Ms.
Myers! The facts! Besides, what do *your* feelings have to do with science teaching?" At that
time, Catherine was a young teacher with less than three years of experience. Science was (and
still is in many ways) a rationalist, intellectual endeavor of finding the most appropriate concepts and theories to describe and explain our world. And part of good science teaching has required teachers to think about their work in terms of the great dichotomies: either science facts
or feelings, rigorous and objective scientific evidence or personal and biased emotions
("demons," as many philosophers describe them). Catherine and her science teaching were
often described (and dismissed) as "touchy-feely," because she allowed emotions to play a for-

mative role. She had always believed that emotions are a part of who she is and are involved with her values, the culture of the school, her decisions, her beliefs, and her actions.

Catherine has been teaching now for twenty-five years. She currently works at an elementary school of 400 students, located in a medium-size university city in Illinois. The school serves a diverse range of children, including students from the surrounding neighborhood, students bused from two affluent areas on opposite sides of the city, and a large population of low-income students who are also bused. Approximately 62 percent of the population is low income. Her classroom "family," as she likes to call her students, is a heterogeneous group with cultural heritages including African American, Latino/a, and European American. Catherine has developed an in-depth integrated inquiry science approach to meet the diverse needs and interests of her students. Through this thematic, project-centered curriculum, students construct their own understandings while experiencing the connectedness between subjects, using authentic materials and activities that are compelling and interesting. Such an approach engages imaginations and enthusiasms and evokes the emotional and aesthetic responses of the children.

Catherine frequently centers her efforts on finding or constructing support for her own beliefs about including emotions in her science teaching and her need to explain her beliefs to multiple audiences, including her students, colleagues, and principal. In the following conversation, Catherine explains her continual effort to work out a rationalization for what she does:

Michalinos: What do you mean when you say that you use emotions in your science teaching?

Catherine: [I describe] how I felt about something we saw or read about, how the room is looking, or how I was trying to figure something out and was having trouble or got frustrated about it. I would tell children, "I don't understand; *this* says *this,* and *this* says *that!* Ha!" That's a feeling, a puzzlement. I talk to them about feelings about my family, about things that happened to me outside of school, about something I learned that got me all excited. . . . [And] I encourage them to share their feelings too, if they want to, and usually they do. . . . I encourage them to experience and feel science, and of course everything else we study. . . .

Michalinos: But although you seem to feel very strongly about your convictions, you have also talked about some discomfort you experience because you have to justify these beliefs to others, including your students, colleagues, and principal. Can you talk more about that?

Catherine: By sharing my emotions and by reflecting on them and on my understanding of students' feelings, I guess I hope to communicate a lot of [the process of] finding out about things and wonder and seeing relationships between other things. I am not trying to insist that everybody feel that way certainly, but to share that that's how I feel about it and to be receptive to how kids are feeling about it. What kinds of things excite us and get us really wanting to question and come over and explore and experiment? At the same time, I always feel the need to justify my beliefs to myself and to others, to rationalize what I am doing. My view of science teaching always changes because of my emotions. If you add on or try something new, you find a different direction to go. You expand the repertoire of experiences. You ask another question. You stop and rethink: OK, is *this* a valuable experience? Do I need to re-structure the experience here? Do I need to think about my questions? Is this a point and time at which it would be useful to introduce some new terminology, to act something out? How do I and my students *feel* about this experience?"

Catherine admits that over the years, she has formulated her pedagogy from her convictions, from what feels right and good to her, but periodically she finds herself in situations in which she has to articulate and implicitly or explicitly, justify her pedagogical choices, such as including feelings in her teaching. She has constructed a belief system about science pedagogy and practice that may include frustration, anxiety, and excitement. This belief system has been modified over the years as she has gained more experiences that have confirmed and refined her beliefs. These reside within Catherine as much as within the context of her teaching. These notions raise some interesting questions: How does Catherine find support to include her emotional ways of knowing (and those of her students) in her science teaching? What is the role of self-reflection in this process, and what form does Catherine's reflection take? This question is crucial, for it is through self-reflection that Catherine finds her answer to her first question. To understand this, we must ask the question, How does Catherine become a self-reflective teacher, what is her history, and how has it shaped this process?

The turning point in Catherine's career that led to her development of reflective practice occurred when she taught kindergarten fifteen years ago. It was then that she saw for the first time how she and her young students could articulate their own views as *felt,* not merely as *thought.* "When I went to kindergarten," says Catherine, "I felt comfortable for the first time talking about feelings. I felt that I didn't need to know all the answers. Also, going to kindergarten, I recognized the incredible need for everything to be hands-on. Feeling comfortable for the first time to say to my students, I don't have all the answers, opened the doors for a deeper reflection on my feelings and my teaching." Catherine still remembers a young African American boy coming to her one day saying, "Ms. Myers, I found this wonderful rock in my backyard. This is the prettiest rock I've ever seen. I want to learn more about my rock." Since that day, Catherine admits, she has had to give up using *reason* as the only way of organizing an activity, of experiencing *knowing,* or reflecting on her teaching. She began to see the countless instances of emotionality in herself and her students: the feelings of success and failure at finishing a science project, the students' curiosity at her announcement of a new science investigation, her frustration when a science conversation with her students seemed to lead nowhere, her own personal passion and interest in exploring sea life and space.

"I remember curiosity as a kid," says Catherine, "being fascinated just by things. And I think for me some of what happens with children is just exploring stuff and thinking about it and wondering with them as if I am a kindergartner or a first grader or a second grader. And I think my guess is that all of us who've had those experiences when we were very young were really mesmerized by watching a worm or a beautiful, colorful rock. And it seems very much so that a place to begin in science education is targeting what students or a teacher remembers or discovers as being interesting or being excited about."

Catherine now feels the need to emphasize the importance of feelings in science as a valuable way of knowing the world. "Emotions," she says "are ways with which we know the world around us." She uses multiple ways and audiences to articulate her beliefs, thoughts, and emotions. She keeps a self-reflective journal (one part of which is an emotional diary), and she often shares various excerpts of it with her students—about things she wonders, things she is excited to learn, or things that frustrate her. She frequently tells the students that our feelings sometimes tell us many things about what we value and that we can use this information to make better decisions. How she and her students feel sometimes determines the direction of their science investigations; if there is frustration and confusion, she tries to alleviate that by infusing activities that create positive feelings and bring back the lost enthusiasm; if there is excitement, she encourages her students to express that in many different ways: role plays, poetry, art, design, music, and dance. Catherine often shares with her students how much she loves science and that she always tries to feel the organisms and the objects she explores. Catherine says that she uses her emotions "to make science more exciting and refreshing" for herself and her students.

The development of her propensity for self-reflection has been fundamental in Catherine's efforts to respond to her dilemma. She is constantly engaged in self-reflection—through writing a journal, sharing her ideas with colleagues and university researchers, attending conferences, and presenting at workshops. By reflection, Catherine means that she tries to become deeply aware of her strengths and weaknesses, her positive and negative emotions, and the ways in which those influence her science teaching. Three years ago, I asked her for the first time how she used her emotions for reflecting on her science teaching. She smiled. "You can't imagine," she said, "how many laughs, raised eyebrows, and weird-looking faces I get from people when I tell them, 'You know, we are humans with emotions, at home with our family and friends, and at school with our students and colleagues.' How can one say that emotions have no place in our teaching!"

As a result of constantly looking for ways to respond to her dilemma, Catherine points out that over the years, she has increased her self-confidence. "I don't think I had a broad enough understanding of what science was back when I was a young teacher," she said once, and then added, "Maybe it was when I freed up to 'Oh, I see that science is everything I do! OK!' . . . Probably the biggest thing was just self-confidence. And in writing and reading more about ways to approach looking at science and thinking about my ideas and sharing my feelings with my students and some of my colleagues. . . . I think all of those experiences with things that made me feel more comfortable and more confident about 'Gee, it's not that I know a great deal more than I knew ten years ago about individual topics.' Maybe this is about thinking more about what I think and how I feel it's important."

"I am not sure if I'll ever find a final resolution to my dilemma of justifying my beliefs about the role of emotions in my teaching," says Catherine. "But the one thing that I know for certain is that in my self-reflection, I can find as much emotion as in my teaching itself."

FOR REFLECTION AND DISCUSSION

1. On the basis of Catherine's story, how does one become a self-reflective teacher?
2. Is there ever a final resolution to Catherine's dilemma? Why or why not? What is the role of self-reflection in encountering this dilemma over the years?
3. What are the relationships between Catherine's emotional being and her needs for justifying her beliefs to others, including her students, colleagues, and principal?
4. Describe particular classroom situations in which you can show how using your emotions can be a part of the process of reflecting on your teaching.

■**COMMENTARY**

"I Love This Rock": Passionate Science and the Myth of Objectivity

Megan Boler

Why is it an oxymoron to engage emotions in the teaching of science? Why would Catherine's principal reprimand her for this courageous work? Since the Enlightenment, science has evolved as the "myth of objectivity." As countless scholars have affirmed over the last three decades, science replaced God's authority in Western cultures and has been reified as an objective, unquestionable authority on matters of nature as well as culture (Harding, 1986; Kuhn, 1962). According to this myth, science does not involve bias, subjectivity, or emotions. This myth depends on value-laden dualisms central to Western thought—dualisms such as mind versus body, reason versus emotion, fact versus fiction, male versus female, and good versus evil. The first term of each dualistic pair is more highly valued in Western culture than the second term. In short, science has been distinguished from emotion to ensure the Western cultural authority of science as "true" and "unpolluted" by the demons of love and emotion.

Catherine's twenty-five years of teaching tell us another story. Her self-reflective practice challenges the myth and necessity of scientific objectivity. Catherine is far from alone in her self-reflective integration of emotions into scientific inquiry. In her ground-breaking books, Evelyn Fox Keller (1983, 1985) documents the work of geneticist Barbara McClintock. Keller documents how this important scientist conducted her scientific work, developing a kinship with what she studied. McClintock defied the mythic Western dualisms that impose divisions between the scientist and her object of study. The scientist's relationship to that which she studies depends on a "respect for difference . . . a capacity for empathy—in short on the highest form of love" (Keller, 1985, p. 164).

What are the values of engaging in emotions as part of the practice of science education? Catherine's story reveals that her self-reflective practice enables her to do the following:

- *Demystify science.* Students can come to see, through the teacher's modeling, that wonder, curiosity, and frustration are important components of scientific knowledge.
- *Encourage active learning.* Students come to see themselves not as passive (objective) viewers but as actively engaged in a mutual relationship with the world they examine.
- *Engage the self as part of the text that is studied.* When we engage self-reflective emotions in our scientific inquiry, we ourselves become an invaluable part of the inquiry process. We become present rather than (fictionally) absent. Self-reflection about where and how we actively engage provides important information not only about what excites or bores us, but also about what is significant in the experiment we are conducting.

Students also benefit from a self-reflective teacher who potentially becomes a more attentive educator: attentive to students' different learning styles, to culturally variant emotional expressions of students, and so on. What a tragedy it would have been if Catherine had not been attentive to the boy who came to class with the rock from his backyard, with which he had fallen in love and wanted to know better! The teacher is not merely pushing students through textbook material, but is dynamically engaged with them in the unfolding process of passionate learning.

Finally, the self-reflective teaching approach offers an invaluable counter to the increasing imposition of state-mandated curricula. Catherine's approach demonstrates how we can engage students in the excitement of education no matter what curricula we are asked to study.

■ **CASE 10.2** ■

Teaching Science the Right Way

Melissa George and Sandra Abell

■ *In this closed case, Emma, a veteran second grade teacher, wants to teach science the "right way." While attending a series of science teacher workshop sessions, she struggles to change her science teaching strategies and bring them into line with the* National Science Education Standards. *Emma's struggles bring her more questions than answers. Emma is a composite of teachers with whom Melissa and Sandra have worked. The case is followed by commentaries from Valarie Akerson and Ruth Leonard, science educators who have also struggled with issues related to standards-based science teaching.*

Emma stood in line to register for the ten-session teacher workshop, *Children's Science.* This workshop promised to help teachers cultivate an understanding of the *National Science Education Standards* and apply them to their classroom teaching. As she stood there, Emma recounted her recent attempts to become a better elementary science teacher. A couple of years ago, her colleague, Linda, a science enthusiast, inspired her to rethink the textbook-based science instruction she had been using with second graders for nearly thirty years. She had attended hands-on workshops the past two summers and had actually had fun learning new science activities. Yet Emma knew that good teaching was not simply a matter of using activities learned in workshops.

Emma was a confident teacher in language arts and mathematics. Proficiency in these areas had been crafted through years of experience, professional development, and personal commitment. To improve her math pedagogy, Emma became involved in the mathematics reform efforts in her district. This dedication had inspired a fellow teacher to nominate her for a national award earlier in the year. Emma's knowledge and application of the ideas in the math reform documents gave her confidence. She believed she was teaching math the right way, according to the vision of the experts. She didn't feel the same sense of confidence about her science teaching. "Science is my weakest area," she told the course leader, Patti, at the registration table. "If you want to do a good job, you avoid the things you are not good at. My weak science background prevents me from being a better teacher. I want to learn to teach science right."

Since her first year of teaching, Emma had struggled with her lack of science content knowledge. She was unsure of the facts, the "right answers" in science. Because of this, she relied on scripted lessons and had difficulty picturing herself trying some of the open-ended inquiry approaches her friend Linda used. When Patti began the workshop by asking the participants to recount their most positive science teaching experiences, Emma responded, "I don't know that I can honestly say that I have had a positive experience. I don't know that I ever did something that I feel was right."

At the end of the first workshop session, Emma was even more confused about the right way to teach science to her second graders. The session had focused on strategies for incorporating inquiry into the classroom. Emma and her colleagues had been given a flashlight and simply told to see what they could find out about light from using it. Patti helped the teachers generate a list of what they found out and a list of what they wanted to know more about. Patti accepted all the comments from the teachers and reminded them that next week they would follow their interests and investigate questions that were meaningful to them. The class had a heated discussion on the definition of inquiry. This inspired Patti to ask the teachers to bring an example of how they might use children's real-world experiences to generate classroom investigations with them to next week's meeting. "Make the example relevant to what you are teaching in your class right now," Patti said. Emma had never been to a workshop that had been so open to incorporating participants' interests and ideas into the schedule. She reread the suggestions for classroom inquiry from the *National Science Education Standards* that Patti had asked the teachers to think about:

> Full inquiry involves students asking a simple question, completing an investigation, answering the question, and presenting the results to others. Student questions might arise from previous investigations, planned classroom activities, or questions students ask each other. (National Research Council, 1996, pp. 121–122)

"Will I ever feel comfortable with my second graders asking questions about science concepts that I know so little about?" she wondered. Emma was also stressed by the assignment Patti had given her and wondered what she was looking for. She lay awake that night thinking about it.

The 10 inches of snow that paralyzed the town and kept school closed for the next two days added to her stress level. However, when school opened again, she was encouraged by how excited the students were about the snow. She came to the next workshop session with an idea to share. "I was thinking about how I might capitalize on the children's excitement about the snow as I begin my weather unit," she said, "and I thought I would send them all out into the snow with a plastic measuring cup and have them find a way to collect a level cup of snow. Then we would observe what happened with the snow over the next couple of days of school. Do you think this would be an appropriate start for a weather unit?"

Patti asked the class what they thought. Many of the participants supported Emma's idea. "Great idea," said a fourth grade teacher. "This activity would be a neat way to use children's real-world experiences in a science lesson as we talked about last week." A third grade teacher agreed, "Kids have a lot of questions about snow. Going out to collect it would get them thinking about precipitation and uncover some of their funny ideas." Patti agreed and said that Emma's idea could also serve as a starting point for inquiry. "How so?" Emma asked. "Think about it," Patti said. "Children will pack their snow into the cups in different ways. The snow in some of your students' cups will melt faster than in others, and snow in some cups will melt into more water than in other cups. These observations will set the stage for classroom investigations like the one we will do in tonight's class."

Emma enjoyed the second session. She felt empowered asking and answering her own questions about light. She wondered how she could structure such an activity in which students design and carry out an investigation in her classroom. She would have to ask Patti more about this, but she had a more practical question first. Emma was determined to find out what an inch of rain meant before she began teaching this concept to her second graders. She had ordered a rain gauge from a supply company and was curious to know how it was standardized. She asked Patti, but Patti couldn't tell her for sure. Patti opened the question up to the other teachers, none of whom could give Emma the right answer. "Well, Emma, you have a need to know. Try the library or the Internet. We'll ask you about this at the next class."

Finding the answer to this question kept Emma busy during the next week. During the next workshop session, Patti asked what Emma had found out. "Well," Emma said, "this has been frustrating. After trying unsuccessfully to locate this information at the library and on the Internet, I finally decided to seek out an expert from the National Weather Service. Guess what? He responded that he did not know either!" "So what did you do?" Patti asked. "Rather than giving up, I decided to focus instead on the issue of standardization, even though it is a math topic." Emma proceeded to share with Patti and the other teachers how she had gathered together several household containers of different shapes and sizes, such as margarine tubs, pill bottles, and pickle jars, and had each child choose a container, measure an inch from the bottom of the container, and mark it with a permanent marker.

"Last Thursday, when it rained, the children set the containers outside, attempting to get an inch of rain in each one. Then I had each child pour his or her rainwater into a 'standard' cup that measured an inch. The children compared the amounts of water in the cups. Of course, the amounts were different, and the children were led in a discussion about the importance of standard measurement," Emma said with excitement. "I couldn't figure out the right way to teach the science part, so I turned it into a math lesson." Patti was perplexed. "Emma, that lesson was a fantastic science lesson. Don't sell yourself short!"

Emma was confused. She wanted to reform her approach to classroom science, teaching the right way, like the vision in the *National Standards,* but she did not know how. She asked herself, "What kind of information can second graders handle? What can they understand? What is worthwhile? What is grade-level appropriate?" She felt that the questions about light that she and the other teachers in the workshop investigated were more like true science. But sometimes she was frustrated with Patti's approach. Patti didn't hand out step-by-step lessons as she had received in other science teaching workshops, and Patti didn't know all the answers. Emma thought back to last week, when she had asked Patti about the clouds. "Come here for a minute and look outside with me," she had asked Patti while pointing at the sky. "What kind of clouds are those?" Patti said she didn't know. "Well, I think they are stratus clouds. At least that is what stratus clouds look like on the computer program I am using in my class. I just wanted to check with you to make sure I was right." Yet Emma admitted to herself that when Patti didn't know the answers to her questions and directed her to resources, she actually felt good. Having to confront Patti's lack of content knowledge afforded Emma the opportunity to gain more confidence in her own ability to acquire the answers.

The following week was a busy one for Emma. Besides teaching all week and attending the science workshop, she had to put the finishing touches on the essay she had written for the national math award. That evening after a long day of teaching, she took out her essay and started reading.

My students are always exploring, thinking about, and sharing our math experiences. I have fostered their curiosity by allowing students to make their own choices. For instance, manipulatives are available at recess for free exploration, which strengthens their prior knowledge. Children are able to work individually and cooperatively in many instances in my math classes. Through group interaction, children are able to gain confidence and skills at the same time. My children learn to collect and present data in various ways. I help them to evaluate their answers with questions asked during an activity. These questions are: How do you know? What has you stuck? Why do you think that? Tell me what you know for sure. I believe children learn best this way.

Rereading her essay, Emma knew she was teaching math the right way. Ironically, she felt uncomfortable teaching science the right way, using inquiry as the reform documents suggested. Emma wondered why it was so hard to experiment with her science teaching approaches.

FOR REFLECTION AND DISCUSSION

1. If Emma is comfortable with reform-minded approaches in her math teaching, why couldn't she be comfortable using them in her science teaching?

2. What are some of the barriers Emma must overcome to change her science teaching?

3. Do you think elementary science teachers should change their teaching strategies to comply with educational reform documents? Why or why not?

4. What are some of the issues that arise when teachers try to make changes in their science teaching strategies?

■ COMMENTARY

Is One "Right" Way the Wrong Way to Think about Teaching Elementary Science?

Valarie L. Akerson

Emma is struggling with issues with which many elementary teachers struggle. Each semester in my science methods courses, I know that one effort I must make is to build my students' confidence in their abilities to use their strengths to learn both content and pedagogical skills to effectively teach science in line with state and national reforms. Emma holds strengths that may be described as typical of elementary teachers—those in literacy and oftentimes mathematics—while her perceived weakness is teaching science. One needs to only look at the *Benchmarks for Scientific Literacy* (American Association for the Advancement of Science, 1993) and see the number of scientific concepts that are to be addressed in grades as young as kindergarten to understand the daunting task facing elementary teachers. They need to teach not only each science content area with strong pedagogy, but every other subject area as well, also attending to the reforms, standards, and benchmarks of those subjects. It is easy to see why Emma and her colleagues find the task overwhelming and why they tend to focus on subject areas such as literacy and mathematics with which they are more comfortable.

However, just because the task of reforming elementary science teaching is difficult does not mean that it is impossible. Any time learning takes place, there is some cognitive struggle, which seems to be what Emma is dealing with right now. Her discomfort with her own students' questions and lack of confidence in her own content knowledge need to be dealt with. She can discover that student questions can become an opportunity to investigate a question as a team and to increase her own content knowledge at the same time (Akerson, Flick, & Lederman, 2000).

Indeed, Emma shows much promise in reforming her science teaching. Her efforts to build on students' knowledge and interests with her snow unit were a very good start. She modeled problem solving with her own efforts to solve the challenge of measurement with the rain gauge. She should be encouraged to persevere in her efforts. With support by her administration and the professional development group, she will continue to make progress. Change does not always progress at the rate we wish, and it often comes much more slowly as we adapt ourselves to new ideas. Emma needs to be commended for her efforts and encouraged to persevere.

Emma's focus on finding "the right way" of teaching science gives the impression that she is searching for a single method for teaching science in line with the reforms. This focus on a single "right" method of teaching science may be related to an alternative belief she holds that there is a single "right" way of doing science. It is not unusual for teachers, even practicing teachers, to hold many alternative conceptions about the nature of science (NOS) (e.g., McComas, 1996). It is obvious from Emma's work in mathematics that she holds a more accurate view of mathematics and encourages students to resolve problems in ways that allow for free exploration and group work. She also asks questions of her students in mathematics that focus them on the evidence they are seeing and the need to justify their responses. If Emma is able to recognize that science teaching might be approached in a similar way (of course, with adjustments to content), she would likely be more confident in her teaching of science. Instruction in elements of NOS, particularly tentativeness, the empirical NOS, and the subjective, theory-laden NOS, along with the view that there is no single scientific method, would improve Emma's conceptions of science and make it less intimidating than trying to teach a body of absolute scientific knowledge through a new method of instruction.

Teacher and Students as Fellow Investigators in Science

Ruth S. Leonard

I believe Emma is on her way to being the science teacher she wishes to become. Her workshop instructor, Patti, is modeling a student-centered approach, and Emma is already using this approach as she teaches mathematics. Recognizing the need to improve and being willing to work on that need are the hallmarks of a good teacher.

The barrier between Emma and her goals is her belief about what science is rather than her knowledge of how to teach it. Emma sees science as a set of key concepts and knowledge, which she doesn't feel comfortable enough with to support student learning. To address this, Patti is modeling for her the role of teacher as fellow investigator. Once Emma sees how she and her students can learn together, she will be well on her way to promoting inquiry in her classroom.

Many people see science as concepts to be learned through rote memorization. Teachers are expected to be keepers of this knowledge. This is a daunting position even for those with a strong science background. Scientists would agree that science is more a way of thinking or looking at the world than a set of rudimentary facts. Science influences and is influenced by the world around us. Understanding these influences and the resulting tentativeness of science is a key to student understanding of what science is and how it affects their lives. This is one reason why including science inquiry is important and appropriate in our classrooms.

Science in the elementary classroom can be more usefully seen as an adventure to be experienced than as a collection of concepts to be passively acquired. Science education reform movements encourage the development of habits of mind to emphasize this process. For example, students could investigate how a variety of household products change the color of litmus paper and then group them accordingly. Other properties of these materials could then be considered from this classification. Alternatively, these same students could be told bases turn litmus blue, acids turn litmus red, and then try it themselves. The first example provides for questions generated by the students that could be used to investigate or "do science" in much greater depth; the second emphasizes only verification without fostering an understanding of the broader implications of the properties.

Emma is comfortable with allowing students to investigate mathematics because it has concrete outcomes that can be evaluated easily. When a teacher is evaluating students' science learning, the variables that are involved produce less than certain outcomes. It is this process of experimenting, however, that provides a richer, more meaningful experience. The tentativeness of experimental outcomes needs to be accepted as a dilemma of the nature of science. By encouraging investigation and questioning, Emma will be allowing science to take place in her classroom, and students will learn more than just concepts; they will develop a better understanding of how science works, as evidence in their investigation of an inch of rainwater.

Relinquishing control of information is one of the keys to making this approach to science education work. Emma feels a need, as most teachers' do, to be in control to promote learning effectively in her classroom. An Advanced Placement Chemistry teacher once shared with me how she accomplished this in a very high-stakes class: "I joined the students on a quest in which we worked together to understand the material that would be on the AP exam."

Testing is always a consideration as teachers guide their students through the year. It isn't possible in most situations just to let students investigate whatever might interest them. But providing interesting situations that spark their curiosity can lead them to question the very ideas that are outlined in the required curriculum. Through this questioning and investigating, students' preconceived ideas become a part of the lesson as well as knowledge they might have that connects with the topic. The opportunity for students to choose their own investigation will spark interest in science and imagination in science, in much the same way as when they pick their own books from the library to read.

■ CASE 10.3 ■

Partnering for Progress in Elementary Science

Janet Carlson Powell and Linda Block-Gandy

■ *Mountain View Elementary School (Adams 12 Five Star District, Broomfield, Colorado) and the University of Colorado have an established partner relationship through the auspices of the Colorado Partnership for Educational Renewal, a member of the National Network for Educational Renewal. This case was written from the perspective of Linda, the science chairperson at Mountain View, and Janet, who was a graduate student in science education at the University of Colorado at the time of the case. Their dilemma came in trying to find a process that would allow for the development of a true partnership between the school and the university. In this case, Janet and Linda focus on their views of how the partnership came to life to improve pre-service and in-service teacher education in science.*

GETTING THE PARTNERSHIP ROLLING

Linda's Voice

It has been my experience as an elementary science educator and classroom teacher that most pre-service and in-service teachers have little background in science and feel uncomfortable teaching science. When Mountain View Elementary received a grant from the Colorado Partnership for Educational Renewal, no one at our school realized that one aspect of the grant was to become an exemplary site for elementary science education in the Denver Metro area. When our entire staff originally applied for this grant, we were told by the school grant writer and our principal that this grant would provide us with needed help from practicum students and student teachers from the University of Colorado at Boulder. No one realized that the grant had four parts: Exemplary Education for All Students, Professional Development, Preservice Teacher Education, and Inquiry. Mountain View's new five-year goal was to become a center where both pre-service teachers from the University of Colorado (CU) and in-service teachers from around the area could observe and participate in the latest science practices. The staff had not really chosen this goal for themselves. It was a condition of the grant, and as the science chairperson, I was given the task to lead the work toward this goal.

The top-down nature of the grant was a problem, especially given the history of change and innovation within our school. Teachers who had taken on other in-house leadership roles had not been taken seriously. The other staff members had either felt threatened by their expertise or thought they themselves knew more than the content area leader and managed to sabotage the work being done. Being a prophet in your own country can be destructive. I believed that if exemplary science education was to succeed, it would be necessary to have someone from the outside initiate and guide our work.

I first identified the science needs of all of the teachers in the building through a survey. Three major issues were identified: lack of comfort with the content being taught, lack of materials and space management, and lack of understanding of the latest pedagogy.

During the first half year of the partnership, CU's Department of Education had no one who could help Mountain View teachers with pedagogical issues. They did help Mountain View's teachers and intern students by providing on-site science content workshops that were conducted by faculty from arts and sciences in the areas of physics, earth science, and chemistry. This seemed to improve teachers' comfort level with content material but did not reflect true qualities of a partnership. By definition, a partnership should include give and take from both parties. We seemed a long way from that definition.

In addition, things were at a standstill with the other identified issues. CU's science methods instructor was on leave, and the other science educators were already committed to other projects. In our partnership meetings, I continued to ask for help. CU eventually found a doctoral student who might be available and interested in working with our staff and practicum students, but this still did not help to clarify what this partnership was going to mean.

Janet's Voice

"People keep telling me to talk to you, so you must be the right person." This was my introduction to the possibility of working as a consultant at Mountain View. I had no idea what the CU partnership director was talking about, and I already had more work than I needed for the fall semester. I was intrigued, however, by the possibility of working in a school that requested help with pedagogy and the adoption of a new science curriculum, so I accepted the invitation to discuss the idea of working at Mountain View with the CU director.

My interest grew when I found out that this elementary school had requested to learn science content the year before and now wanted to improve its teachers' teaching skills. But because I had a full-time assistantship and was taking my comprehensive exams for my doctoral degree that semester, I told the partnership director that I would consider working at Mountain View only if I went out to the school one day every other week. If they could live with those parameters, then we could continue the conversation. In addition, I wasn't convinced that they needed me. After all, if they were reflective enough to realize they needed to improve their approach to teaching, weren't they reflective enough to "fix it"? I wasn't really expecting this job to go anywhere because, on the basis of what I had heard, it just didn't seem that they needed me in the equation. At this point in the story, it is important to realize that I had no idea that I was joining a "partnership."

I met with Linda, as a representative of the science design team, to discuss Mountain View's perceived needs in science education. After she and I agreed that we were philosophically compatible and could work together, she went back to the design team to recommend working with me.

Within a few weeks, the school agreed to work with my restricted schedule, and I started visiting every other week. I was full of expectations that people would be running up to me asking for advice and counsel about their science teaching. After all, they had indicated on their survey that they were concerned about materials management and did not have a full understanding of inquiry or a constructivist approach to teaching science. The first several visits to the school were like visits to a cloister. I went to my table in the library at the appointed hour, and there I sat. Although this was a nice opportunity to get caught up on my reading, I really didn't think this was what anyone had in mind when they requested that someone from CU come work with them on pedagogy.

After I had voiced my frustrations to Linda, we decided that I could get a better handle on the situation if I knew firsthand how people were teaching science. With this idea in mind, I talked to the Mountain View partnership liaison, and he agreed to find volunteers at each grade level who would let me observe them teaching science. We had now entered into the high-risk category of partnership activity. It is one thing to invite a pedagogical expert into your school or allow practicum students into the classrooms; it is altogether different to let that expert into your classroom to watch you teach. But eight brave souls let me do just that.

THE NATURE OF SCIENCE TEACHING WHEN WE STARTED

Linda's Voice

The Mountain View staff had a long history of teaching science, so we did not need to conquer the traditional barrier at the elementary school of finding time to teach science. However, most of the teaching was thematic and activity-based, rather than constructivist and inquiry-oriented. Most of the teachers had a buy-in to a district integrated science and social studies program that was conceptually based but not inquiry based. They tended to teach this program in an interactive but teacher-centered manner. They continually added activities because they were fun or interesting but mistook these additions for a conceptually coherent approach to curriculum. The school district was also looking at new science programs, and some of the staff were piloting new programs, while others were still using the district integrated program. We needed someone to pull us together and help us to define our vision of exemplary science.

I'm sure Janet's first year of sitting around was boring for her, but the staff soon knew that she wasn't going away. As they became comfortable with her presence at Mountain View, a few staff members started asking for help. Simultaneously, while working with individual teachers, Janet facilitated meetings at which the staff developed a mission statement and goals for the school to accomplish. Once this direction was set by the staff, with me as a participant, the tone was set. The staff was on the path toward determining its own route for defining exemplary science education. This was a turning point for us, and it is interesting to note that the first indication that we were headed toward a partnership was when the staff decided that Janet, the university person, had something to offer that we did not have internally. This created the need for a relationship.

Janet's Voice

I watched 184 minutes of science teaching. Overall, I saw a lot of good teaching and a real dedication to making sure the children had a positive experience with science. Yet the kids were actively engaged with "science stuff" for only 26 percent of the time. The teaching was dominated by teacher talk, seat work, and teacher demonstrations the rest of the time. I wasn't convinced that this was what the Mountain View staff wanted out of their science instruction.

I went to a meeting of the science design team and presented a summary of the observations after asking them what they thought science teaching ought to look like in their school. Their vision and the reality of science teaching and learning at Mountain View did not match.

This dichotomy set up a lively discussion that led to a two-month process of developing a vision statement of science education at Mountain View.

> To be an exemplary school in science education, Mountain View will:
> - Provide a supportive and comfortable atmosphere for learning and teaching science.
> - Promote curiosity, discovery, and questioning.
> - Ensure that all teachers and students are successful in science.
> - Encourage students and teachers to transfer scientific problem-solving and critical-thinking skills to all academic areas.

The teachers worked with me to define concrete actions that could help us accomplish each bulleted item in the vision. It took the whole semester to get this far, but I finally felt that I knew what my job was and how we were going to move toward a two-way partnership!

Unfortunately, the original funding for my position ran out at this point. But by this time, I was committed to Mountain View, and the teachers finally knew why I was there and what I could do. I was willing to volunteer my time for the spring, but the ingenuity of both CU and Mountain View administrators kept me from having to do that. During the spring semester, I also found out that I would be teaching the elementary science methods class at CU and that some of those students would complete their practicum at Mountain View. The teaching team at CU and the staff at Mountain View worked with me to coordinate the placement of practicum students from my class in rooms where teachers were trying to implement the vision statement, which was consistent with the emphasis in the methods class. We were now on the way to a concrete, understandable form of a partnership.

IMPLEMENTING THE CHANGES TO IMPROVE SCIENCE TEACHING

Linda's Voice

We used the vision statement to guide us through the selection of a new science curriculum in the spring. As part of the adoption process, the staff was next asked to attend a science workshop before school started. Although the curriculum that we adopted was agreed to by the majority of teachers, there were some strong resistors as well as some who had little or no knowledge of the new program. The summer workshop was designed to familiarize teachers with key components of the curriculum and exemplary science teaching as defined by the *National Science Education Standards* and our own vision statement.

I was able to receive funding from the district for the workshop and provide each teacher with a $100 materials stipend. Then Janet and I planned the workshop so that I managed the logistics and she modeled and taught the sessions on pedagogy. This helped to increase the teachers' trust in Janet as someone who did understand what it meant to teach elementary school science. And although we had made steady progress through the school year, the summer workshop proved to be a turning point in the teachers' understanding of the budding partnership. The playing field was leveled, with everyone having a common understanding of the goals of the curriculum and acceptance of Janet and her role. In addition, we now had a concrete means of involving the practicum students in school-based experiences that were consistent with the emphasis in their science methods class.

The next big leap was the implementation of *grand rounds,* a suggestion generated at a partnership meeting. We borrowed the term from the medical profession and adapted a model used at a university in Texas so that we could set up opportunities for the teachers to watch either Janet or another teacher conduct a science lesson and then debrief the lesson. We had the practicum students cover teachers' classes, so a group of ten to fourteen teachers were able to watch a science lesson in action. Janet then facilitated discussion around the lessons and highlighted the good science going on at Mountain View.

Janet's Voice

My first year with Mountain View involved a lot of abstract activities that graduate students are good at, such as observing others teaching and reporting the results, developing vision statements, and tracking down research articles upon request. I think there was a time for this type of activity, but I don't think practices changed much that first year. In fact, my presence in the hallway outside classrooms only seemed to make people nervous, and we really did not have much of a partnership.

Our summer workshop helped us turn the corner in how teachers perceived me. All of a sudden I wasn't that abstract university person, but someone who could translate theory into practice in a meaningful manner. This change in perception, coupled with meaningful placements for the practicum students, now meant that all members of the partnership were giving and receiving.

A number of teachers were very nervous about using the new curriculum but now viewed me as a resource person. During the fall, I answered questions about everything from assessment to keeping chameleons alive. I covered classes so that teachers could go to meetings. I met with teachers during their planning time to decipher the content and strategies in this new curriculum. Despite my sense of being helpful, I still didn't feel that we had a plan of action for improving science instruction.

The associate director of the partnership suggested that we try grand rounds at our November partnership meeting; this proved to be another turning point for us in the development of a true partnership. We had the grand rounds up and running within two weeks. The practicum students covered classes, and ten teachers came to watch me teach a kindergarten science lesson emphasizing the role of questioning strategies as a means of helping students develop their own understanding of science phenomenon. It was the most nerve-wracking teaching experience I'd had in some time. As a former secondary teacher, kindergarten was not my forte, nor was I thrilled at the prospect of failing in front of all these teachers when it had taken me over a year to gain their trust. However, kindergartners being the wonderful people they are, the lesson went well, and we spent over an hour debriefing it. We all agreed that it was a staff development strategy worth trying again.

We now do grand rounds once a month and have shifted to the teachers teaching their own kids, though I still lead the debriefing session at the end of school. These sessions have opened the door to lively discussions of questioning, inquiry, and gender equity. The combination of a common, concrete experience followed by an intellectual discussion has prompted a number of teachers to reflect on their own teaching. Now, instead of turning the other way when they see me in the hall or teacher's lounge, the teachers are actually coming up to me and sharing their successes and their frustrations. It has been two very fast years, but I think we finally have a partnership! The teachers offer invaluable practical, real-world situations in which the practicum students can see ideas from methods put into place, the practicum students have many opportunities to teach science, the university is setting up research projects to examine the partnership, the teachers get support for teaching science, and the kids are learning more science.

KEY POINTS WE HAVE LEARNED ABOUT GETTING PARTNERSHIPS TO WORK

We think that change is occurring at Mountain View and at the University of Colorado. In our two years as partners in science education, we have found several key elements that, in our view, seem essential to the success of a partnership:

1. Time, money, and space for the partnership relationship to develop
2. Support from all layers of administration at the school, district, and university
3. A common vision among all those instigating the change
4. That benefits are seen and realized by both the school and university

We are both somewhat worried about the future of the partnership that has developed. Linda will be on sabbatical leave for the coming school year, and Janet is leaving the state to start a new job. We feel there is a commitment from both the school and the district to continue the work that has begun. Discussions are underway right now about how to adjust to our departures and keep the strength of the partnership alive.

FOR REFLECTION AND DISCUSSION

1. What elements do you think are important to a school–university partnership?
2. Whom do you see as the essential players in a school–university partnership?
3. How would you benefit from a school–university partnership?
4. What do you think it would mean to be an exemplary site for elementary science education?
5. How could a school–university partnership help an elementary school to become an exemplary site for science education?

▪ C O M M E N T A R Y

Reflections on the Messy Work of School–University Partnerships

Linda A. Molner

Janet and Linda's story of an evolving partner/professional development school relationship illustrates the often messy work that teacher educators and schools undertake as they form school–university collaborations. The case highlights three conditions and their accompanying challenges that contribute to successful partnerships: they take time to develop, participants engage in frequent negotiation of common goals and mutual interests, and teachers and teacher educators must be willing to take risks in their new roles. My comments and observations as the director of this and other CU Boulder partnership projects address each of these themes.

SUCCESSFUL PARTNERSHIPS
TAKE TIME TO DEVELOP

When members from two often discrepant institutions, such as the school and the university, attempt joint renewal, some bumping together of the two cultures is in order (Goodlad, 1993), and developing understanding takes time. Linda and Janet describe a relationship that required a getting-to-know-you period. The teachers at the school had previously worked with outstanding science professors from the university in developing content expertise in chemistry, physics, and earth science. But these interactions were transient ones; the professors left the school when the workshops ended. Janet, by contrast, was to become a permanent member of the school community. As such, she had to negotiate her way through an existing culture, develop teacher and student trust, and collaborate with the staff and students on their goals for improved science instruction.

Our experience tells us that some less structured period of "messing around," in which school and university interests are explored and plans developed, is a precondition to later success. It is important for participants to face and resolve sensitive problems without giving up (e.g., finding ways for Janet to collaborate effectively with Mountain View teachers), a process that inevitably engenders trust. In fact, other facets of the Mountain View partner school relationship (pre-service teacher placements and science methods assignments, professional study groups on the moral dimensions of teaching, seminars for pre-service and in-service teachers) involved some trial and error and frequent communication.

PARTICIPANTS ENGAGE IN FREQUENT
NEGOTIATION OF COMMON GOALS AND
MUTUAL INTERESTS

The school's goal of creating constructivist, inquiry-oriented science instruction required teacher planning and commitment, new pedagogy, and frequent practice. Many of these approaches eventually found their way into the curriculum taught on campus. As Mountain View teachers became more expert in science and more involved with elementary teacher candidates placed at the school for their science/mathematics/ educational psychology course, they renegotiated some of the curricula and classroom-based assignments with campus instructors. Likewise, the university's interest in promulgating curricula in the teacher education program that addressed equity and democracy in schools eventually became a topic for yearlong teacher inquiry at the school.

TEACHERS AND TEACHER EDUCATORS MUST BE WILLING TO TAKE RISKS IN THEIR NEW ROLES

In a recent review of the costs and benefits associated with school–university partnerships, Bullough et al. (1999) note that changes in teachers' and teacher educators' roles almost always produce uncertainty. But the collaborative norms and dispositions toward professional growth that the school nurtured assuaged much of this anxiety. As Mountain View evolved as a community of inquiry encouraged by an innovative principal and site coordinator, teachers began to take risks. In the first year of the partnership, teachers, many of whom had never visited another classroom, formed peer coaching pairs to observe each other's teaching. This eventually led to the grand rounds, in which larger groups of teachers observed a teacher's science lessons and reflected on them afterward. The majority of the staff invited pre-service teacher candidates into their classrooms and found themselves performing new roles as coaches and mentors. This required the teachers to think aloud about their science and mathematics instruction, answer questions, and share their daily successes and failures.

Janet became a member of this inquiring community and openly admitted her apprehension about becoming the "science expert" in elementary classrooms. With Linda's guidance and coaching, Janet allowed teacher and student scrutiny of her own science instruction and expertise and, in her way, modeled for both the pre-service and experienced educators processes of teaching and reflecting on practice in which all good teachers regularly engage. Janet, Linda, and the Mountain View teachers became what Sandholtz and Finan (1998) term "border spanners" as they successfully adapted to new roles that had previously been reserved for members of either school or university settings.

The conditions that Janet and Linda identified as prerequisite to the partnership's progress certainly helped to create a site for the simultaneous renewal of a school and teacher preparation program. Even with Janet's move and Linda's leave of absence, I suspect that the collaboration, with its occasional but inevitable disorder, will continue to thrive. With Janet and Linda's help, Mountain View has become, in Goodlad's (1994) terms, a healthy school with mission and identity, a school that is "making it."

References

Akerson, V. L., Flick, L. B., & Lederman, N. G. (2000). The influence of primary children's ideas in science on teaching practice. *Journal of Research in Science Teaching, 37*(4), 363–385.

American Association for the Advancement of Science. (1993). *Benchmarks for science literacy: A Project 2061 report.* New York: Oxford University Press.

Bullough, R. V., Birrell, J. R., Young, J., Clarke, D. C., Erickson, L., Earle, R. S., Campbell, J., Hansen, L., & Egan, M. W. (1999). Paradise unrealized: Teacher educators and the costs and benefits of school/university partnerships. *Journal of Teacher Education, 50,* 381–390.

Darling-Hammond, L. (1996, March). The quiet revolution rethinking teacher development. *Educational Leadership,* pp. 4–10.

Goodlad, J. I. (1993). School-university partnerships and partner schools. *Educational Policy, 7*(1), 24–29.

Goodlad, J. I. (1994). *What schools are for.* Indianapolis, IN: Phi Delta Kappan.

Harding, S. (1986). *The science question in feminism.* Ithaca, NY: Cornell University Press.

Keller, E. F. (1983). *A feeling for the organism: The life and works of Barbara McClintock.* New York: Freeman.

Keller, E. F. (1985). *Reflections on gender and science.* New Haven, CT: Yale University Press.

Kuhn, T. (1962). *The structure of scientific revolution.* Chicago: Chicago University Press.

McComas, W. (1996). Ten myths of science: Reexamining what we think we know about the nature of science. *School Science and Mathematics, 91*(1), 10–16.

National Center for Education Statistics. (1999). *Teacher quality: A report on the preparation and qualifications of public school teachers.* Washington, DC: U.S. Government Printing Office.

National Research Council. (1996). *National science education standards.* Washington, DC: National Academy Press.

Sandholtz, J. H., & Finan, E. C. (1998). Blurring the boundaries to promote school-university partnerships. *Journal of Teacher Education, 49,* 13–25.

Resources to Consider

Boler, M. (1999). *Feeling power: Emotions and education.* New York: Routledge.

This book includes discussions of theorizing emotions in education as well as case studies that show the role of emotions in pre-service education programs. It also contains a fascinating discussion about the nature of contemporary emotional literacy curricula.

Eisenhower National Clearinghouse. *Ideas that work: Science professional development.* Available at: http://www.enc.org/professional/ideas/science/documents

Nested within the Eisenhower National Clearinghouse site, this web page presents information about professional development strategies and links to numerous professional development resources. The contents of this page are greatly influenced by the work of Susan Loucks-Horsley, former Director of the National Institute for Science Education's Professional Development Project.

Loucks-Horsley, S., Hewson, P. W., Love, N., & Stiles, K. E. (1998). *Designing professional development for teachers of science and mathematics.* Thousand Oaks, CA: Corwin Press.

The design, implementation, and support of professional development for science and mathematics teachers is the focus of this book. The book includes a framework for designing professional development, a discussion of knowledge that supports professional development, strategies for professional learning, and an analysis of contextual factors and critical issues that influence professional development in science and mathematics.

Marx, R. W., Freeman, J. G., Krajcik, J. S., & Blomenfeld, P. C. (1998). Professional development of science teachers. In B. J. Fraser & K. G. Tobin (Eds.), *International handbook of science education* (pp. 667–680). Dordrecht, The Netherlands: Kluwer Academic Press.

These authors trace the history of professional development in science education and discuss current approaches. They suggest an alternative model to professional development based on collaboration with others, enactment of new practices in classrooms, extended effort to initiate change, and reflection on practice.

Sergiovanni, T. J. (2000). *The lifeworld of leadership: Creating culture, community and personal meaning in our schools.* San Francisco, CA: Jossey-Bass.

Sergiovanni contributes to the discourse on school reform and renewal through an exploration of the lifeworlds that are essential to schooling in the twenty-first century.

Trumbull, D. J. (1999). *The new science teacher: Cultivating good practice.* New York: Teachers College Press.

The stories of six new science teachers serve as the backdrop for examining the role and purpose of reflective practice in learning to teach as a lifelong endeavor.

11

Writing and Living the Case

The science teaching and learning cases highlighted in the previous chapters are stories that reflect the lifeworlds of elementary teachers and their students. They illustrate educational dilemmas and challenges in which teachers need to make daily decisions within specific situations and contexts. And they are narratives that bring to light the complicated aspects of learning to teach science through stories that capture the tensions embedded within the everyday realities of the classroom. The cases in this book were not developed to represent exemplary models, particular theoretical positions, or established norms of practice. Indeed, the notion of cases as exemplars of practice is somewhat paradoxical. On the one hand, the various cases might seem to suggest a norm toward which all elementary teachers of science should clearly be moving. On the other hand, the cases illustrate the diversity of learning goals, contexts for science teaching and learning, and experiences that are encountered daily in the lives of teachers. It is this flexibility of contexts and interpretations that enables the cases in this book to serve as powerful learning opportunities for teachers throughout the course of their professional development.

We envision that the cases in this book will be used in ways that challenge traditional notions of authority in science teaching and learning. A case approach to learning stands in stark contrast to models of professional development that emphasize theories and questions external to the lives of teachers. It represents a vision of teaching as a web of researchable moments and teachers as professionals with the skills and desires to question their own practices and assumptions to understand their own situations. At the heart of the case approach is the belief that meaningful learning can be understood only in the context of our individual and collective histories, in the zone where information about the discipline of science intersects with personal experiences and understandings. Whether you are a beginning or experienced elementary teacher, writing and responding to cases can create opportunities for you to connect the act of science teaching with the cognition and feelings that surround it. This chapter is intended to provide you with some guidelines for writing and sharing cases and commentaries that foster reflection and discussion on questions of importance to elementary science teaching and learning. Although we do not advocate a single approach to case writing, our own experience has shown that some introductory guidelines can help teachers better understand the value of, and processes involved in, writing and interpreting cases.

GETTING STARTED: FINDING A QUESTION TO LOVE

Teachers' questions are often born of frustrations that create feelings of uncertainty and dissatisfaction. Although many of the questions encountered on a daily basis are general in nature, others are specific to the teaching of science. These questions are often messy, may reflect ethical overtones, and occur over long periods of time. For the most part, these questions are not likely to have neat and tidy solutions. When we consider that the root word of *question* is *quest,* it is not surprising that an intriguing question may be the start of a journey that leads to a new vision of science teaching and learning in your classroom.

You might wonder, What is a question worth asking? A meaningful question begins with observations of the world around you—your classroom, the students, other teachers, and all aspects of the learning environment. Curiosity is a natural part of human behavior. Do not be afraid to be curious! Likewise, a good question is one that leads you to ask even more questions. Howe and Nichols (2001) suggest that "one way to get started is to think back over the past week and recall incidents that occurred during a science class that you felt uneasy about, that remained unresolved or that were resolved in a way that was not satisfactory to you" (p. 112). As you let your questions evolve, here are some guidelines that may be helpful:

- Keep a journal. Make time to re-read and reflect on your journal entries.
- Be open to the researchable moment. Science teaching is full of teachable and researchable moments. In the previous cases, you may have read about some of these teachable and researchable moments that were at the heart of teachers' dilemmas.
- Watch for patterns. Pay close attention to the things that seem to happen over and over again in your classroom.
- Ask "I wonder" questions about science teaching and learning.

- Realize that your questions will unfold and shift over time, a reflection of the inherent uncertainty and complexity of teaching.
- Keep your questions open-ended to allow for multiple possibilities. Share these questions with colleagues or even your students as you let them stew in your mind.
- Put yourself in the place of a child in your classroom. Sometimes meaningful questions emerge by considering a perspective that is different from your own.

THE POWER OF CASE WRITING

Writing a case provides an opportunity for you to further define and explore a dilemma of your own choosing. By its very nature, the writing process will provide you with practice in framing and interpreting problematic classroom events. Although the idea of writing about a classroom dilemma might seem intimidating at first, the experience can serve as a powerful tool for organizing your thoughts in the face of uncertainty. Your written case can become a stored record that you can visit and revisit as new information becomes available.

Your case can also be a source of inspiration for other teachers as they strive to make sense of their own science teaching and learning experiences. In this sense, your written case can be the site for a shared experience that teachers can examine and critique as a group. If you are like most teachers, you may experience, at some point, a sense of isolation that engenders a belief that dilemmas and challenges are unique to your own classroom. Thus, the opportunity to write and share a case can support the development of teachers as a community of learners who "practice framing problems, generating various solutions to those problems, choosing among alternative solutions, and reflecting on implications of their choice" (Borko & Putnam, 1998, p. 50).

In many ways, the process of developing a written case resembles that of baking a cake. Both processes depend on a variety of ingredients that are added in various amounts and different sequences. Just as no two cakes are ever the same, teachers' case narratives will reflect great diversity in their representation of classroom dilemmas. As teachers identify writing styles that enable them to effectively communicate experience, they cross boundaries of traditional inquiry. In this sense, teachers as writers and readers of cases advance innovative research in the field of science education. There is no "correct" way to write a case, and we encourage teachers to experiment with different formats and writing styles. We have also adapted some guidelines initially developed by Kagan and Tippins (1991) as a template for introducing case writing as a professional development experience for both prospective and practicing science teachers. We ask teachers to develop written cases using open or closed writing formats. Teachers share and exchange these narratives with colleagues, who write solutions or responses that examine the issues highlighted in each case. We emphasize our belief that no case is every really closed.

WRITING AN OPEN CASE

Initial Considerations

1. Establish a safe environment for the writing of cases. New and experienced teachers alike are vulnerable when sharing sacred stories of the classroom. Care must be taken to ensure that their written case materials will not be used without permission.

2. Emphasize the importance of the writing process, not just the final case product.
3. Cases should reflect a realistic view of the complexity of teaching that does not over-simplify the messy nature of classroom dilemmas.
4. Mundane, everyday experiences should not be overlooked as potential source materials for cases (Hansen, 1997).
5. Written cases should emphasize the human dimensions of teaching and learning that invoke intentions and feelings that are often at the heart of classroom dilemmas.
6. Cases should be of reasonable length to facilitate opportunities for group discussion.
7. A summary or abstract of the case can be useful in orienting the reader.

Guidelines

Use a real or imaginary classroom situation as the basis for developing your case. You may choose to enhance a real situation with imaginary details. Your case should include a clear description of the dilemma or challenge. Your case may include any or all of the following components:

- Description of the teacher
- Teacher's background and/or experiences
- Description of the classroom, school, or community
- Description of the students
- Teacher's feelings and intentions
- Students' feelings and intentions
- Actual or imaginary dialogue
- Description of other relevant parties (e.g., parents, principals, other teachers)

Do not include a solution, outcomes, or morals in your case. You may use as many or as few of these components as you like, and you may arrange them in any order. There is no correct way to write an open case.

WRITING SOLUTIONS TO AN OPEN CASE

Guidelines

Exchange open cases with colleagues who teach similar subjects or grade levels. Write a response to the case in which you comment on any of the following:

- Your interpretation of the dilemma or challenge
- The solutions you recommend
- An explanation of why you think your solutions are viable
- Any morals or lessons you think you can draw from your reading and interpretation of the case

Your response may include any, all, or none of the following elements:

- Theories about science teaching and learning
- Theories about human behavior

- Your own experiences as a student, teacher, or parent
- Experiences of friends or colleagues
- Common sense
- Reference to any component of the case itself

There is no correct way to write solutions to an open case.

WRITING A CLOSED CASE

Guidelines

Use a real or imaginary classroom situation. You may choose to enhance a real situation with imaginary details. Your case should include the following components: a clear description of the dilemma or challenge and a clear description of the solutions. Your case may include any or all of the following components:

- Description of the teacher
- Teacher's background and/or experiences
- Description of classroom, school, or community
- Description of students
- Teacher's feelings and intentions
- Dialogue
- Description of other relevant parties (e.g., parents, principals, other teachers)
- Outcome(s) (How did the solutions work?)
- Lessons or morals that can be drawn from the case

You may use as many or as few of these components as you like, and you may arrange them in any order.

WRITING RESPONSES TO A CLOSED CASE

Guidelines

Exchange closed cases with a colleague who teaches similar subjects or grade levels. Write a response in which you comment on any of the following.

- Your interpretation of the dilemmas and/or challenges (Do you agree or disagree with the case author?)
- Your evaluation of the solutions
- Your justification of the solutions
- Your opinion concerning the viability of any morals or lessons drawn by the case author

Your response may include any, all, or none of the following:

- Theories about science teaching and learning
- Theories about human behavior

- Your own experiences as a student, teacher, or parent
- Experiences of friends or colleagues
- Common sense
- References to any components of the case itself

There is no correct way to write responses to a closed case.

References

Borko, H., & Putnam, R. T. (1998). The role of context in teacher learning and teacher education. In *Contextual teaching and learning: Preparing teachers to enhance student success in the workplace and beyond* (Information Series No. 376, pp. 33–66). Columbus, OH: ERIC Clearinghouse on Adult, Career, and Vocational Education Center on Education and Training for Employment in Colleges of Education.

Hansen, A. J. (1997). Writing cases for teaching: Observations of a practitioner. *Phi Delta Kappan, 78,* 398–401.

Howe, A. C., & Nichols, S. E. (2001). *Case studies in elementary science: Learning from experience.* Upper Saddle River, NJ: Merrill/Prentice Hall.

Kagan, D. M., & Tippins, D. J. (1991). How teachers' classroom cases reflect their pedagogical beliefs. *Journal of Teacher Education, 42,* 281–291.

Appendix

Case-Based Teaching Resources

Granwood, G. E., & Parkay, F. W. (1989). *Case studies for teacher decision making.* New York: Random House.

Harvard-Smithsonian Center for Astrophysics. (1997). *Video case studies in science education.* Burlington, VT: Annenberg/CPB.

Kleinfeld, J. (Ed.). (1989). *Teaching cases in cross-cultural education.* Fairbanks: University of Alaska.

Kleinfeld, J., & Yerian, S. (Eds.). (1995). *Gender tales: Tensions in the schools.* New York: St. Martin's Press.

Koballa, T. R., & Tippins, D. J. (Eds.) (2000). *Cases in middle and secondary science education.* Upper Saddle River, NJ: Merrill.

Kowalski, T. J., Weaver, R. A., & Henson, K. T. (1994). *Case studies of beginning teachers.* New York: Longman.

Lundeberg, M. A., Levin, B. B., & Harrington, H. L. (Eds.). (1999). *Who learns what from cases and how? The research base for teaching and learning with cases.* Mahwah, NJ: Lawrence Erlbaum Associates.

Schifter, D. (Ed.). (1996). What's happening in math class?: *Envisioning new practices through teacher narratives.* New York: Teachers College Press.

Shulman, J. H., & Colbert, J. A. (1987, November). *The mentor teacher casebook.* Eugene, OR: University of Oregon, ERIC Clearinghouse on Educational Management; San Francisco, CA: Far West Laboratory for Educational Research and Development.

Shulman, J. H., & Colbert, J. A. (Eds.). (1988, July). *The intern teacher casebook.* Eugene, OR: University of Oregon, Far West Laboratory for Educational Research and Development.

Shulman, J. H., & Mesa-Bains, A. (Eds.). (1993). *Diversity in the classroom: A casebook for teachers and teacher educators.* Hillsdale, NJ: Research for Better Schools and Lawrence Erlbaum Associates.

Shulman, L. S. (1992). Toward a pedagogy of cases. In J. Shulman (Ed.)., *Case methods in teacher education* (pp. 1–32). New York: Teachers College Press.

Shulman, L. S. (1996). Just in case: Reflections on learning from experience. In J. A. Colbert, P. Desberg, & K. Trimbel (Eds.), *The case for education: Contemporary approaches for using case methods* (pp. 197–217). Boston: Allyn & Bacon.

Silverman, R., & Welty, W. M. (1993). *Primis case studies for teacher problem solving.* New York: McGraw-Hill.

Silverman, R., Welty, W. M., & Lyon, S. (1991). *Case studies for teacher problem solving.* New York: McGraw-Hill.

Wasserman, S. (1993). *Getting down to cases: Learning to teach with case studies.* New York: Teachers College Press.

Wasserman, S. (1994). *Introduction to case method teaching: A guide to the galaxy.* New York: Teachers College Press.

Index

Credits

Photo, p. 32: Will Hart.

"Animatter," p. 38: Copyright © Russell Edson. Reprinted by permission of Russell Edson.

Photo, p. 129: David Young-Wolff/PhotoEdit.

Photo, p. 162: Play School's Association.

Excerpt, pp. 208–211: From *Cases in Middle and Secondary Science Education: The Promise and Dilemmas* by T. R. Koballa, Jr., and D. J. Tippins, © 2000. Reprinted by permisssion of Pearson Education, Inc., Upper Saddle River, NJ.